CARRY TIGER

to

MOUNTAIN

CARRY TIGER

to

MOUNTAIN

The Tao of Activism and Leadership

STEPHEN LEGAULT

Arsenal Pulp Press
Vancouver

ARSENAL PULP PRESS
Suite 200, 341 Water Street
Vancouver, BC
Canada V6B 1B8
arsenalpulp.com

The publisher gratefully acknowledges the support of the Canada Council for the Arts and
the British Columbia Arts Council for its publishing program, and the Government of Canada through the Book Publishing Industry Development Program for its publishing activities.

Front cover photograph by Stephen Legault
Back cover photographs by Joshua Berson and Matt Jackson
Illustrations by Mark Holmes
Text and cover design by Shyla Seller

Printed and bound in Canada on recycled paper

Library and Archives Canada Cataloguing in Publication:

Legault, Stephen, 1971-

   Carry tiger to mountain : the Tao of activism and leadership / Stephen Legault.

Includes index.
ISBN 1-55152-200-4

   1. Taoism. 2. Social justice--Religious aspects--Taoism. 3. Leadership--Religious aspects-
-Taoism. I. Title.

BL1923.L43 2006   299.5'1417   C2006-900336-X

ISBN-13 978-1-55152-200-5

More information can be found at *www.CarryTigertoMountain.net*

The author will donate a portion of the proceeds of the sale of this book to
the Hollyhock Scholarship Fund. This fund makes it possible for individuals in
need of financial support to participate in programs at the Hollyhock retreat
centre on Cortes Island in British Columbia. Hollyhock exists to inspire, nourish, and support people who are making the world better.

For my boys:

Rio Bergen
Rivers and mountains without end
Born January 25, 2002

&

Silas Morgen
Dawn's man of the woods
Born July 19, 2005

& with a deep bow to the "Old Boy,"
Lao Tzu

Contents

FOREWORD

Dr. Jim Butler

In the 1970s, there were probably more Americans and Canadians initially exposed to and influenced by the teachings of Taoism than there were to Buddhism, Zen Buddhism, Hinduism, Shintoism, or any other Eastern religion or philosophy. This awareness of Taoism came from a remarkable television movie and subsequent weekly TV series, *Kung Fu*, that became a global phenomenon. David Carradine played Kwai Chang Caine, a man of peace, raised as a child to be a Taoist monk at a Shaolin Temple in China, where he was taught remarkable martial arts skills.

The story of his travels through the violent, racially unjust American West was intercut with flashbacks to his Taoist lessons as a child and the wisdom of his teachers Master Kan and the blind Master Po (played respectively by Philip Ahn and Keye Luke). *Kung Fu* presented a spellbinding alternative to the usual television westerns when it first appeared in February 1972, and it triggered a tidal wave of popular interest in martial arts, including Aikido and Tai Chi Chuan.

Like many others, I was enthralled by the character of this wandering Shaolin monk. This led me to dabble in most Eastern religions over the years through readings, lectures, and workshops, and later I spent time with teachers in wats, temples, and Zen gardens. In Thailand I was ordained a Buddhist monk, but in practice, as an environmentalist and a professor who created and taught a university course on environmental advocacy at the University of Alberta, I try to honour and embrace the best of what all of these religions have to offer, especially with their relevance to my relationship to nature and my ecological underpinnings. But the *Tao te Ching* has been an influence on me ever since a woman I dated in college, who later became my wife, first introduced me to her own copy and encouraged me to read it.

The *Tao te Ching* has become a source of inspiration for grounding oneself and connecting in harmony with the energies of nature and the earth. In my understanding of the Tao, I see these energies becoming manifest in viable ecological systems and abundant dynamic biodiversity that not merely struggle to persist but flourish, evolve, and diversify. All of this nourishes, in turn, the human spirit and the evolution of its own path to a more holistic spirituality. In Taoism, that path is referred to as the "way of water," a path of flowing and accepting. The power of water is not in its individualness but its unity and persistence. Water journeys across the landscape into streams and rivers until it returns to the mighty ocean where even the illusion of the individuality of a drop of water is lost because it never existed in the first place. That's Taoism, more or less, in a nutshell.

The *Tao te Ching* is all about harmony, and environmentalists are all about the preservation and restoration of harmony. In Taoism, living in harmony with the Tao is to be in *wu wei*, which is a state of unity and oneness with no sense of personal separation. Wisdom in Chinese Taoism is "to conform to the rhythm of the universe, to the natural order." In the Shinto religion of Japan, evil is defined as that which disrupts the natural order of things; therefore, what is good is that which restores order and harmony. Aldo Leopold, a father of the North American conservation and wilderness movements, believed that environmental destruction of the land was really a moral issue of right vs. wrong. He seemed to support the Taoist perceptive in his land ethic when he wrote that "a thing is right when it tends to preserve the integrity, stability, and beauty of the biotic community; it is wrong when it tends otherwise."

Stephen Legault has chosen some wonderful symbolism in his title of *Carry Tiger to Mountain*. The charismatic power and mysticism in both tigers and mountains is why they are two of the most common objects to be painted in Chinese art. Mountains symbolize the eternal Tao: harmony, happiness, and oneness of nature. Every mountain had its own deity. The mountain images represent the peace of the cosmic order and were inspiring symbols of veneration. To the conservation biologist, mountains are the wild refugium for many rare and symbolic wildlife, from grizzly bears and golden eagles to fragile cloud forest wildflowers. Tigers in eastern symbolism are revered, respected, and feared for their courage and bravery. It is said that their image alone has the power to drive away the demons. They are a guardian spirit of agriculture, and in China are considered the greatest living power on earth.

In my work over the years, I have crossed paths with wild tigers in the Liang Shui Reserve in the Lesser Hinggan Mountains of Heilongjiang, China, Khao Yai in the central mountains of Thailand, and Gunung Leuser National Park in Northern Sumatra. In a most unusual event in the Orangutan Rehabilitation Centre at Bukit Lawang, the head ranger and I moved unarmed and on foot through a thick bamboo forest following the blood trail of an orangutan dragged by a Sumatra tiger who had proven a repeat predator on the gullible, formerly captive, orangutans being rehabilitated to the jungle. We both came to a stop for a rather large and annoyed king cobra. This in itself was adventure enough and fully stimulating. But it was the next event, still in proximity to the cobra, that covered my arms and legs in goosebumps and made the hair rise on the back of my neck. We were motionless and silent, giving the snake right of way. A twig snapped in the silence of the bamboo jungle. Again it happened. The sound came from just ahead of us where the drag path was leading. Our eyes met; the ranger gestured that we quickly return and took the lead. I no longer knew where the king cobra was, nor cared. It was inconsequential. Everything else in the world was suddenly inconsequential. Tigers have that effect.

"Carry Tiger to Mountain" is a movement in Tai Chi Chuan, one where you turn to face your opponent who is behind you. Defenders of the earth assume similar challenges, adapting to uncertainty, wearying confrontations, and adversaries who are often faceless individuals concealed behind the blackened windows of corporate skyscrapers and who impose their might in whatever form money and influence can buy. But these adversaries only project the illusion of strength. They never achieve the power or stealth of a tiger. They neither seek nor drink from the springs where tigers nourish themselves. Alien to the way of Tao, they are, and remain, at a disadvantage.

The reader of the *Tao te Ching* is reminded that meditation, centeredness, and introspection become the pathway to restore sacredness and power to the mountain, the symbolic site of wisdom and inspiration, from where all is determined. We learn that we must do the "inside work," i.e., turn within ourselves, before we can properly do the outside work.

Authorship of the *Tao te Ching* is attributed to the Taoist sage, Lao Tzu (which means "Old Master"), but probably represents contributions from other sages who preceded him. *Tao te Ching* translates as a "classic work" (ching) which deals with "the way it is" (Tao, pronounced dow as in dowel) meaning not the "path" but the primal source of it all, the oneness and nature of reality. "Te" is pronounced closer to dur (rhymes with fur) and while popularly translated as "virtue" in modern times, it originally referred to a more complex concept – the potential power of being at the correct place in the right state of mind and at the right moment.

When Eastern religions and philosophies actively advocate reform of injustice whether in social, political, or environmental issues, they are said to be "engaged." "Engaged Buddhism," a liberation movement in Asia, is symbolized in the famous photo of the Buddhist monk Thich Quang Duc, who set himself on fire on a public Saigon street on June 11, 1963. Although more than 2,000 years old, the message of the *Tao te Ching* is timeless, with deep relevance to the turbulence of our times. The language of the *Tao te Ching* is the language of the sage advocate, guiding and directing the ruler. This is a mountain sage who is not in seclusion but is very much participating in the events of the period.

The work has been widely read and translated over the years, with each translator finding and emphasizing additional themes, insights, and a new relevance for their time. Stephen delves into the passages of the *Tao te Ching* and provides a fresh, worthy, and insightful exposition of this timeless classic. It will give you one more necessary book to carry in your daypack or backpack into the mountains for reflective reading. It will strengthen your resolve while it mellows your chi. It will make you wonder whether you should wear your waffle-soled hiking boots or your meditation sandals into the mountains. You will pause and be revitalized beside the waters where tigers themselves find nourishment.

1

GRASP BIRD'S TAIL

An Introduction to the Tao of Activism and Leadership

Let's get this straight right from the start: I know enough about the *Tao te Ching* to understand that writing a book about it is risky business, for two main reasons. The first is:

> The way that can be spoken
> is not the only Way
> (*Tao*, 1)

And the second is:

> Those who know don't speak
> Those who speak don't know
> (*Tao*, 56)

The *Tao te Ching* is a text, originally written in ancient Chinese, which translates roughly to mean "the Way and its Virtue." Other translators decipher this as "the Way and its Power." Still others call it "The Classic Book of the Supreme Reality (Tao) and its Perfect

Manifestation (Te)."[1] Rolls off the tongue, doesn't it?

The *Tao te Ching* is the second most translated book in the world, next to the Bible. There are more than 250 English translations of this ancient tome alone, with many more in nearly every Western language and, of course, Mandarin and Cantonese. While few translators or scholars agree on the literal definition of the *Tao te Ching*, how to order the chapters, and what the translation of each phrase is, all seem to agree on its purpose: to help guide people towards a better way of living.

So I started out with the intent of keeping this book *relatively* short, heeding the earlier passage from the *Tao te Ching* about "knowing" and "not speaking." Alas, I take some solace in how others have interpreted Lao Tzu's famous line. "He who knows doesn't talk, but words are no hindrance for him. He uses them as he would use gardening tools," says Stephen Mitchell in the notes to his 1988 version of the *Tao te Ching*.[2] According to Mitchell, even Lao Tzu was criticized by other Taoists for running on at the mouth with his book of 5,000 characters. It seems that you really *can't* win.

Let me start by saying simply that this book is my own interpretation of the *Tao te Ching*, as applied to activism, one of my life-long passions. Throughout, I refer to activists and advocates interchangeably. The *Concise Oxford Dictionary* defines an advocate as "a person who supports or speaks in favour" and activism as "a policy of vigorous action in a cause." It is my belief that everyone has a cause they would advocate for. It may be something as innocent as a six-year-old advocating for fewer vegetables at dinner time, or as dangerous and courageous as being an advocate for democracy and freedom of religion in mainland China. Whatever your kind of activism – to write firebrand letters to the editor, to march in the streets, to blockade logging roads – my hope is that the *Tao te Ching* will speak to you.

Some advocates take a very different path altogether. A growing number of activists are starting businesses as a means to achieve social and environmental change. People like Gary Hirshberg and

---

1. Lao Tzu, *Tao te Ching: The Definitive Edition*, trans. Jonathan Star, New York: Penguin, 2001, p. 2

2. Lao Tzu, *Tao te Ching: A New English Version*, trans. Stephen Mitchell, New York: Harper Perennial, 1988, p. 86

Samuel Kaymen – the New Hampshire-based founders of Stonyfield Farm, makers of organic milk products – who, from the vantage of being the fourth largest yogurt producer in North America, advocate on issues as diverse as climate change, women's health, food security, and organics; or Kipchoge Spencer of Xtracycle, located in North San Juan, California, whose business builds and customizes "sport utility bikes" with the goal of creating a bicycle lifestyle around the world. Spencer is also the co-founder of Worldbike, a non-profit organization that focuses on creating economic opportunities by allowing people in Africa to move themselves, their goods, and their families using human power.

"Business should be the great breeding ground of the spirit," says Joel Solomon, co-founder of Vancouver, British Columbia's Renewal Partners. "But business and spirit have been allowed to become separate. In that lies the root of many problems in society."

Joel Solomon and business partner Carol Newell are philanthropists and entrepreneurs who started the Endswell Foundation to support environmental charities, and Renewal Partners, an early stage venture capital company that has helped spawn more than fifty environmentally and socially progressive businesses in British Columbia and across North America. These advocates use their position within the business community to create wide, sweeping changes that favour society, culture, and the health of our planet.

"There is no excuse for employing ruthless ethics while you make money," says Solomon, "and then go to your place of worship to be forgiven." Solomon is an advocate for aligning our values with our system of commerce and our business practices. There are hundreds upon hundreds of businesses emerging across North America and around the world, led by inspirational entrepreneurs who would describe themselves first as advocates and secondly as business people.

In my book (and it's my book, after all), if you have something that you believe in enough to speak up for, to lend your voice and your passion to, then you are an activist. You don't need to be on TV every night or on a picket line to be an activist; all you need is to love something – freedom, democracy, children, the Earth, those who have no voice in society – and a desire to give your voice to that cause. It is you that I will be addressing throughout *Carry Tiger to Mountain*.

As the subtitle of this book states, this is also the Tao of leadership as it specifically applies to those who have something that they are advocating for, whether it's in the front office or on the front lines. Many advocates come into the social justice or environmental movements seeking leadership, and soon find themselves reluctant leaders. The same is true for owners of ethically driven businesses.[3] And while I don't dwell on leadership in every chapter of *Carry Tiger to Mountain*, without a firm grasp on the *Tao te Ching*'s central tenants of leadership – trust, restraint, conviction – many of the *Tao*'s lessons for activists will be lost.

No One Way for the One Way

Writing a book about the Tao is risky because there is no single way to perceive what some translators call the *One Way of the Tao*. (That little paradox will make sense later.) In writing this book, I've studied a dozen different translations of the *Tao te Ching*, and another dozen books about Taoist philosophy and Tai Chi, and they all differ in sometimes subtle and sometimes dramatic ways. Although some treat it as such, the *Tao te Ching* is not solely a religious doctrine with strict rules and concise application. One of the things that I like most about the *Tao te Ching*, in fact, is that it is *not* a religious book. It is deeply spiritual and holy, but it is not a book about religion. It has no deity. People of many faiths can and do look to the *Tao* for guidance without fear or hesitation. It does not challenge the supremacy of any other God. It does not say *this* way is the *only* way. In fact, it says the opposite. The *Tao* simply seeks to help us follow a path through life that is virtuous and fulfilling, with love, courage, restraint, and compassion as our guides.

The *Tao* is a book of philosophy about how to live your life and

---

3. The term ethically driven business is of my own making. It's a catch phrase I use in my work to describe businesses that are pursuing a triple bottom line: taking care of people, the planet, and profits. While corporate social responsibility is the buzz in nearly every business sector, few businesses can honestly say that they are driven by progressive and transparent ethics.

manage your affairs with virtue. One recent publication interprets *Tao te Ching* as "Making this Life Significant."[4] Both in history and in modern practice, Taoists have based a theology on the writing of Lao Tzu and his contemporaries, and the practice of Taoist internal alchemy, martial arts, and meditation. In this book, I don't fuss too much with doctrine or its religious application, but rather am concerned with how the *Tao te Ching* can be used to help us activists protect and restore what we love.

Carry Tiger to Mountain is not a translation of the *Tao te Ching*, but an interpretation of others' translations. On my best days, I can struggle with English – ancient Chinese is well beyond my capability. The translations (or interpretations of translations in some cases) by Thomas Cleary, Stephen Mitchell, Brian Browne Walker, John C.H. Wu, Jonathan Star, and Gia-Fu Feng and Jane English, have been my constant companions. I have read others in passing, and have found dozens of translations in the public domain on the Internet.

I have chosen the more traditional spelling of *Tao te Ching* over *Daodejing* – which is favoured by some scholars – for the simple sake of ease and familiarity for the reader. Though *Tao* and *te* are pronounced somewhere between *Dao de* and *Tao te*, I'm not here to educate readers on the subtleties of vernacular and the history of the Tao's translation. For the same reason, I refer to Lao Tzu rather than Laozi, and Chuang Tzu – one of Lao Tzu's contemporaries – rather than Zhuangzi.

Throughout *Carry Tiger to Mountain*, I interchange *Tao te Ching* with The Way and its Virtue. I've also used the words The Way and The Tao to mean the same thing. Also, the *Tao te Ching* is sometimes referred to simply as The Lao Tzu, after the sage who is believed to have penned the original text. And while *Tao* (with italics) means the *Tao te Ching*, Tao (no italics) simply means life, the universe, and everything, as it is understood by Taoists and lay practitioners alike. (I'm sorry if that's confusing. Just plough ahead and trust that it will make sense as you read on.)

---

4. Lao Tzu, *Dao De Jing, A Philosophical Translation*, trans. Roger T. Ames and David L. Hall, New York: Ballantine, 2003

Who Was Lao Tzu?

Just as there is "no one way" to interpret the *Tao*, likewise there is no agreement on who the author actually was. A sage from the age of Confucius living in China between 200 and 700 years BC, a man named Lao Tzu is widely *believed* to be the principal author. It is said that upon witnessing the decline of society during the Warring States Period in China, Lao Tzu, the keeper of the royal archives in the state of Chou, set off for the mountains to live apart from society as a hermit. He rode a buffalo. Or possibly an ox.

Before letting him leave, a guard at the gates to the city (or, in other versions of the story, at the western pass through the mountains out of Chou) asked the wise man to write down a little of what he knew to be true of the world. The result was the *Tao te Ching*. We are left with the impression of Lao Tzu clambering down from his steed, jotting a few notes on some handy parchment or bamboo like we might prattle off the shopping list, and then disappearing into the west. As one of his key pieces of advice suggests, he did his work and then stepped aside, and it has indeed lasted "forever."

It may be that over the millennia others have added to or augmented the original text. It also has been suggested that Lao Tzu was never just a single man, but that the *Tao te Ching* emerged from a small legion of scribes. The name Lao Tzu means "The Old Master" or "The Old Boy," and some wonder if anyone could have had such a name. Whatever the case may be, the *Tao* has endured long enough to be considered among the wisest books ever written. Whoever Lao Tzu was, she/he/they gave us just enough, and then no more.

Recently, I read a new translation of the *Tao te Ching* by Robert G. Henricks, who bases his version on recently discovered Mawant-tui texts that appear to be the oldest version of the *Tao te Ching* uncovered so far. Henricks has made subtle changes to how we perceive the *Tao te Ching*, the first of which is to change its name to *Te-Tao Ching* to represent a reordering of the *Tao*'s eighty-one verses.

Just as I thought that maybe the last word had been written about which way is the right way for the One Way, I read another translation, this one featuring "recently discovered bamboo texts" by Roger T. Ames and David L. Hall that provide new insight into the *Tao te Ching*. This serves only to underline my first argument: when a book is as shrouded in mystery and antiquity as the *Tao te Ching*, we can never expect to know a definitive *Tao*.

No doubt a debate will carry on between different camps around the various translations of the *Tao te Ching* about which ones are better and which more closely reflect the point of view of the author or authors of the original version. While I have been distracted by this debate, I don't find it particularly compelling. First, given the mystery around the origin of the *Tao te Ching*, its author, and the possibility that it predates the transition from oral history to written history in ancient China, we won't ever be certain which version is the most accurate.

Second, and I think everybody is in agreement here, the *Tao te Ching* says:

> The name that can be named
> is not the only name
> (*Tao*, 1)

Even with this ambiguity, it is widely understood that the *Tao te Ching* is 2,500 years old, give or take a few hundred years. Like accounts of the author, the exact date of creation for the *Tao* varies widely from one source to the next. But generally it is agreed that the book was written some time between the second and seventh century BC, though I strongly suspect that its folksy wisdom had been passed through ancient Chinese culture and society as lore and narrative long before it was committed to paper. If Lao Tzu was indeed the first to write it down, then we might assume that as the keeper of the records of the province of Chou, he had access to a great deal of recorded history which may have found its way into the *Tao te Ching*.

The *Tao te Ching* is the force of nature in the universe. It is what guides us on our path towards virtue, and it is the force of life that sustains us on our journey through the stars. For anybody to say definitively that their interpretation of the *Tao te Ching* is the true way of reading and understanding it is contrary to the very teaching of the Way and its Virtue. The Tao is a way, a process, a pathway, not a state or destination.

In addition to the interpretation of others' translations, *Carry Tiger to Mountain* contains nine chapters that attempt to apply the teachings of the *Tao te Ching* to our work as advocates, whatever your cause or mode of activism might be. I hope these lessons will be as applicable to negotiators trying to secure protection of Canada's endangered boreal forest as they are to *Customers Who Care* participants at the Co-operative Bank of the United Kingdom as they work on issues like trade justice and climate change.

The Tao is Out of Doors

To understand the *Tao te Ching,* we must put the text aside and step out into the world and experience it. For me, the best places to see the living Tao is in our children playing in the woods or at the playground; in the graceful, slow-motion dance of a heron along a river bank; or in the curl of the water itself as it slips over rocks and rounds the bend in the brook and disappears from sight.

I first read the *Tao te Ching* in my last years of high school around 1988. It was the Penguin Classic edition translated by D.C. Lau. This introduction corresponded with my first experiences as an advocate for the environment.

Though I did not know it then, the two fit well together, and over the past decade and a half, I've tried my best to apply some of the lessons I've gleaned from the *Tao te Ching* to my conservation work. I was driven to speak out against the threats to the places I loved, at that time a tiny woodlot near my home in north Burlington, Ontario. I read the *Tao* because intuitively I sensed in its lessons that which would help me be a better person, and hence, a more effective spokesperson for things wild, even if they were only remnant second growth forests being cut to make way for Highway 407.

Carry Tiger to Mountain was conceived during my second season as a Park Naturalist at Lake Louise in Banff National Park, Alberta in 1993. I was hiking over Wasatch Pass, its rough terrain strewn with snow-covered boulders. At that time this book was about the outdoors – an attempt to marry an interpretation of the *Tao te Ching* for people who love the mountains with the *Tao's* physical form – Tai Chi, which I'd dabbled with – which I believed could bring grace to the mountain experience. (Tai Chi's balancing postures kept me from falling on my face more than once in the high country.)

Over the next few years, though, as I grew ever more involved with the effort to protect the mountains that I had adopted as my home, *Carry Tiger to Mountain* started to become a way for me to apply the *Tao* to my efforts as an activist.

Since 1996, when I left the Park Service – or more aptly, when it left me – I've made my living working with conservation groups. In 1999, I started, with high school acquaintance Kevin Scott, a national conservation organization called Wildcanada.net that I led full time until the beginning of June, 2005. During this period I made many, many mistakes, but I got a few things right too, and I learned many important personal lessons from each experience, whether good or bad. These experiences have in some way elucidated aspects of the *Tao te Ching* and how we might attempt to incorporate its quiet wisdom in our efforts, whatever the cause our business or organization might have: homelessness, child poverty, famine, labour, the environment.

I ask that you indulge me in some retrospection throughout this book as I look at my experiences as an activist, the lessons learned from these efforts, and their relevance to the study of the *Tao te Ching*. I find that I learn best when people tell me about experiences that they have had incorporating abstract concepts into day-to-day practice. I offer some examples from my experience in that spirit.

There are many themes in the *Tao te Ching* that the seasoned advocate will find familiar, and budding ones might heed, such as:

> We call the time we spend *doing* productive
> but it is the time when we are *not doing* that gives
> > birth to our best ideas
> (*Tao*, 11)

or

> Rush into anything
> and you will slip and fall
> Try to hold things still

and you will lose your grip
(*Tao*, 64)

Much of what we take as contemporary thought was born many thousands of years ago. This knowledge comes back to us through the cycles that Taoists believe link all elements of the world together, called *wu hsing*.[5] Later, I discuss what I call body memory. I believe that we can learn to unlock the memories that the matter in our bodies have of their past configurations as rock, soil, forests, and most certainly as water. This is a relief to me. It means that I don't have to learn everything anew, but simply be silent long enough to remember it.

The *Tao te Ching and the Tai Chi Tu*

To understand how we might apply these lessons from the *Tao* to the development of our strategy and the management of conflict and crisis, we'll need to look at some underlying ideas of the *Tao te Ching*.

Many people are familiar with the common Taoist symbol for yin and yang. This symbol is sometimes called the Tai Chi, or Tai Chi Tu, which is modestly translated to mean "the supreme ultimate." I've seen it used as a logo for everything from surf wear to a steak house. The symbol is older than the *Tao te Ching*. Some Taoist historians believe that its origin is with the *I Ching* – the book of changes – whose teachings predate Lao Tzu by several hundred years, though its origin in oral history, like that of the Lao Tzu book, is not well known to the west.

Although commonly taken to represent balance and harmony,

---

5. My use of *wu hsing* and other words from the Chinese are taken from Alan Watts' beautiful book *Tao: The Watercourse Way*, published by Pantheon Books in 1975. I am deeply grateful for Alan Watts' work.

the Tai Chi, or yin and yang symbol, is not about two separate things living together, but about different elements of the same thing. "The key to the relationship between yang and yin is called *hsiang sheng*, mutual arising or inseparability," says Alan Watts in his book *Tao: The Watercourse Way*. [6]

In our daily lives, we often try to obliterate this relationship. We want health without sickness. We want riches without being poor. But harmony is found in the tension between the two. They arise out of one another. They define one another. The polarity is natural.

Because the Tai Chi represents the whole or the complete universe, there is the implication that demise is as natural as salvation. I've struggled with the repercussions this might have for my work: ecological demise is simply a natural part of the yin-yang equation.

In places throughout the *Tao*, there is the suggestion that nature should be left to take its own course, and that the events of the world are unfolding as they are intended. For example, verse ten asks, "Can you accept that even for the most vital matters the way of the Tao is to let events run their course?"

The yin-yang polarity that demands balance and harmony through the marriage of opposite sides of the equation could be said to predetermine the horrors, human suffering, and ecological devastation that we fight each day. For there to be balance, we must have both affluence and poverty, one could argue. The world is simply evolving as it should.

Given this, why go on fighting? If the universe is unfolding as it should, why struggle against it?

Cloudwalking Owl explains: "I think a subtle and profound issue is at work here. I believe that Western society has a bias towards *substance* (i.e., things) and Daoism has a bias towards *process* (i.e., actions.) What this means is that whenever Westerners look at a situation we try to find the thing behind it, whether it be the atoms that make up a rock or the "soul" that makes up our spirit. Instead, Taoists look at a situation in order to understand the process. This means that they look at the interplay between yin and yang, or the five elements, when looking at physical things.

"This bias towards process as opposed to substance gives Taoists

---

6. Alan Watts, *Tao: The Watercourse Way*, New York: Pantheon Books, 1975, p. 22

a head start, in my humble opinion, when it comes to understanding things like ecology and activism, because it gets them thinking from the point of view of systems analysis instead of right and wrong, or people's innate tendencies."[7]

You and I are a part of the balance of nature. We too are instruments of the Way and its Virtue, and our lives are intended to be a part of the sometimes awful, sometimes beautiful struggle to keep this world we love so dearly in harmony.

Given this, can we hope to achieve our goals? Eliminate poverty? Stop or reverse climate change? I believe so. The polarity that keeps all the elements of the universe and this tiny corner of it that we call Earth in harmony is deeply and profoundly out of whack. It will be our life's work, and the life's work of our children and their children, to return balance and harmony to the world we occupy. As concerned citizens we are the counterforce to issues such as rampant development, exploitation of children, and the criminal misuse of power around the world.

Balance is not a static point. In the real world, balance is a matter of daily change. When you try to balance on one foot, you are constantly making subtle adjustments to stay upright. While working on our various activities, that balance swings as if on a pendulum. When we look at the Tai Chi Tu as it was originally conceived – the movement of the sun across the sky, casting longer and shorter shadows, easily but constantly changing with the passage of the year – we can imagine that by embracing the balance of the Tai Chi, we can accept nearly constant change. We must move with such change rather than against it if we are to be effective in restoring some equilibrium in a world so acutely tilted towards strife.

Our job as activists is to slow that pendulum down. As it swings towards injustice, we must position ourselves in a way that we can use our energy, our conviction, our compassion, and our love to impede the pendulum's momentum. Can we stop it? No. Try and we will be knocked aside. Can we slow it down or even use its own force to change its direction? Yes.

Some would argue that if the Tai Chi dictates that all things

---

7. Cloudwalking Owl is a Taoist and activist with whom I have corresponded over the course of writing this book. He has given me frank and insightful feedback, some of which I have added directly to the text as quotes.

will come to a balance, then there is no need for us to do our work as activists. In time, matters will simply find a point of equilibrium. But remember that we are part of a harmony that exists far beyond our tiny blue planet whose time frame is unknown to us. Preserving life here on Earth and protecting what we love on this planet is not the work of some benign force in of the universe. It is *our* work. Balance is ours to find: it may be millennia before the pendulum begins its slow progress back towards ecological and social justice, and our children cannot wait that long for clean air to breathe and clean water to drink.

Thinking about our struggle in this way has resulted in an important change in how I perceive my work. Winning our fight no longer means merely finding a solution. Rather, I now accept that the struggle will never be over. Our role is to hold in check those forces which continually threaten to destroy that which we care for.

Talk of balance often divides activists, who fear compromise and trade-offs. As advocates, we find ourselves in a world in which further arbitration is not an option. Many of the people I have worked with over the last decade or more of conservation activism agree that we cannot spare even an inch of land that is undeveloped, unspoiled by pollution, or protected from clear-cuts, oil and gas development, mining, or commercialization. Nearly all agree that we need to reclaim much of what has been spoiled.

Where is *hsiang sheng* – the mutual arising – to be found in this predicament? The harder those who would destroy what is beautiful and precious and essential to life on Earth push, the more of us who care for this planet and all its creatures will stand up. Our terrible predicament as a species, and our will and ability to solve the myriad challenges we face, arise mutually of one another. They are inseparable.

But as discussed in the title chapter of this book, we must be cautious of how we approach these life-threatening problems. "Be an advocate with love, and you wield a great sword," advises Lao Tzu in verse sixty-seven of the *Tao te Ching*. Unless we remember to take Lao Tzu's advice, we risk further exasperating this inseparability between opposing forces. Accepting this is one of the most difficult tasks civil society faces today.

Alan Watts might advise us to take solace in the principle of mutual arising, saying of the two sides of the yin and yang polarity: "There is never the ultimate possibility that either one will win over the other, for they are more like lovers wrestling than enemies fighting."[8]

Accepting this intellectually is easier than being on the front lines of various twenty-first century causes, such as the fight against climate change or the astounding loss of biodiversity – the very fabric of life – that is occurring world-wide. When it is human dignity or lives we are fighting for, it's not easy to accept that the oppressor and the oppressed are part of the same equation, shifting back and forth to find some kind of balance.

But following the teachings of Lao Tzu is not an intellectual exercise; it's an emotional and ultimately spiritual leap of faith. We simply have to trust that this balance exists and that we, as advocates, are part of the *Tao's* way of finding that balance. Accepting that balance does not necessarily mean equal or even just.

If for a moment we were to think about what we really want, we might discover that finding a place where darkness does not threaten to win over light, where evil does not threaten to win over good, isn't half bad. My life's work is to protect the environment that my family, friends, and co-habitants on this planet depend on for life. I'd like to reverse climate change so that it doesn't impact life on Earth one iota. Is that going to happen? Right now, I'd settle for reducing its impact to a point were we can simply survive.

Our work is to toil not just with our heads, but with our hearts, in a way that respects the polarity present in the world, in a way that uses the force that our opponents exert to ultimately shift the balancing point towards justice. If the universe does in fact tilt towards justice, as some have argued, then our task is to find a sufficient fulcrum to pry it loose.

The Tao te Ching *Will Challenge Us as Advocates*

For the activist, there are some challenging ideas in the *Tao*, and at times I've struggled with how to interpret them. How, for example,

---

8. Alan Watts, *Tao: The Watercourse Way*, New York: Pantheon Books, 1975, p. 23

can a busy person incorporate "non-being" into their efforts to protect endangered species, clean up toxic waste, or advocate for the homeless?

After reading the *Tao* countless times, I'm still not certain what non-being is. Or isn't, as the case may be. As I've said, I'm just learning these things myself.

There are other ideas in the *Tao* that challenge the common way of thinking about advocacy. For example:

> Do not force action,
> Instead allow action to arise on its own
> and follow its course
> (*Tao*, 48)

As advocates, we buzz around, busy as bees. We hasten to action, striving to gain the advantage over those who oppose us. The *Tao te Ching* suggests "doing by not doing." That's a tough concept for many to comprehend, driven as we are by real world deadlines, crises, and grief. However, when I think about the times that I have enjoyed even limited success, it's been when I deliberately stood back from "the action" and observed the course of events as if detached from them. Often making a decision about what course of action to take is weighted with emotion, ego, anger, or fear. The *Tao* might suggest that by stepping back, the correct course of action will "arise of its own accord." We can then follow it with ease.

Another head-scratcher is:

> The sage leader knows that force and conflict
>   always lead to defeat
> Even the most effective campaign leaves bitter
>   feelings
> and a desire for retribution in the hearts of the
>   defeated
> Lasting victories are not won this way
> (*Tao*, 31)

This has been a particularly difficult lesson for me to learn. My response to conflict has most often been more conflict. Something that you care about is threatened? React quickly, with force, and maintain that pressure as long as you can. My friend Brock Evans' statement "Endless pressure, endlessly applied" has been my own battle cry for more than a decade. But what I've failed to understand is that pressure need not mean conflict or force. And while the *Tao* accepts that sometimes we must engage in conflict, it advises us to do so with a heavy heart, accepting that by doing so, we have already lost something precious.

The *Tao* is full of wise advice for planning, campaign development, strategy, and tactics:

> Sound planning leaves no evidence of a design
> Careful strategy makes people think they arrived
>   by chance
> Refined creativity allows for intuition
> Deliberate calculation appears random
> (*Tao*, 27)

There is even advice on fundraising in the *Tao*, though those lessons may be the hardest of all to accept.

Throughout this book, I write about civil society and the application of the *Tao te Ching* to our work and daily lives. I make references to what I think are some things that we do as activists that pit us against the natural flow of energy in the world, against the course of the Tao. At times I might sound critical. If you recognize yourself in any of the examples I present – if you see in yourself some of the traits that I suggest run counter to the Way and its Virtue – be gentle with yourself. We are all learning, growing, changing, and challenging the constraints that have held us back as a movement and as civil society. I write about my own experiences here to illustrate that we are all evolving as advocates. Our goal is to become better at what we do so we can protect and restore what we love in this world. Sometimes we have to tackle some really difficult questions and face things about ourselves that make us uncomfortable.

Do not be afraid. You are not alone.

The Tao of Escher

Trying to understand the *Tao te Ching* is sort of like trying to find the starting point in an M.C. Escher print. Escher was the Dutch graphic artist who depicted so-called impossible structures such as the famous *Ascending and Descending* and *Waterfall*. The lithographs are enigmatic, and at once tickle the brain and challenge our perspective. In *Ascending and Descending*, we look down at a rooftop set of stairs with men marching in both directions, up and down. Follow one set of men with the eye as they march and the stairs go up, turn ninety degrees and climb, turn ninety degrees and climb again, and then again, and suddenly you're back at the start, going up ever further. Follow the other set of men in the opposite direction and they are forever going down, around and around the four corners of the stairwell. There is no start and no finish, and the harder you look at the image, the more difficult it becomes to comprehend.

I think it's best to be the bemused observer, pictured in the famous 1960 lithograph, resting on your elbows, somewhat detached and watchful.[9] Like Escher, the *Tao te Ching* is both unknowable and simplistically insightful at the same time. The trick to understanding its paradoxical nature is not to try too hard.

Grasp Bird's Tail

Thinking about the *Tao te Ching* and hoping to live by the Way and its Virtue is a lot like trying to grasp a bird by the tail. You might come away with a few feathers, but more often than not, the bird flits away, leaving you standing and staring up at the sky. Some intuitively know that the harder you try to grasp the bird's tail, the faster the bird will fly.

Some have learned that the best approach is to simply let the bird come to you.

In Taoist Tai Chi, Grasp Bird's Tail is a form often repeated. The gentle pivot of the hips, the drawing back of the hands as if firing a bow, and the firm but restrained push forward with the hands feels like the effort to grasp the Tao. I've named each of the short inter-

---

9. For examples of M.C. Escher's "impossible structures," visit *mcescher.com*.

pretive essays in this book after a Tai Chi movement as a way to illustrate that understanding the *Tao te Ching* as it applies to our life's work – as it applies to life itself – is about moving physically through the ideas, as well as mentally and emotionally. (My good friend Mark Holmes has also provided some interpretive illustrations to start each chapter).

I explain further in the chapter by the same name why I chose *Carry Tiger to Mountain* as the title for this book. The truth is, I didn't really choose the title, it chose me. From the very moment of conception, those have been the words my body and my mind held as its title for this book. The movement Carry Tiger to Mountain captures the strength, courage, and restraint I think is needed to embrace the challenging ideas the *Tao te Ching* presents us as advocates. As Dr. Jim Butler explains in his Foreword, tigers and mountains are two of the most common and powerful symbols given to us by ancient China – symbols of harmony, happiness, and oneness of nature and courage and bravery. Plus, as an added bonus, it sounds pretty cool.

"Playing" Tai Chi, as author and Tai Chi practitioner Trevor Carolan calls it, has provided me with a way of understanding the *Tao te Ching* not just in my head, but in my body.[10] As I explain in the chapter called "Wave Hands Like Clouds," it's through Tai Chi that I have been able to understand some of the principles of the *Tao te Ching* more clearly, and sort through how they can help me in my work as an activist.

As you read this book, I encourage you to put it down often to move, to practice Yoga, to dance, to run, to walk along a forested path, or sit by an urban creek or stream. The author won't be insulted if your copy of this book has mud on it and has been warped and faded by the sun and stained by salt water. In fact, it will be the greatest compliment a reader could provide.

I want to repeat that this book is not a translation of the *Tao te Ching*. I have made subtle but important changes to the text to adapt for the subject of activism; it is an interpretation. I encourage readers to seek out other translations of the *Tao te Ching* that ring true for them. When you find one, you'll need to read it many times. And sometimes reading it won't be enough.

---

10. Trevor Carolan, *Return to Stillness: Twenty Years with a Tai Chi Master*, New York: Marlow & Company, 2003.

"Even with a complete understanding of the text," says Jonathan Star in the notes to his translation of the *Tao te Ching*, "some sections still do not make sense – and I realized that they were not supposed to."[11]

The meaning is not in the text itself, but in where that text leads us. It's not good enough to read the *Tao te Ching*: we must experience it in everything we do. Many people who have never heard of the Way and its Virtue follow its path every day. "I like to believe," says Brock Evans, Chair of the US Endangered Species Coalition, "that for the most part in my own approach to the issues, my lobbying at all levels, and certainly in my personal life, I have indeed followed the Tao – even without knowing that that's what I was doing."

The *Tao te Ching* "was never meant to fully explain the mysteries of the universe, only to allude to them," says Jonathan Star.[12]

Chuang Tzu, a contemporary of Lao Tzu who is believed to have lived around 250 BC, said, "the world values books, and thinks that in so doing it is valuing Tao. But books contain words only ... these words are worthless as long as that which gives them value is not held in honour."[13]

Reading about the Tao will not reveal it. Talking about the Tao will not communicate it. Thinking about the Tao will not instill it in the heart or mind. All of these things merely prime the pump. If you hadn't picked this book up, you might not have ever heard of the *Tao te Ching* or Lao Tzu, but you could very well know the Tao, and the teachings of the Old Boy. You'd have another name for it. Or maybe – best of all – you'd simply live the Way and its Virtue. It would be a part of your work. It would be a part of your family.

If my publisher and my own ego would let me, I'd have you open this book and find only an invitation to visit the nearest patch of unspoiled nature. You might walk along a forested trail to a place where there was a creek or river, maybe with a waterfall or a small set of rapids. There you could sit or jump around or dance or sleep and slowly find the nameless thing that Lao Tzu called the Way. May-

---

11. Lao Tzu, *Tao te Ching: The Definitive Edition*, trans. Jonathan Star, New York: Penguin, 2001, p. 2

12. Ibid, p. 3

13. Thomas Merton, *The Way of Chuang Tzu*, New York: New Directions Press, 1965, p. 82

be you would get it in an instant, maybe it would take much, much longer. And maybe you'd find a way to take it back with you to your home, your community centre, your neighbour's kitchen, your office, or your boardroom, and weave it into your work.

But sometimes we can drift from this natural way of living and we need some words, even if only the counsel of a good friend or mentor, to remind us that we've veered from our path.

Pages with words on them are two-dimensional, and the ideas on those pages connect in what appears to be a linear fashion. This is illusion. The Tao is not two-dimensional. It's not even three-dimensional: it has no dimensions at all.

The world is the Tao, and you are part of the world, and so you are the Way and its Virtue. To use it, you need to do nothing; to harness its power, you need only let go of it.

Carry Tiger to Mountain is a love letter to people who are trying to make the world a better place. It has been written out of love: love for people, for my colleagues whose struggles I share, and for matters that are important to us, whether we are leaders of large international human rights organizations or conservation groups, business leaders who struggle to guard their bottom line while being outspoken advocates for human rights, fair trade, and the environment, or simply caring citizens gathered around a kitchen table trying to save what we love about this Earth.

It is my greatest hope that *Carry Tiger to Mountain* will help others be happier in their work and more successful in their efforts to safeguard that which we hold dear.

2

THE *TAO TE CHING* FOR ACTIVISTS

1

The way that can be spoken
is not the only Way
The name that can be named
is not the only name

The Tao is both known and unknown
Embrace the unknown as both a start and a finish
Embrace the known as both a beginning and an end

Free from a desired outcome, you can realize your potential
Locked in a preconceived notion, you see only consequences

Both potential and consequence
are born from the same source
This source is called the Way

The mystery within this mystery
is the root of all our efforts

2

When you see your way as the only way
other ways of doing things go unobserved
When you see your cause as the only just cause
the efforts of others become unjust

By defining victory
we also define defeat

Being and non-being are opposite, but equal
The difficult effort helps to define the easy
Misfortune reveals opportunity
Your failures demonstrate the importance of your successes

Therefore the sage activist
acts without doing a thing
and guides her colleagues without uttering a word
Triumph and troubles present themselves and she lets them come
They disappear and she lets go

The sage activist has, but doesn't cling to, anything
She takes action but doesn't pre-determine the outcome
When she is finished, she forgets her accomplishments
And so doing, she is remembered for them always

3

If you heap praise upon a great person
other people become less important
If you seek to build an empire of your organization
others will compete with you for power and resources

The sage activist leads
by freeing people of expectations
and opening their hearts
by dissolving their personal ambition
and strengthening their passion
He helps his colleagues let go of prospects for victory and success
and casts doubt over the best-laid plans
so that what is not seen and not spoken
can be revealed of its own accord

Sometimes the best action to take
is to take no action
and to embrace the unexpected as it occurs

4

The Way is like a mountain spring
always flowing but never running dry
The path with the most promise is like the sky above
filled with stars beyond counting

Blunting sharpness
untangling the string
softening harshness
settling the ripples in the pond

The true Way is within us
We must wait with patience
for it to reveal itself
for it is older than all the stars in the sky

5

The Way doesn't take sides
It isn't aware of our struggles
The sage activist learns not to see issues as black and white
but instead understands that her opponents are people too, capable
      of love

The Way is like the ocean
From above, all we see are waves
but below there is a vast, infinite life
and though its shape may change, its form holds fast

The more closely you follow the Way, the easier it becomes to trail
The more you try to understand it, the harder it becomes to grasp

Trust yourself
Keep focused on the centre

6

The Tao is the source of all of our efforts
It is both empty and full of infinite potential
From it we can derive all we need to achieve our goals

We have everything that we need within us
We can choose to use that potential any way we want

7

The Way has always been, and will always be
How is that?
It is within every living thing
thus it has always been
It will continue to live in all creatures forever
that is why it will always be

The sage activist does not take the lead
that is why she is a true leader
She remains unattached to desired outcomes
that is why she is never disappointed
Because the sage activist has let go of expectation and ego
she is able to be confident and content

8

Our finest efforts will flow like a river
Rocks, boulders, even a dam, in time, will succumb to the current
We can learn to act with such patience and perseverance
In doing so, be like the Tao

In planning, keep things simple
In strategy, be flexible and anticipate
In conflict, be fair, open-minded, and honourable
In managing, let go of the need to control
In work, engage only so long as your efforts are fulfilling
In action, be ever aware of your timing
In life, keep a balance, avoiding overwork and burnout

When working with others
resist the urge to compete, and focus instead on co-operation
and you will win the greatest respect

9

If you try to do too much
you will fail at all things
If you don't achieve a balance between your work and your rest
you will not be an effective advocate
If the only thing that matters is success and victory
you will find nothing but disappointment
If you seek only the approval of others
you will never be fulfilled

Do your work well, and then step aside
This is the way of the Tao

10

Can you focus on the task at hand and keep to your purpose?
Can you stay relaxed and supple in your efforts
as a little child at play?
Can you clear your mind of distractions
until your purpose and vision become clear?
Can you love people and provide guidance
without being overbearing and dominating?
Can you accept that even for the most vital matters
the way of the Tao is to let events run their course?
Can you find the wisdom to provide your heart and mind with
    the leeway
to make the difficult decisions that you cannot?

Creating and guiding
Having without owning
Letting go of expectations
Leading without controlling
This is the way of the Tao

11

The bicycle glides on two wheels
but it is the hole at each wheel's centre
that makes it move

We fashion a cup from clay
but it is the space inside the cup
that we drink from

We make our offices from four walls and a roof
but it is in the empty space which we work

Being has form
but non-being has usefulness

We call the time we spend *doing* productive
but it is the time when we are *not doing* that gives birth to our best
ideas

12

Too much to see and we will go blind
Too much to hear and we grow deaf
Too much to taste and things become flavourless
Too much thinking and our minds grow numb
Too many ambitions and our hearts grow weary

The sage activist watches the world around her
but trusts the world within her
She is guided by her heart and not her eyes
and so she sees the world as it really is

13

Be as wary of success as failure
Hope and fear are phantoms of the organizations we lead

What does this mean, be as wary of success as failure?
Both success and failure can bring ruin to your efforts
Plan to manage your success as carefully as you plan to avoid
    failure

What does this mean that hope and fear are phantoms
of the organizations we lead?
We think of ourselves as the organizations we lead
but these bodies are merely the vehicle to accomplish our work
When we stop clinging to them, we can abandon many fears

Love the earth, its creatures, and its people as you love yourself
Have faith that your love will guide you
Be willing to give your life to that passion
The Way will be revealed by your love

14

In straining to see, we go blind
In hoping to hear, we go deaf
In reaching to hold, we slip and fall

The sun is not bright
the night not dark
That which we are seeking has no name
and is always just out of reach, around the bend in the trail

Chasing it, it has no back
Confronting it, it has no face

You will never reach it
but it is within you
like your breath, your heart beating
It is your greatest gift

To understand where your journey started
is the beginning of your path towards the Way

15

Our mentors were wise and insightful advocates
We cannot describe their ways
we can only describe how they appeared

They were as careful as a person crossing a river in flood
They were as alert as if surrounded by their opponents
They were as courteous as one who is seeking support
They could flow like a melting glacier
They could be shaped like a mound of clay
They were empty as a starless sky
They were like the sun on a cloudy day

Do you have the patience to wait for the clouds to clear
and for the sun to cast its light on things to make them seen?
Can you wait for the right action to present itself
and then know what must be done?

The sage activist doesn't seek fulfillment
and because she is not distracted by her ego
she can seize opportunities as they arise
She is completely still until the moment of action

16

Strive for emptiness and openness
Practice being still
Be at ease
When turmoil swirls around you
be as the stone in the river's flow
Allow the waters to come and go
          come and go

Be still
Wait for the right moment to act

All of our work has a common source
All of our effort returns us to that point
If you know this in your heart
you will be patient
tolerant of others
respectful of their opinions
amused by the uproar
able to respond with dignity

Knowing that the Tao is the source of our efforts
we can have faith that we will not fail

17

The mark of a good leader
is that his colleagues do not require his attention
Next best is a leader who is loved
After that, one who is feared
And worst of all, one who is hated

Trust that the people you work with
are able and worthy of your confidence
and they will exceed your expectations

Lead by example
Do your work and be humble about your accomplishments
When you have finished, and your colleagues say
"Look at what we accomplished all by ourselves"
Then you will be a leader

18

When we lose the Way
we rely on policies and procedures for guidance
When we stop relying on our intuition
we resort to clever strategies and formulas for success

When an organization loses the Way
its leaders become sanctimonious
and its staff and volunteers merely dutiful

When the movement loses the Way
we carry on as a matter of routine
without passion or hope

19

Stop your attempts at complexity and cleverness
and you will be one hundred times happier
Abandon cumbersome rules and procedures
and people will know to do the right thing
Relinquish the desire for gain and advancement
and people will stop pushing each other out of the way

If you believe more is needed, seek to do less
Focus on the simple and hold onto the centre
Let things follow their own paths

20

Ease your thinking, and the answers will arise on their own
Is there a difference between victory and defeat?
Is there a difference between the beginning and the end?
Must I celebrate what others honour?
Must I dread what others fear?
What a fool I have been

Some people get very excited
as if they were at a victory party
I stand aside
remaining calm

Some people lack for nothing
I stand back, alone
without the clutter to distract me from my purpose

Some people are radiant
I seem dull
Some people are sharp
I seem blunt
Some people fly straight as an arrow
I wander
appearing aimless, lost

I am different than many people around me
I see that the true path is not so obvious
and so instead I follow the Tao

21

What gives us our strength, our power as activists
is the gift of the Tao within us
Always keep your heart centred on the Way

But the Tao is ungraspable
How can we keep our hearts centred on the Way?
By not being attached to it

But the Tao is mysterious and hidden by shadows
How can we see it to follow its path?
By looking away from it

The Tao was at the centre of the universe
before the universe began
It is a part of all things
To know the Tao
know yourself
You have everything you need to follow the Way within you

22

If you want to become complete
first accept that you are unfinishable
If you wish to follow a sure path
first accept that the Way is winding
If you want to be fulfilled
first relinquish your ego
If you wish to succeed
first accept failure

By following the Way, the sage activist
becomes a leader for others to follow

But he does not make a spectacle of himself
so that others can see his example
He doesn't try to prove himself
so then people can trust him
He does not boast or exhibit pride
so others can give him credit due

He does not overuse his influence
and so it will last forever

He does not compete with others
so people feel comfortable sharing with him
He abandons who he is
so others see themselves in his actions

Surrender and be victorious
Give everything up, and gain everything

23

When you speak, do so clearly
and then remain quiet
Be like nature
A tempest doesn't last all day
Afternoon heat is followed by a thundershower

Open yourself to following the Way
and you are already on its path
Open yourself to understanding
and you will have already found it
Open yourself to defeat
and you will already have surmounted it

Have faith in the Tao
and others will have faith in you

Trust yourself and you will not fail

24

Reach too high and you will fall
Run too fast and you will trip
Shine too bright and you will burn out
Speak too loudly and you will go deaf
Boast too much and you will lose worth
Exercise excessive pride and you will be shunned
Exert power over others and you will become powerless
Cling to your efforts and they will vanish before your eyes

To do your work and then let go is the way of the Tao

25

Before the birth of the universe
something formless and without definition prevailed
Alone, empty
vast, boundless
It was the centre from which
all things emerged
It has no name
We call it Tao

The Tao is great
The universe is great
The earth is great
All creatures are great
All creatures follow the Earth
The Earth flows through the universe
The universe moves towards the centre of the Tao
And the Tao is at the centre of all things

26

A great weight gives birth to lightness
Stillness is the source of action

Thus the sage activist can execute complex actions
without moving or losing her inner peace
Regardless of distractions
she stays centred and focused

Why would a great activist
reveal his weakness to all the world?
If you allow yourself to be easily distracted
you will lose the focus of your purpose
If you let impatience drive you to indiscriminate action
you will lose your hold on the centre

27

Sound planning leaves no evidence of a design
Careful strategy makes people think they arrived by chance
Refined creativity allows for intuition
Deliberate calculation appears random

The sage leader is available to all people
and turns no one away
For him, all situations are opportunities
to learn, grow, and guide people towards the Tao
When no opportunity is wasted
you are following the true path

For what is a challenge but a sage leader's opportunity?
People of strong and weak moral fibre are but opportunities for
        each other to learn
Only by accepting the gift of another's teaching can we learn by it
Forget this, and you will lose the path, regardless of how clever
        you are
It is a principle of the Tao

28

Know the male
yet follow the female
Be like a river flowing to the sea
steady, unswerving in its path to
a childlike state of peace

Know the white
yet follow the black
Follow the simple patterns of the world
and follow unerringly the path of the Tao
to surpass all that you dreamed was possible

Understand attachment
yet remain unattached
Accept things as they are
and the Tao will well up inside you
and you will return to the origin of the Way

Returning to the origin of the Way
We become the Uncarved Block
Some leaders among us carve up the block
and with a few pieces try to solve the world's problems
But the sage leader holds the block in one simple piece

Simplicity is the root of many things
some of which, in the master's hands
can be used to create monumental change

Start by doing little
to accomplish much

29

The world is sacred and holy
Do not interfere with its creatures and patterns

Try to change it to suit your needs and you will destroy it
Try to hold onto it and it will slip from your grasp
The world cannot be improved upon
It is perfect

Know that for everything there is a time
To be a leader
to follow
To take action
to stand still
To be strong
to fade
To be cautious
to take a risk

Know the difference between the extremes
Accept things as they come to you
Do not try to control them

Let go
Avoid excess, extremes, and complacency

30

Rely on the Tao in leadership and you will not force others to
    follow your lead
Nor will you attempt to defeat your opponents by attacking
    them personally
For every force there is a counterforce
Even when done for a noble cause
a personal attack will backfire
For every action, there is a reaction

The sage activist does his work well
and knows when to stop
He knows when a win is a win
He knows that he cannot control even the simplest elements of the
    universe
and that by trying, he is working against the Tao
He is confident without displaying ego
He is content without requiring the approval of others
He accepts himself, so is accepted by others

31

The sage leader knows that force and conflict always lead to defeat
Even the most effective campaign leaves bitter feelings
and a desire for retribution in the hearts of the defeated
Lasting victories are not won this way

Only as the final measure should forceful tactics be employed
Accept that afterwards you will find no favour among the defeated
Wield what power you have with restraint and you will be respected
Victory from force always has consequences

Always remember that your opponent is human like you
Treat him with love and compassion

After you have completed your campaign
do not be boastful, proud, or egotistical
Simply step back and be watchful

To fight is to have already been defeated
Better to avoid battle and take your enemy whole

To grow too fast is to hasten your demise
Be as careful with your success as with your failure

The sage leader regards victory and defeat the same way
from both dire consequences are possible

32

The Way cannot be perceived
Smaller than a mite
pods of blue whales swim within it
Its strength is so vast

If the world's leaders
could be centred on the Way
the earth and its creatures would be in harmony
People would have enough to eat
No nations would war
No child would suffer

Names and labels don't last
Every plan comes to an end
Knowing when to stop
you can avoid the pitfalls of going too far

In the end, there will be Tao
as at the end of its journey
a river empties into the sea

33

Knowing what others will do is intelligence
Knowing what you will do is wisdom
Controlling others is force
Controlling yourself is real power

Know that you have enough
and you will have it

Find your true role and play it
and you will endure

When you have come to the end, leave with grace
and your efforts will be remembered forever

34

The Way and its Power are everywhere
within and around you
All of our efforts are born from it
yet the Tao did not create them
The Tao guides our work
yet it doesn't claim the rewards
The Tao feeds our efforts
but it doesn't boast about them

The Tao has no wish for greatness
Thus, it is truly great

35

The sage activist holds onto the centre of the Tao
and can navigate even the darkest storm
Though there is pain and suffering in the world
the sage sees harmony and peace
because she follows the Way

Unlike wine, good food, or music
the Tao is dull and colourless
But it is because of its simplicity that it endures

36

To reduce, first make great
To weaken, first make strong
To cast aside, first embrace
To take, first give

This is called subtle insight

This is the universal truth
The soft overcomes the hard
The slow overtakes the fast

Keep your strategy and tactics hidden
Show only the results

37

The Way does nothing
but by it, all things are done

If our leaders were to keep the Tao at their centre
the world and its creatures would be at peace
Nature would be in balance
People would be content with simplicity

With simplicity
would come freedom from desire

With freedom from desire
would come tranquility

38

The sage activist shuns power
and thus is powerful
The ordinary person desires power
and finds herself powerless

The sage activist does nothing
yet nothing remains undone
The ordinary person is always doing
and there is always more to do

Those who act of out service
leave nothing undone
Those who act out of kindness
always leave something undone
Those who act out of a sense of justice
leave many things undone
Those who act out of moral righteousness
turn to brute force when they do not get their way

Failing to follow the Tao
we turn to virtue
Failing to follow virtue
we turn to morality
Failing to follow morality
we turn to justice
Failing to follow justice
we turn to ceremony
If we have to resort to mere ceremony
we have truly lost our way

Ceremony and ritual are the hallmarks of moral victories
and moral victories are but a shadow of real progress

The sage activist focuses on the fruit and not the flower

39

Following the Tao
the Earth will be renewed
the people will be fed
the oppressed will be set free
the children will laugh and play
content with themselves and
the Way and its Power
caught in the endless patterns of renewal

Lose touch with the Tao
and the Earth will fall into ruin
the people will starve
oppression and hatred will grow
our children will come to great harm

See the Earth's creatures and all humanity as part of the Tao
each working together in a seamless cycle

Sage activists refer to themselves as servants
They do not seek fame and praise
but rather allow themselves to be like the canyon walls
shaped by the ceaseless coursing of wind and water

40

To take a step back is to follow the Tao
To meet hatred and force with love and yielding
this the way of the Tao

Start with being
return to non-being

41

When the sage activist hears of the Tao
he strives to follow its path
When some others hear of the Tao
they regard it with scepticism
When the fool hears of the Tao
he laughs out loud, so preposterous it sounds
If he did not, it would not be the Way

And so it is said
The path towards the light seems dark
The road forward leads back
The shortest route appears to be the longest
What seems easy is hard
Real power yields
The pure appear flawed
Resolve seems supple
Clarity appears clouded
The path to victory seems to lead to defeat
The moment of resolution seems to end in loss
The solution for the most complex problem is the simplest

The Tao is never where you seek it
but through it all things are possible

42

The Tao gave birth to the beginning
The beginning gave birth to yin and yang
Yin and yang gave birth to the sky, the Earth, and its creatures
These three gave birth to all things

All things keep light behind
and dark ahead
The sage activist combines these
and finds perfect harmony

Many people fear their failures
being helpless
lacking greatness
but the sage activist cherishes these
In fact, she uses those very words to describe herself

Remember this: winning and losing both have costs
By always attacking, you will always be attacked

43

Softness overcomes hard
like a canyon wall slowly yielding to water
Only that without substance penetrates an impervious barrier
That is the value of non-being

The sage leader
lets silence be her teacher
lets stillness be her action

44

Fame or integrity: which do you choose?
Wealth or happiness: which do you want?
Success or failure: which will bring you to ruin?

Seek praise from others and you will never be satisfied
Rely only on money for your wealth and you will always be poor

Know when you have enough to accomplish your goals
and you will succeed
Know when to stop
and you will always move forward
Seek nothing
and you will find everything you need

45

Perfection appears imperfect
Fullness seems empty
The sage activist understands this
therefore he is not bound by limitations

The simplest path seems most crooked
The wisest tactics seem uncomplicated
Eloquence seems plain

The sage activist allows events to unfold
He knows how to gently shape things as they come
and step aside to avoid others
He lets the Tao guide him

46

When an organization is in harmony with the Tao
it shares openly with others, prizing above all the others' successes
When an organization is out of harmony with the Tao
it hoards and competes and tries to stifle friends and foe alike

As leaders these three are our greatest sins
        desire, greed, selfishness

Fear drives us to make mistakes
and creates a culture of scarcity
Do not be afraid
and you will flourish

Know that there is enough
and there will be

47

Without ever leaving your home
you can know all the ways of the world
Without looking out your window
you can see the heart of the Tao

The more you strive
the less you succeed

The sage activist knows the path to success without having set
        foot on it
and achieves her goals without doing more than is called for

48

Learning means adding knowledge
Wisdom means leaving knowing behind
To follow the Tao
surrender ideas and beliefs

Do not force action
Instead allow action to arise on its own
and follow its course

The more you interfere
the less is accomplished

Abandon your ambitions
surrender personal motives
and you will succeed beyond your imagination

49

The sage leader follows her colleagues
and takes on their concerns as her own

She treats both friends and enemies
as if they were brothers and sisters

She trusts both friends and enemies
as if they were the same

The sage leader stands back
and lets others take the lead
They look at her with wonder
but she only smiles and stands aside

50

The sage activist abandons possession
of the projects, programs, and organizations he builds
He knows that they will all run their course
and he has no stake in the outcome of his efforts
He has nothing to hold onto
and therefore has nothing to hold him back from success
Every moment he can give what is needed to succeed

He does not fear the piercing horns of failure
or the sharp claws of defeat
Because he has embraced them
they can find no place to wound him

He holds nothing back
and therefore, come success or failure
he has done his best
and then can step aside

51

All things on earth
are an expression of the Tao and te
The Tao gives birth to them
te guides them and gives them virtue
The world around shapes and perfects them
Knowing or otherwise
we all follow the Tao

The Tao gives rise to all that we do
it guides our work
informs our thoughts
directs our strategy
steers our tactics
honours both victory and defeat

Following the Tao we should
create without holding on
work without expectation
lead without controlling

To guide without directing
is to follow the Way and its Virtue

52

In the beginning was the Tao
All our efforts issue forth from it
everything returns to it

To get to the root of a challenge
recognize its origin by understanding its consequences
Trace it back to the source of the trouble
Focus your energy on the source, not the manifestations

If you allow yourself to judge others
and let yourself be caught up in wanting more
you will never achieve your goals
If you cast off judgments
and accept that there is enough
you will move beyond winning to true success

Appreciate small gains, and you will make great strides
Know when to yield to opposition, and you will overcome
     challenge
Know that to see far, you must look deeply within
This is called internal insight

53

Because the sage activist has a little sense
she creates simple strategies that are easy to follow
Her only fear is to be led astray by those
who like to make things more complex than necessary

Know when you have strayed from the simple path
and move slowly back to the centre

When we treat the Earth
    as if we were not one of its creatures
When we treat our children
    as if we were not once children ourselves
When we treat the poor
    as if they were not our brothers and sisters
When we treat ourselves
    as if we were not kin to the whole universe
This is a true crime
and is counter to all that the Tao can teach

54

Root our work firmly in the Tao
and it will not be pulled up easily
Embrace the Tao in our work
and it will not slip away
Its legacy will be passed on to future generations

Let the Tao be a part of your life
and you will know peace
Let the Tao be a part of your family
and you will know joy
Let the Tao be a part of your community
and it will be an example for others to follow
Let the Tao be part of the world
and things will find their balance

How will you know that the world works like this?
Simply watch

55

Those who are in harmony with the Tao
are like infants
whose bones and muscles are soft
but resolve and strength are great
The child doesn't know about the union of yin and yang
the basis of its own vital power
and so it always has power to wield

To know this harmony is to know the deepest satisfaction
a full life, a gentle heart

The sage activist is like a child
letting things come and go
without interfering or trying to control them
He doesn't force things or dwell on the results
and therefore is always able to move beyond them

He knows that anticipation leads to disappointment

56

Those who know don't speak
Those who speak don't know

Close your mouth
Dim your senses
Dull your sharpness
Untangle your lines
Soften your gaze
Settle the mud in your waters
and find your true identity

Be like the Tao
It can't be sought after or shunned
It can't be helped or harmed
praised or insulted
It is always giving itself away
and therefore is inexhaustible

57

To be a sage leader
you must learn the Way and its Power
Stop trying to manage everything
Let go of complex plans and strategies
and your goals and objectives will be accomplished with ease

The more complex your rules
the less likely people will follow them
The more you attack
the more time you will spend defending
The more intricate your strategies
the less likely they will be carried out

Therefore, the sage activist knows
I don't interfere
and people know the best path to follow
I stick to the simple plan
and it is accomplished without fuss
I do not hold onto power or control
and the people will follow me
I let go of expectations
and things fall into place

58

Lead with tolerance
and your colleagues will perform well
Lead with rigidity
and they will flee

Bad things can be born of good intent
Good things can come from bad

If you try to exert too much control
things slip through your grasp

The sage leader serves as an example
and does not impose her ideals and methods on others

Therefore, the sage
        cuts without wounding
            strikes without bruising
                    carves without leaving a mark

59

For managing an organization well
there is nothing better than restraint

The sage leader lets go
of his own concept of how things should be done
He accepts others' ideas
and saturated with compassion
stands solid like a rock wall
yields like a field of grass

He sets no hard and fast rules
so he can take advantage
of every opportunity that comes his way

He can accomplish anything
because he has stopped trying to accomplish everything

Letting go of his own desires
he embraces the needs of his colleagues as his own

60

Running a complex organization
is like frying a small fish
Turn it too many times and it will fall apart

Start by centering your organization in the Tao
and preoccupation with petty things and infighting will not
   take hold
Not that they won't be present
but you will be able to sweep them aside when they appear

Give pettiness nothing to take root in
and it will not find the energy to grow

61

When an organization grows and gains power
it should become like the ocean
so that all streams will run downhill to it
The larger the organization grows
the lower it should stoop in humility
Trusting the Tao
it will never need to be defensive

The organization that embodies humility will endure
The organization that holds its focus will succeed

Though our enemies might tower over us
stoop low before them to defeat them

Act with humility
Take care of your colleagues and volunteers
Avoid meddling in the affairs others
and you will be a light to guide the way

62

The Tao is a well that can never be pumped dry
The sage leader treasures it
The fool seeks shelter in it

Good deeds and virtue can be accomplished following the Tao
but just because you stray from your course
doesn't mean that you can't return again
The Tao values everyone equally

So, when a new leader steps forward
others might ply her with tales of their successes
and the merits of this strategy or that
You alone must say nothing
and in doing so, teach her of the Tao

When the sage leader is one with the Tao
what she seeks she will find
and when she errs, she is forgiven

63

Act without taking action
Work by being still
Consider prosperity as a dearth
Consider meagre resources as plentiful
Face your challenges directly, and at their beginning
while they are still surmountable
accomplish a mighty feat
by taking one step at a time

Heal wounds with gentle cures

The sage activist never strives for grandeur
thus his accomplishments are all grand
When he is confronted with a challenge
he stops and gives himself to it
He forgets his own ego and pride
He never underestimates the contest
and so his challenges seem easy to overcome

64

What is grounded is easy to stand upon
What is near is easy to grasp
What is obvious is easy to understand
What is clear is easy to see

Prevent conflict before it arises
Start by putting in place simple plans
The greatest flood
started as a single drop of rain
The hardest journey of many miles
can only be completed after taking the first step

Rush into anything
and you will slip and fall
Try to hold things still
and you will lose your grip
Force a project to completion before its time
and you will lose any hope of finishing
Failing to plan for your success can mean failure

The sage activist takes action
by letting the right course appear on its own
She stays calm
in the face of calamity
She expects nothing
and therefore cannot be disappointed
She learns to unlearn
preconceived notions and ways of doing things
She reminds her colleagues
of who they are
and caring for nothing but the Tao
cares for all things

65

The sage leader
doesn't try to teach his colleagues
but helps them only to follow the Tao on their own

If you think that you have all the answers
you are in fact the most ignorant of all
When you realize how much more you have to learn
you can finally start to see the Way

To learn how to lead
avoid having all the answers
Follow the simplest plans
and know when you have won

The sage leader
simply lets others find their way
on their own

66

Creeks empty into rivers, and rivers into the sea
because one is lower than the other
Thus humility makes us strong

To be a sage leader of people
bend down before them
honour them
follow their advice

The sage leads
but his colleagues do not feel exploited
He strides ahead of them
but they do not feel left behind

He competes with no one
so no one feels threatened by his leadership

67

Some may think that these lessons are simple-minded or foolish
Others might suggest that they are unattainable
But for the sage activist who knows herself
what seems foolish is wise
And for the sage leader who surrenders to a simple lesson
she is already following the Way

The Tao has just three lessons
restraint, compassion, and love
These are the three treasures

With love you can be courageous
With compassion you can accept all things
With restraint you can lead

To be courageous without love
to try and accept all things without first surrendering to them
To lead without bending low with humility
is to fail

Of these three, love is the most important
Be an advocate with love, and you wield a great sword
Defend the earth and all its creatures with love
and you will be a mighty shield

68

The sage activist
never gloats over her victory
and does not allow herself to act out of anger
The sage leader
prefers to win without causing shame or bitterness
and lead her colleagues by serving them

This is the virtue of humility
This is the power of harnessing the strength of others
This is the value of love

69

The best strategists say
"It is better not to make the first move
but to wait and see what your opponent does
It is better to take a step back in confidence
than to creep forward in doubt"

This is said to be moving forward without advancing
pushing your opponent back without aggression

The worst mistake the sage advocate can make
is to underestimate your opponent
When this occurs, you abandon your three treasures:
        restraint, compassion, and love

If you must enter into conflict
know that the side which acts out of love
with simple plans
and with a humble heart
will succeed

70

The Tao is easy to understand
and to apply to your efforts
Yet try to grasp it with your intellect
or recite it as rules
and you will be confounded

These teachings are simply part of the world
and nobody can fully know them

To start, understand yourself
and keep your heart wide open

71

The more information we have
the less we understand
Know that you know too much
and you can begin to learn

When you tire of so much knowledge
you can start on the path to wisdom

72

When your colleagues regard you as an equal
you can be a leader
When they no longer need you to lead
you will have done your work well

If your opponents and friends fear your power
you have no power to wield

The sage leader knows himself
but does not boast
The sage leader loves himself
but is not vain

Lead by following, teach by learning
and you will find heaven in your heart

73

Act with courage out of daring
    and you will fail
Act with courage out of love
    and you will succeed
Of these two acts of courage
one is beneficial
the other is harmful
The Tao prevents some things
but which things we will never know
Even the most wise among us cannot tell

This is the way of the Tao
It overcomes without competing
It is silent but speaks volumes
It arrives without being called
Plans for all circumstances without haste

Its net stretches across the world
and though its mesh is wide
nothing on earth or in heaven slips through it

74

The sage activist realizes that all things are in flux
and so she does not try to hold too long to one tactic
If she is not afraid of failure
there is nothing that she won't try in order to succeed

The sage leader realizes that punishment
leads only to further disorder among her colleagues
If she judges too quickly, or harshly
she will only create mistrust and anger

The sage knows that trying to direct a course of action
is like trying to use the master carpenter's tools
More than likely you will cut your hand
and be no further ahead with your efforts

75

Don't overwork your colleagues
and they will give you more than you could ever hope for
Don't interfere in their day-to-day efforts
and they will work hard to reward your trust

Do not take your efforts too seriously
lest those around you disregard them entirely

When leading
act for the benefit of others
Trust them, let them follow their own course

76

All living things are soft and flexible
All things in death are hard and brittle

The hard and the brittle will be broken
the soft and flexible will endure

In conflict, bend and flow
and you will endure and triumph

Be humble and bend
Be watchful and flow

77

The Way is like a bow
When drawn it is in perfect balance
its lower tip drawn up
its upper tip drawn down

The Tao seeks balance
adding and subtracting
to keep the world in harmony

Often people are out of balance
taking from where there is little
and rewarding those with much

To follow the Tao is to always have more to give

So the sage acts without expectation
succeeds without recognition
and steps aside when his work has been done

78

Water is as soft as anything on earth
yet mountains and canyons have been sculpted by its force

Thus the soft overcomes the hard
the yielding overpowers the rigid
Though a fact of nature
this truth is difficult to put into day-to-day practice

The sage leader knows
by taking on the difficult and menial tasks
she becomes the one who achieves her goals

By facing challenges head on
she can understand them better and surmount them

Often the opposite of what seems to be true is correct

79

After a conflict
someone will remain hurt
and that will stand in the way of future agreements

The sage activist hopes to do more for others
than what they can do for him

Fulfill your obligations, correct your mistakes

The Tao does not take sides
It always favours those with a virtuous heart

80

Keep your organization small
Focus on its people, not its capital
Enjoy your work
and make time for play
Stay close to home
and focus on improving, not growing
Though you might have power
never display it openly
Ensure your colleagues have clear responsibilities
that are simple and straightforward
so that they can be accomplished without frustration
and so they will feel fulfilled before starting the next task

And though it might be easy to take on new programs
when you grow tired of the old ones
stay focused and finish your work

81

Straight talk isn't colourful
Colourful speech isn't straightforward

The sage doesn't need to prove herself
Those who must prove themselves are not wise

The truth is simple
Follow complex paths and you will become lost

The sage activist lets things go
and all things come back to her
She improves by giving herself to others
and grows by giving herself away

The way of the Tao
Succeed by not forcing
Lead by not contending

3

CARRY TIGER TO MOUNTAIN

The Three Treasures: Restraint, Compassion, Love

The Tao has just three lessons:
restraint, compassion, and love
These are the three treasures

With love you can be courageous
With compassion you can accept all things
With restraint you can lead
(*Tao*, 67)

When I began as an activist, I didn't have three treasures, I had one. It was simple. I had to win. How I won didn't matter as much as winning itself did.

Like many who come to the defence of the planet, my entrance to the conservation movement was motivated by negative forces: anger, rage, and fear. I was sixteen years old and living in Burlington, Ontario. My family had recently been disrupted by the divorce of my parents, and I was a temperamental and sullen teenager. The only healthy outlet I had for my anger was photography. Through the lens and in the darkroom, I was able to channel my anger and produce something constructive and sometimes even beautiful out of my emotional roller coaster. But I was a landscape photographer living in a place without much landscape: the over-built suburbia that rings Toronto.

I did find one wild place close to home. My walk to school each day was through a small patch of woods that had been spared the saws and the bulldozers for reasons I didn't yet understand. In time, I came to know those woods as intimately as any person could. More days than my teachers would have liked, I didn't make it to school, or skipped out early and instead explored and photographed this tiny patch of forest. The woods became my confidante. I knew every bend in the tiny creek that emerged from a culvert near the town-houses where my mother, my sister, and I lived. (My father, wishing to be close to his family, bought a townhouse just across the road.) I knew each path, each tiny hill, each stand of giant white pine, each grove of sun-splashed maples.

Those woods became my refuge and my salvation during a turbulent adolescence.

I knew many of the individual trees, and even named a giant American Beech Phaedrus after the protagonist from *Zen and the Art of Motorcycle Maintenance*. Phaedrus was the centre of those woods for me, from which the rest of the forest rolled away in all directions. In the summer, when it was so hot that the rest of the world wilted, I could go into the woods where it was cool. The light that fell to the forest floor refracted and filtered down through layers and layers of lime green leaves. It was dim there among the opulent growth; the eyes and the body could rest in relative peace. The sound of cars on Upper Middle Road was damped by the foliage; it came to the ears the way sound does through childhood sleep on long cross-country drives.

I grew protective of those woods. Once, I found bundles of the local weekly newspaper dumped in the creek in the middle of that forest by someone who was too lazy to deliver them, but who had had enough energy to drag them half a kilometre into the woods for disposal. Enraged, I called the newspaper and made threats that I could never carry out. Later on, dripping and mud-splattered, I hauled those sodden newspapers out of the woods to be recycled.

With few exceptions, I enjoyed those woods undisturbed through much of my high school life. But one morning, I discovered some men working at the edge of the forest. They were erecting a large sign where Upper Middle Road passed through two patches of the remnant woodland. After school, I walked home along the road to see what they had been doing. I approached the four-by-six-foot marker as one might approach a pit full of snakes. In the glare of the afternoon sun, I read the notice and learned that the woods would soon be cleared for the passage of a major highway.

Sometime later, men entered the woods with axes and theodolites and survey stakes and hacked a line from one edge of the forest to the other. It was a hot summer day, and I crept into the woods to watch the men do their work – something which I came to know later as bearing witness, a form of non-violent protest. I watched them go about their business and felt a cool hatred towards them for what they were taking from me.

But witnessing wasn't enough for a hot-tempered teenager. That night I returned, pulled up the survey stakes, snapped them in two, and tossed them into the brush. Then I stripped the flagging tape from the undergrowth and pushed it into a trash can. I felt an exhilarating rush of adrenaline as I undertook this action, though I knew that my night work would not stop the construction. At best, it might delay it for a few days.

I wasn't doing it to stop the building of the road or to stave off the clearing of the forest. I was doing it because I was angry and wounded, and I wanted to make someone's life miserable: I wanted to make a statement.

I did it because I couldn't think of anything else to do.

On three consecutive nights I went into the woods to undo the day's work, but on the fourth night I returned to find that the survey crew had hacked their markings directly into the trees. There was nothing more I could do. I sat in the woods that night and watched the sun dip, casting light the colour of honey through the forest. I felt the spirit of that forest slip away. Phaedrus still rose tall and stalwart amid the pines and maples and other elephantine beech, but whatever voice he once had was rendered silent.

I felt anger. It wasn't white-hot rage, just a grey sadness and an exasperation that started a journey that has lasted more than half my life. Though I didn't recognize it at the time, I also felt fear: a fear that what's crucial for our survival – not just the clean air and water, but the wildness that brings sanity – is being threatened by our backward notion of progress.

These things gave birth to my activism. They fuelled me through the creation of my high school's first environmental club, and the makeover of my college's Earth Issues Club. And so on. I was the portrait of the angry young activist – seething at times, letting the hurt that I felt for the Earth, struggling under the weight of humanity, propel me forward. These emotions made me want only one thing: to win, at any cost.

Sometime since, I began to see that to win at any cost put the price way too high. It's not that I no longer want to win. Now, with two children and undeniably in my mid-thirties, I want to win even more. The stakes are so much higher now. But to win at any cost is no longer an option. Now, to win so that the victory lasts is my goal. To win so that in five, ten, or twenty years, we don't have to fight the same battles all over again is more important to me than achieving a temporary victory.

The blindness that is born of anger and fear often eclipses the best way forward. We're so busy channelling our negative energies towards those we perceive as our enemy that we fail to see the solutions to the problems we are confronting. We forgo strategy for an opportunity to embarrass our opponents. We sacrifice long-term victory for short-term satisfaction.

"By my calculations," says blogger Kate Dugas, "there is one 'root cause.' It is the crux of our suffering: Fear. It manifests in countless ways – violence, greed, people being so knotted up that we don't listen to one another, people being so frightened that we can't express love for one another. Until we decide to stop holding on for dear life to everything around us, we will be choosing to allow fear to become the very fabric of our experience, blinding us, harming us, causing us to harm each other."[1]

I don't remember exactly *when* this started to change for me, but I remember *why*. It was my study of the *Tao te Ching* that led to that awareness. Though the *Tao te Ching* has been a part of my study

---

1. Kate Dugas, *Kate's Thoughts for the Day,* published online at *katesthoughtsfortheday.blogspot. com,* 2005

for nearly two decades, it's only been in the last few years that this simple message has resonated:

> To be courageous without love
> to try and accept all things without first
>   surrendering to them
> to lead without bending low with humility
> is to fail
>
> Of these three, love is the most important
> Be an advocate with love, and you wield a great
>   sword
> Defend the earth and all its creatures with love
> and you will be a mighty shield
> (*Tao*, 67)

The three treasures – restraint, compassion, and love – form the backbone of this book. For those of us accustomed to responding to the crises of the world with anger, for those of us motivated by the fear of loss, for those of us suffering from the pain of having been wounded during our lives, learning to act with restraint, compassion, and love will be a lifetime's work. For me the journey is just beginning.

Let's start with restraint.

Daring Not to Be First

Restraint is sometimes known as "daring not to be first" in various translations of the *Tao te Ching*. Ostensibly, it requires us to control our own ego, to step aside while allowing others to step forward. A key element of restraint is patience.

One of the many things my children are teaching me is patience. When our first son Rio was born, I said that he was my little Taoist master. He is full of the Tao. One minute he's dancing around, singing and laughing; the next, he's wailing his lungs out. Now he's ecstatic, now he's furious; he is always in the moment. Our children are great teachers about the Way and its Virtue.

Learning to be patient has not been easy for me. Many times I've said sanctimoniously that "I am not a patient man," as if that would somehow petition people not to try what little patience I possess! At the root of my own impatience are two things: a lack of confidence that other people can complete a task as I would like to see it done, and a fear that time is not on our side, that we must move quickly if we are to save what we love in this world. You see that once again ego and fear obscures my way forward.

"Do you have the patience to wait for the clouds to clear, and for the sun to cast its light on things to make them seen?" asks Lao Tzu.

It takes time for a child to learn how to navigate through the world. My job as a father is to give my children that time, and to gently guide them as they learn. It's also my job as a father to know that there are many ways to arrive at those lessons, that my way isn't the only way. And so I am learning patience from my sons as we discover these lessons together.

Patience is an important element of practising restraint.

> Our finest efforts will flow like a river
> Rocks, boulders, even a dam, in time, will succumb
>   to the current
> We can learn to act with such patience and
>   perseverance
> In doing so, be like the Tao
> (*Tao*, 8)

Together, patience and perseverance form a yin-yang equilibrium. Patience is the yin side of the equation, the feminine (not to be confused with female) or dark side of the Tai Chi symbol. Here, we are able to hold back and allow others to learn and grow and teach us new ways of acting and accomplishing our mutual goals. Perseverance is the yang side of the equation, the masculine (again, not to be confused with male) or light side, where we know when it is time to give a little nudge, to apply some pressure at just the right moment, so that we keep things moving and on track.

Through meditation, a lifelong yoga practice, and the guidance of experienced spiritual teachers, Jason Mogus has recently learned to exercise patience and restraint while leading Communicopia, an ethically driven branding and technology company that helps leading socially responsible companies and non-profits like Loreto Bay Company, Capers Community Markets, and the BC Cancer Foundation tell their stories and engage with people online. Like many determined entrepreneurs, Mogus confesses that his big personality tends to drive his business to the exclusion of his staff's equal participation in making decisions and setting directions. But he says that recently he has learned to step back to allow others to shape the conversations about the directions the company should take, and has found that this creates space for others to bring new and innovative ideas to the table. "Isn't it hard," I asked him, "to show patience and restraint?" He laughed and said no: "It's the easiest thing in the world to be present, trust life, and say nothing unless deeply moved to contribute."

Until we develop that patience, finding and following the Way will be difficult. The path is not obvious. It doesn't yield to our demands for quick solutions and easy answers. Without some patience you might read the *Tao te Ching* and unceremoniously toss it aside: its paradoxical riddles do not yield to impatient inquiries.

> The true Way is within us
> We must wait with patience
> for it to reveal itself
> for it is older than all the stars in the sky
> (*Tao*, 4)

I struggle with this. For more than half my life, I've been fighting to protect nature. I have a profound need to do so because without nature I could not survive. We all depend on the natural world. That *should* – but often doesn't – go without saying. It is nature that I cling to as my sanctuary. As a child, this was true. Never was it more true than when I was a teenager, struggling with life's growing pains. And as an adult, nature has been my talisman. I want my own children to have it as a sanctuary. Already Rio is most free and alive when we are on a beach, buffeted by the on-shore winds, running and exploring. Silas in time will follow his older brother on greater and greater adventures.

So I feel this crushing urgency to protect it. Telling myself that I must be patient is one of my greatest challenges.

"If you let impatience drive you to indiscriminate action you will lose your hold on the centre," says Lao Tzu. He reminds us that impatience – giving in to the sense of urgency that drives us recklessly forward – does not actually solve the world's problems. He says: "Reach too high and you will fall. Run too fast and you will trip."

When we act rashly, we make mistakes. My friend Bart Robinson liked to say when he was the co-ordinator of the Yellowstone to Yukon Conservation Initiative: "Speed kills."

Through patience coupled with perseverance, we might exercise one of Lao Tzu's three treasures, restraint. Restraint is referred to as "daring not to be first," or "presuming not to be at the head of the world" in some translations of the *Tao te Ching*.[2] (In the chapter on leadership, we'll discuss this concept more fully.)

A good example emerging in the environmental movement is *who* speaks to the media about certain issues. When organizations have something to say, they often send a sole spokesperson to speak to the media. When I was volunteering for a coalition of organizations trying to protect Kananaskis Country – a 4,200-square-kilometre region of mountains and foothills, grizzly bears and wolves west of Calgary, Alberta – from oil and gas development, logging, off-highway vehicle use, and industrial tourism, I was on radio, TV, or in the newspaper almost every week for years! At first, I played this role because there was no one else to do it. But soon it became a matter of pride. I became the "go to" person for the media, not

---

2. In the four main translations that I have used for *Carry Tiger to Mountain*, the interpretations of "the three treasures" vary widely. Jonathan Star lists them as love, moderation, and humility. Gia-Fu Feng and Jane English call them mercy, economy, and "daring not to be ahead of others." Brian Browne Walker calls them "motherly love," economy, and "daring not to be first in the world." Stephen Mitchell says they are "simplicity, patience, compassion." Others call them "mercy, frugality, and not presuming to be at the head of the world." As in many cases in interpreting the *Tao te Ching* as it might apply to and help activists, I chose language that is close to what I believe is the true meaning of Lao Tzu's words while providing what I think activists need to hear most.

just on Kananaskis, but on many other issues. The media knew I was good for a quote, and as a result I became well-known in my community. I loved it. It fed my ego.

I sought this notoriety not solely for its own sake, but also as a way to powerfully leverage decisions from the provincial government about the future of Kananaskis Country. But in retrospect, my prominence in the campaign did not serve it over the long term. I couldn't continue as spokesperson after I took a full-time position as executive director of Wildcanada.net, and there was no one else who could speak publicly to the issues.

Had I spent more of my time helping others in the campaign develop their media savvy rather than hoarding the media spotlight myself, I might have helped keep the pressure on the Alberta government longer, with even better results. We made great gains in protection for Kananaskis Country, but as leaders we should be thinking about how our service will be reflected as subsequent generations of activists take up our cause.

It was a mistake I rectified while at Wildcanada.net, where I stepped aside and allowed other talented staff to become spokespersons for the organization. The environmental movement is also learning this lesson; landowners and ranchers, municipal politicians, outdoor enthusiasts, anglers, and even celebrities are often spokespersons on various environmental issues. In doing so, organizations present a more believable face to the public, build alliances with folks who share the same values, and redefine a sense of leadership that will have a lasting impact on the movement's future.

This is an act of restraint. It feels good to be recognized as an authority, and to be sought out for our opinion. But real strength comes in handing attention to others, demonstrating that we are diverse, and that it's not just "the same old angry redhead" on the TV every night.

Restraint can take many forms. As activists we wonder when to claim victory and promote our success in order to build on the political power that comes with our achievements. Lao Tzu says:

> After you have completed your campaign,
> do not be boastful, proud, or egotistical

> Simply step back and be watchful
> (*Tao*, 31)

This flies in the face of much of our thinking. I used to advise, "When you win, let people know." Winning builds momentum, but only if your opponents fear your winning track record. Winning builds support, both from philanthropic foundations and from the general public. People like to back a winner. And winning builds confidence and morale. So why would Lao Tzu suggest to "simply step back and be watchful"?

Being boastful, proud, or egotistical about our successes tends to harden the resolve of those we oppose. This is quite the opposite effect we are aiming for. There are times when we need to demonstrate our power by pointing to what we can accomplish. When trying to convince corporate decision-makers that failure to meet our demands for reform will result in market action against them, we can point to our past successes. It gives us integrity, and provides us with an opportunity to "capture our enemy whole" by making a credible threat, and possibly avoiding a fight altogether. The concept of capturing your enemy whole is taken from the *Tao te Ching*, but also from Sun Tzu's Taoist treaty *The Art of War*.

If we are boastful or arrogant about our successes, those who oppose us may become entrenched. Can we use our success to build a "credible threat" while exercising the restraint needed to honour our three treasures? Yes, we can.

> When you speak, do so clearly
> and then remain quiet
> Be like nature
> A tempest doesn't last all day
> Afternoon heat is followed by a thundershower
> (*Tao*, 23)

Celebrate your success, but do so with humility. Say your piece, and then say no more. Be respectful of your opponent, and when it comes time to present an ultimatum in your next campaign, you can do so from a position of strength. Your opponent will know that you have exercised restraint in your previous endeavours, and can negotiate with you knowing that you will do the same again.

More will be said on this in the chapter "Step Up to Seven Stars." For now, let's remember that restraint is a cornerstone of the Tao; that to "succeed by not forcing" and to "lead by not contending" is one of the riddles that we must unravel in our attempt to follow the Way.

And remember that Lao Tzu says to "simply step back and be watchful." Be watchful. Winning isn't enough. Ensuring that we don't backslide after we've made progress on our campaigns is equally important. We need to keep our eye on our victories so that we don't have to win them all over again. That's why, after we've won, we might respectfully step back and be attentive to any challenges that arise.

Compassion

The second treasure of the *Tao te Ching* is compassion. The dictionary defines compassion as "deep awareness of the suffering of another coupled with the wish to relieve it." Lao Tzu describes the sage as being "saturated with compassion."

How do we apply that compassion in our daily work as advocates? I think there are three outlets: our colleagues, those who we meet in passing on a daily basis, and those we regard as our opponents.

Here is what His Holiness the XIV Dalai Lama says about compassion:

> Genuine compassion and attachment are
> contradictory. According to the Buddhist practice,
> to develop genuine compassion you must first
> practice the meditation of equalization and
> equanimity, detaching oneself from those people
> who are very close to you. Then, you must
> remove negative feelings toward your enemies.
> All sentient beings should be looked on as equal.
> On that basis, you can gradually develop genuine
> compassion for all of them. It must be said that
> genuine compassion is not like pity or a feeling that

113

others are somehow lower than yourself. Rather,
with genuine compassion you view others as more
important than yourself.[3]

It's easy for us to regard our colleagues with compassion. Those who we work with are akin to us. We understand their troubles because we share those difficulties with them. We struggle and sacrifice together.

If we're in a position of authority in an organization, being "saturated with compassion" is an important part of the job we do on a day-to-day basis. I believe that the basis of compassion is simply trying to understand the essence of other people's lives: their jobs, sorrows, triumphs, setbacks. At the best of times, and when under the gentle guidance of a skilled leader, our work together might be a place where we try to heal from whatever wounds we have suffered. By seeking first to understand, we can then extend our guidance to help alleviate that suffering.

Don't get me wrong. I'm not advocating the office or the boardroom table as a Gestalt therapy session. I generally shun primal screaming during staff meetings and advise against replacing your computer work station with a Freudian couch. I'm merely suggesting that we pay attention. If we know the people who we work with well, we can see when they are experiencing grief. We can help them to understand our compassion for them with simple gestures and the reassurance that we all suffer from time to time.

I believe that many of us activists were drawn to our movement because of our suffering. I know of some working in Vancouver's impoverished downtown east side who have lived on the street themselves, and whose pain and suffering during that time propelled them to take on the plight of the homeless. And children of addicts sometimes turn to advocacy to do for humanity what they could not for their parents.

Sometimes our suffering is completely unrelated, but we choose advocacy as the vehicle for our healing.

That's a lot of suffering for a movement to bear, and it can some-

---

3. His Holiness the Dalai Lama, *The Art of Living: A Guide to Contentment, Joy and Fulfillment*, London: Thorsons, an imprint of HarperCollins, 2001, p. 101

times become overwhelming. The depression and despair that at times can become rampant in our movement is born of this suffering.

Suffering *can* cause us to act out of fear. Our hearts *can* grow heavy with the weight of the world: we've lost another campaign to protect ancient forests; our effort to get people off the streets hasn't worked and it's twenty below zero. We fear the consequences. People might die. We take it personally.

Fortunately, we have an almost unlimited capacity for compassion which we can use to enable our friends and those we work with to rise above our suffering and work effectively to protect what we love. As leaders, we can act out compassionately to help our colleagues use their suffering to become stronger advocates, and helping them find a way to act with courage, not fear.

Again, the Dalai Lama:

> I also think that the greater the force of your
> altruistic attitude toward sentient beings, the
> more courageous you become. The greater your
> courage, the less you feel prone to discouragement
> and loss of hope. Therefore, compassion is also
> a source of inner strength. With increased inner
> strength it is possible to develop firm determination
> and with determination there is a greater chance of
> success, no matter what the obstacles there
> may be.[4]

Lao Tzu said much the same thing 2,500 years ago:

> Act with courage out of daring
>   and you will fail
> Act with courage out of love
>   and you will succeed
> (*Tao*, 73)

It's easy to be compassionate with friends and colleagues. Most of us find this to be a natural extension of our daily lives. But what about acquaintances? What about with strangers?

---

4. Ibid, p. 120

At the post office, I practice compassion; sometimes at the bank as well. I'm not always successful. Waiting in line tries my patience (and I am not a patient man, remember). In these circumstances, it's easy for me to forget the humanity around me and become impatient or short with people.

Recently I started saying something in my head before engaging with people even in these casual settings. The word I say is *Namaste*. It's from the Hindu tradition which means, "The spirit in me greets the spirit in you," or "The divine in me greets the divine in you."

"The gesture *Namaste* represents the belief that there is a Divine spark within each of us that is located in the heart chakra," says Aadil Palkhivala. "The gesture is an acknowledgment of the soul in one by the soul in another. 'Nama' means bow, 'as' means I, and 'te' means you. Therefore, *Namaste* literally means 'bow me you' or 'I bow to you.'"[5]

According to the Hindu tradition, it recognizes the equality of all, and pays honour to the sacredness of one another. It is generally performed with a deep bow and with hands pressed together as if in prayer.

When I'm greeting the bank teller or a postal clerk, I generally say it to myself, omitting any prostration.

The thought that we are equal and that each of us is sacred helps me check any impatience I might be feeling. It helps me to be compassionate at best, and friendly at the very least. If I was feeling tired or frustrated beforehand – maybe things were going badly at the office, or some bad piece of news just arrived – I often come away feeling better for having extended a little bit of love and friendship towards people I come in contact with casually.

Compassion with friends, colleagues, and even strangers is one thing; compassion towards those we consider our opponent is another altogether. Lao Tzu says:

> Always remember that your opponent is human
>   like you
> Treat him with love and compassion
> (*Tao*, 31)

---

5. Aadil Palkhivala, writing in the online version of the *Yoga Journal*, yogajournal.com.

First, we cannot be compassionate with those we consider to be our enemy. It may be that in warfare the word enemy is appropriate, but not in the work we do as activists. The dictionary describes an enemy as "one who feels hatred toward, intends injury to, or opposes the interests of another; a foe."

It goes without saying that we often oppose the interests of another, but I believe there is no room for hatred in our work as activists. And there is definitely no room for the intent to injure.

Anger might be what fuels our work as activists when we first suffer the loss of something important to us. When someone we love dies on the job and we become activists for workplace safety, or when a stranger is imprisoned or killed for political beliefs and we take up their case seeking justice, anger might be our initial motivation, but it will not help us carry on the cause for long. Anger and rage burn white hot, but they do not last, and when they have burned out, there is nothing left to propel us forward.

If we can replace anger with compassion, the way we approach our challenges as activists changes.

I consider those on the other side of the equation my opponents. I oppose them, simply put.

Stroller Diplomacy

In the 1990s, Karen Mahon was one of the leaders in the campaign to protect ancient forests on the coast of British Columbia. Karen was a firebrand activist who campaigned internationally in her effort to protect the cloud-soaked old growth forests and the wild creatures who lived in them. Campaigning with Greenpeace Canada, Karen helped orchestrate international pressure on the BC government and on logging companies such as Weyerhaeuser and MacMillan Bloedel, which were logging the old growth forests at breakneck speed. The two sides in the acrimonious debate were completely polarized. In the mid-1990s, the dispute was bitter and divisive with no end in sight.

In their effort to win protection of British Columbia's old growth forests, Greenpeace had sought to create a dichotomous distinction between itself and MacMillan Bloedel, with Greenpeace wearing the white hat, and MacBlo the black. In an effort to repair an internationally tarred image, the forestry giant hired Linda Cody to respond to the environmentalists. Linda quickly became a vice-president at the company, and as Karen puts it, her job was to "make us go away." The two women never spoke except in heated exchanges in the media.

And then one warm Sunday morning, Karen – a new mother – was walking to her neighbourhood café in the west side of Vancouver when she had an encounter that changed the way she advocated for the forests.

As Karen tells it, "I had a brand new Peg Perego stroller. It was navy blue with white polka dots. I was out to get a cup of coffee. That's when I saw Linda Cody walking towards me on the same side of the street. And she was pushing a Peg Perego stroller too!" Karen was certain that Linda had seen her, so it was too late to make a dash across the busy street.

Linda was with her husband, and when they were finally face to face, she turned and said, "Hugh, I'd like you to meet my archenemy from Greenpeace, Karen Mahon."

They stood on the street and chatted. It turned out that the women lived two blocks from one another. Their children were the same age. They frequented the same local "mother's" café. Linda invited Karen to meet her for coffee as a way of toning down the rhetoric that had reached a fevered pitch on both sides of the debate. "I told her I'd have to get back to her," Karen says. "They were threatening to sue us, after all."

But the two women did have coffee, which began a dialogue that eventually led to agreements between MacBlo and Greenpeace on a number of important forestry issues. Karen and Linda came to regard each other with compassion, the kind of understanding that comes from shared motivations as human beings. That chance meeting on a Sunday afternoon in Vancouver led to what is now known as "stroller diplomacy."

Sometime later, Karen left Greenpeace, the stress of the international campaign to protect BC's forests taking its toll on her health. But she didn't leave the movement. Today, she is the executive director of the Hollyhock Leadership Institute, and she, along with the Institute's talented staff, is teaching a new generation of activists to be effective *and* compassionate at the same time.

Hating our opponents will not help us solve the problems that motivate us as activists. It will only breed more contempt and lead to misunderstanding. None of this helps us. And, in the long run, it causes us harm, and it causes our movement great damage.

We make mistakes when we act out of anger or hatred. We speak rashly; we present ourselves poorly to the public. Very few of us are motivated by the anger of others. The first time I watched a tape of myself being interviewed on television, my own anger was palpable. I remember thinking, that guy is crazy! If *I* could feel it, certainly others could. I made a conscious effort after that to be more calm and compassionate when giving interviews. I didn't start thumbing crystals or wearing beads; I just tried to take the edge off my anger by being conscious of it.

It would be naïve to assume that if we set aside our anger or hatred, others will naturally follow suit. Those who have been on a picket line or have blockaded a logging road know that hatred can be visited upon us even if we project love and compassion. Sometimes such hatred even results in physical harm.

I know a man who was once assaulted after taking part in a peaceful protest. Though capable of defending himself rather well, he chose not to fight the two thugs who then beat him up. This is an extreme case where we choose to counter force with compassion. What might we learn from it? When two forces oppose each other, each must push harder to outdo the other.

What are we to do when confronted with violence and hatred?

L.O.V.E.

In the late 1960s, Brock Evans was leading the fight to protect ancient forests in the Pacific Northwest. Brock is one of the patriarchs of North America's movement to protect wilderness, wildlife, and the human connection to all that is wild. He has been a mentor to generations of advocates. He is humble and unassuming as a friend while fierce and uncompromising as an adversary.

Brock's efforts in the Pacific Northwest eventually led to the creation of Cascades National Park and many other advances in protection of areas in Washington, Oregon, and California. At the time,

Brock was working for David Brower as the Sierra Club's Pacific Northwest representative, and was organizing volunteers to attend Forest Service hearings into the future of the region's magnificent Sitka spruce and rugged mountains. Dozens of passionate, fearless speakers appeared at the hearings to speak in defence of the unique and threatened landscape, often times driving hundreds of miles, taking no pay, and suffering the insults and jeers of those who disagreed with them.

During the course of the hearings, Brock became friends with the Wenatchee National Forest's supervisor. Although on opposite sides of the debate, the men respected each other enough that one night after the hearings, they sat down at a local bar for a beer or two. As Brock tells it, he noticed that the Forest Service supervisor was drinking a little faster than he was, and he let him get ahead in the bottle count.

Unable to contain his curiosity any longer, the supervisor leaned over to Brock and in a raspy voice said, "Evans, I don't get it. I don't understand what your people have going for them. They drive hundreds of miles. They volunteer. They are passionate and committed. What do they have that our people don't?"

Brock said, "I don't think you'll understand it."

But the supervisor persisted.

Brock said, "If you really want to know, I'll spell it out. It's really very simple. It's just four letters: L.O.V.E. Love."

What draws us to defend places like Cascades National Park in Washington State, or to risk our lives defending those suffering from disease and famine in war-torn Africa, is sometimes a complex mixture of love and anger, passion and fear.

No matter what propels us to become activists in the first place, it is love that sustains and nurtures us over the long term. Hatred burns too hot to last, and fear has an insidious way of burrowing into our hearts and souls and stealing from us our ability to act out of courage. Only our love for the places we are trying to protect, our love for one another, can provide the fuel to sustain a lifetime of effective activism.

"Some day, after we have mastered the winds, the waves, the tides and gravity, we shall harness the energies of love," said French philosopher and Jesuit priest Pierre Teilhard de Chardin. "Then, for the second time in the history of the world, man will have discovered fire."

Jonathan Star translates the third treasure of the *Tao te Ching* as love. According to Star, many Ancient Chinese characters have multiple meanings. In his *Definitive Edition* of the *Tao te Ching* he translates the character for "tz'u" found in verse sixty-seven as "love / deep love / affection / compassion" and elsewhere as being "loving / affectionate / compassionate / merciful."[6]

Others say the third treasure is "motherly love."

A few years ago, I attended a leadership training course offered by the Hollyhock Leadership Institute. The training took place at Hollyhock on Cortes Island, off the coast of British Columbia. I'll talk about this again later because no other single place on Earth has been as important to my growth as a leader and an activist as Hollyhock has.

The Leadership Institute offered sessions on communications and campaign strategy and working with First Nations people. There was no session at that leadership institute on love, no "Using Love to protect the Earth, 101." But after a week with other dedicated and inspirational activists learning together, struggling with difficult ideas and sometimes failing, but always supporting each other, we were asked to write something on a piece of paper that would be mailed to us in six months. It's an idea that tickles me; getting a note from your past self in the present. I thought about it for a moment, and instead of writing something I drew this:

When I received that letter from myself six months later, I did indeed need to be reminded to "move forward with more love." There has never been a moment in my life as an activist that I haven't needed to be reminded of that.

If we are acting out of anger or fear, we can become convinced

---

6. Lao Tzu, *Tao te Ching: The Definitive Edition*, trans. Jonathan Star, New York: Penguin, p. 232-33

that nearly anything is justifiable in our work to protect what we love. Anger and fear lead us to believe that we must win at any cost. While advocating for wild places and the wild creatures who live there, I have come across activists who believe that we must win at any cost. I was once criticized for choosing not to link Wildcanada. net's website to a site that promoted hatred towards US Fish and Wildlife Service personnel over the issue of wolf control in the United States. And while I think the Fish and Wildlife Service do a pretty rotten job protecting wolves in the US, I'm not going to be party to the rancorous anger that some promote towards them.

Simply put, I no longer believe that the ends justify the means. I say this for two reasons. First, I haven't seen any evidence that personal attacks, violence, or hatred have any positive effect. Second, I believe that the opposite is true: that the means can shape the eventual end. The Dalai Lama provides an excellent example of this. Nobody has greater reason for hatred than his Holiness. But what does the Dalai Lama advocate? Love and compassion.

The *Tao te Ching* says:

> To take a step back is to follow the Tao
> To meet hatred and force with love and yielding
> this is the way of the Tao
> (*Tao*, 40)

If the Dalai Lama can advocate with love after so many of his compatriots have died as a result of Chinese rule, surely we can use love in our own work.

When acting out of love, we treat our opponents as equals regardless of the outcome of our campaigns. We can and continue to disagree with them, and we can work hard to ensure that what we believe to be right prevails, but throughout the effort, and even after it is over, we must remember Lao Tzu's three treasures.

Anger is a natural emotion. My son Rio reminds me of this. When something doesn't go his way, he gets angry, and then he lets it go. If we didn't feel anger over the flawed decisions that our leaders make about climate change, or decisions to engage in illegal and diversionary wars against sovereign nations, I'd be worried. But feeling anger is one thing; acting out of anger is another. We can exercise restraint when we feel anger and channel that energy so that instead we can act out of love.

Here's an inspirational example from Salt Spring Island, British Columbia. As on many of the Gulf Islands in BC, logging threatens the natural ecosystem and the way of life of many islanders. Developers come to the island and buy up private land, opting to clear-cut log it. Many local residents oppose such logging because of its impact on local wildlife populations, on alternative economies such as agriculture and tourism, on the island's fragile water supply. Early in this decade, the debate on Salt Spring reached a fevered pitch when the developer who wanted to log a sensitive piece of land came to the island to meet with local activists about his plans. It would have been understandable if he was greeted with jeers and anger. But he wasn't. He was welcomed by local conservation and community activists with open arms.

There are many who would feel downright vexed by such a display for one's opponent. Don't express your love in a way that makes you feel uncomfortable. Hugs are not for everyone. (Here I am thinking of my friends who work with the ranching community in Wyoming, Montana, and Alberta....) But what you hold in your heart is revealed on your face, and in your body language, your tone of voice, what you say, and how you treat others.

After a lengthy and creative campaign that included a Lady Godiva-inspired horseback ride through the streets of Vancouver, Salt Spring Island residents celebrated the protection of many parts of their island. The effort to protect many special places on Salt Spring and throughout the Gulf Islands continues, but it is much bolstered by the compassionate stance of island residents.

Remember, we are trying to resolve our battles so we won't have to fight them again in a few years' time. This simply won't happen if there is bitterness or anger on either side, or if a party feels vengeful or hard-done-by.

> The sage activist
> never gloats over her victory

and does not allow herself to act out of anger
The sage leader
prefers to win without causing shame or bitterness
and lead her colleagues by serving them

This is the virtue of humility,
This is the power of harnessing the strength of
     others
This is the value of love
(*Tao*, 68)

Looking Inward

So far in this chapter on the three treasures, our focus has been out-ward. Consider also ourselves: do we exercise restraint in how we treat our own bodies and hearts? Do we extend compassion – the awareness of our own suffering and our wish to relieve it – to our-selves? Do we love ourselves?

As advocates we must be selfless. I know many brilliant people who could make bags of money in the corporate sector, but who have chosen to dedicate themselves instead to their causes. The hours are long, the pay sucks, and rarely do we achieve the sort of absolute victory that allows us to feel pride and satisfaction that we have accomplished our mission. But it is also true that we can be our own worst critics. We take our losses personally. We berate ourselves over certain decisions. In short, we beat ourselves up, sometimes far worse than our harshest opponents do.

"Love the earth, its creatures, and its people as you love your-self," advises Lao Tzu. As we walk the sometimes obscured path towards being advocates with love as our sword and compassion as our shield, we must first turn our love inwards.

This dilemma was on my mind when I was back in Burlington a few years ago, visiting family and doing some work in nearby To-ronto. I had some free time one afternoon, and as I'm given to fits of nostalgia, I went for a drive in my old neighbourhood.

Driving past the houses where my family lived after the divorce, I could see the dark forest beyond. I needed to walk in those woods again. I parked the car and hopped the fence that separated Upper

Middle Road from the woods and felt again their familiar coolness.

I had to find Phaedrus, the stalwart beech that was the centre of these woods for me. But the four-lane highway had cut the woods into two tracts. The new opening in the formerly dense canopy allowed a lot more light into the woods, creating a tangle of new undergrowth. Where once I could stroll across the forest floor without impediment, now I had to push my way through tall shrubs. The creek was nothing more than a dry ditch, its water diverted into culverts for the sake of the highway. There were few sounds save the hiss and groan of cars.

When I was young, I could walk to Phaedrus from any point in the woods and arrive at his base unerringly. Maybe fifteen years was too long to be away. Maybe I was disoriented by the fragmentation of this already tiny remnant of forest.

I wandered in circles for a while, marvelling at how a place once so familiar could become so foreign. And then when I was certain that I wouldn't find Phaedrus, he was before me. Still impressive, he had lost several huge branches that lay in tatters among the new dense undergrowth. Looking up, I couldn't tell how much life was left in this old beech.

I'm not given to displays of ceremony or ritual, but I did press my hands against Phaedrus that afternoon. I gave thanks for the shelter and sanctuary that he and his dominion gave me as a troubled teen, and for the path that he had set me on.

Remembering how we came to be activists helps us to honour our journey, keeps alive the flame and passion that we felt in the beginning as we struggle through the present. Underneath the fear and anger that sometimes drive us to take up a cause, there is something that is often forgotten amidst the petty issues of bureaucracy or organizational politics. It is our anchor to our purpose as activists. It is love.

4

RETREAT TO RIDE TIGER

Acting without Action

Do not force action,
instead allow action to arise on its own
and follow its course
(*Tao*, 48)

The sun hasn't yet pierced the horizon when I walk down from the lodge at Hollyhock, on Cortes Island, to the sand and pebble beach. I step lightly over the logs and driftwood that separate the beach from the grounds and orchard, and find a place to sit quietly amid the driftwood as the day begins. I sip a tall cup of tea and watch a great blue heron sweep like a prehistoric vision across the sky. After a few minutes I kick off my Tevas, root my feet in the sand, and bow toward the ocean. I practice Tai Chi, breathing in deeply the ocean air, taking it into my lungs and into every cell in my body.

I come to Retreat to Ride Tiger and I see in it a metaphor. I step back, push my hands to either side palms out, press, and pause. Then, from that stillness the way forward seems clear, and I move ahead, following the natural course of action as it presents itself. The sun splits the morning cloud and bathes the beach in honey-coloured light. From the stillness of the night, the day begins.

Sometimes we must step back from our daily activities in order to see the best course to take. As activists, we are people of action. An activist acts. Some of us fear that if we are not busy doing something for our cause, we are backsliding. That fear is made all the more complex by our ego and a perverse tendency we have as activists to drive ourselves relentlessly, even to the point of self-destruction. Sometimes the best course may be to take no action. Sometimes, taking no action at all is the way to accomplish our goals.

This is another of Lao Tzu's paradoxes: "And so it is said: The path towards the light seems dark ... real power yields ... resolve seems supple."

I know that some of my colleagues will scratch their heads at this notion. "You want us to sit back and do nothing? Just let things happen? That loose screw in your head seems to finally have jiggled free." They may be right. Not acting is anathema to advocates with a sense of urgency and duty. But after many years, I am beginning to see what Lao Tzu means when he says that "action is born from stillness."

We in civil society are very good at *doing* things – at inserting ourselves, sometimes aggressively, into the debate at every point. I'm suggesting that we are capable of acting more strategically, more effectively, if first we step back.

There are two elements to Lao Tzu's "action without action." The first is allowing action to arise of its own accord. The second is taking appropriate action when it does. Like Tai Chi's Retreat to Ride Tiger, there is a time to step back and pause, and a time to push forward and act in an appropriate way.

Understanding the concept of no-action or action-without-acting will be easier outside, so here I will issue an invitation to you. After you have read this chapter, please put this book down and go outdoors and find some free-flowing water – the ocean, a creek, a river or lake – even a reasonably clean ditch with some run-off will do.

If you want to understand the concept of action without acting, you will need to watch how water moves across the face of the Earth.

As a high school student, I used to sit on the bank of a tiny creek in that woodlot behind our townhouse and watch the water that mysteriously emerged from a culvert beneath our housing complex. On a number of occasions, I tried to find the source and destination of that water, without success. It appeared from a culvert and disappeared under a four-lane road from which it never re-emerged. But there it was, cutting through the tiny swath of woods, sparkling on the rocks, and tripping over the roots of silver maple, American beech, and white pine, only to disappear once again under the road and down into the storm sewers of the city.

For a kilometre or so, however, it was the creek it had been before the City of Burlington expanded, entombing it below concrete and condominiums.

It's proof that no matter where you live, you'll find some free-flowing water. That's where you should go when you wish to understand the concept of *wu wei* – action without acting.

Before we moved to Toronto's suburbs, my family and I lived in the rural Ontario community of Porcupine, just outside of Timmins. There was a small creek that trickled through my family's property there; it wove between large, spreading willows near the back of our land, and then was hedged by aspens and smaller shrubs as it cut towards our house. In the summer, my friends and I built crude forts in the arms of one of the larger trees, and closer to home, my father cut a log in half and bridged the tiny creek. I would sometimes sit on that rough bridge and dangle a fishing line there. It was a great place to be a child.

Children understand the power of water. They are drawn to it. And though the lessons are not explicit at the time, from it we learn many of life's teachings. These lessons are often taught with gentle patience, as my creek taught me about stillness.

Sometimes they are not so gentle. In Porcupine in the spring, when several feet of snow still covered the ground, I was quite terrified of the engorged ditches that lined the street we lived on. To a timid little boy, the water's power was frightening. I knew nothing would stand in its way, certainly not my flesh, as it answered gravity's call to Hudson's Bay, 700 kilometres to the north.

Of Its Own Accord

As adults, we can remember water's lessons as long as we listen.

The first practice is to allow the right action to arise of its own accord.

> The sage activist allows events to unfold
> He knows how to gently shape things as they come
> and step aside to avoid others
> He lets the Tao guide him
> (*Tao*, 45)

Always being in motion, always taking some action, eclipses the mind's ability to see a new, creative path forward. Sometimes we must stand back, allowing space for the right action to "arise of its own accord." Then we can seize opportunities that can only be created when we provide enough mental and physical space. This element of *wu wei* is not so much about doing nothing as about not always being busy.

Alan Watts starts the chapter on *wu wei* in his book *Tao: The Watercourse Way* by quoting Gia-Fu Feng and Jane English's translation of the *Tao te Ching*:

"'The Tao does nothing, and yet nothing is left undone.' These famous words of Lao Tzu obviously cannot be taken in their literal sense, for the principle of 'non-action' is not to be considered inertia, laziness, laissez-faire, or mere passivity. Among the several meanings of *wei* are to be, to do, to make, to practice.... But in the context of Taoist writings it quite clearly means forcing, meddling, and artifice – in other words, trying to act against the grain. Thus *wu wei* as 'not forcing' is what we mean by going with the grain...."[1]

Chuang Tzu, a contemporary of Lao Tzu who contributed significantly to the body of Taoist literature, elaborates on Lao Tzu's entreaty to allow action to arise of its own accord, saying, "The non-action of the wise man is not inaction," but instead is "the level of heaven and earth." In other words, we should find stillness and balance before we act. Stillness, says Chuang Tzu, is the source of our

---

1. Alan Watts, *Tao: The Watercourse Way*, New York: Pantheon Books, 1975, p. 75-76

action. From it grows our appropriate response to the events of the world. But it is only from this stillness that we find the correct action to take. "So from the sage's emptiness, stillness arises. From stillness, action. From action, attainment."[2]

"The Chinese, and Taoist, term which we translate as nature is *tzu-jan*, meaning the spontaneous, that which is so of itself," says Alan Watts.[3] *Tzu-jan*, then, is the natural response to things; it is the appropriate action arising of its own accord.

But our conditioning rebels against this natural way. Something in us needs to control the outcome and the course of events, even though much of nature rejects that notion. In expending so much energy – both physical and mental – attempting to control situations, we exhaust ourselves, leaving little else for the things that we can do something about.

"I claim not to have controlled events," said President Abraham Lincoln at the close of the American Civil War, "but confess plainly that events have controlled me."[4] We can rarely control events, but we can always control how we respond to them. That is, if we reserve our energy by not trying to control what is beyond our reach.

In our working lives, we hurry from one activity to the next. But are we really making more progress when we're always rushing ahead?

Better to be still, and allow action to stem from that stillness. A better use of our time between periods of action would be to step out of the office or away from the home computer and take a walk or go for a bike ride.

> Be still
> Wait for the right moment to act
>
> All of our work has a common source
> All of our effort returns us to that point
> If you know this in your heart

---

2. Thomas Merton, *The Way of Chuang Tzu*, New York: New Directions Press, 1965, p. 80

3. Alan Watts, *Tao: The Watercourse Way*, New York: Pantheon Books, 1975, p. 42

4. Abraham Lincoln, "Letter to Alberta G. Hodges," April 4, 1864, *http://showcase.netins.net/web/creative/lincoln/speeches/hodges.htm*

you will be patient
tolerant of others
respectful of their opinions
amused by the uproar
able to respond with dignity
(*Tao*, 16)

Lao Tzu says that the sage who practices *wu wei* "can accomplish anything, because he has stopped trying to accomplish everything."

Think of a time when you stepped back from the chaos around you and let your own response to the situation "arise of its own accord." What was the outcome?

I know that my best ideas come when I take time out in my day to step back. That's when the elusive way forward suddenly becomes clear.

When recently I stepped out of the formal leadership role that I held for six years, I noticed almost immediately that I gained a clarity of thought not possible during the intensity of the previous period. Instead of fretting about cash flows and deadlines, I was able to see broader issues that had always perplexed me and the movement that I serve, but that had been overlooked because of my constant motion. Stepping back gave me a much clearer picture of the wider, systemic problems we faced.

We need to find ways to allow our leaders to see the big picture without having to relinquish their leadership roles. This should be germane to the role of leaders, not incidental to it.

Allowing the right action to rise of its own accord also entails knowing the difference between doing enough and doing too much: enough to accomplish the task, but not so much that more than what is needed is said, or that the moment is lost. Sometimes we feel when talking that we should have stopped a few sentences, or a few minutes, sooner. Good reporters have learned the trick of silence as a prompt, knowing that their interviewee will keep talking to fill that void, and often reveal more than they intend. We need to learn that trick too.

There are times when the right action to take is to take no action at all. We can be lured into a debate over petty issues by our opponents as a means of discrediting our cause or distracting us from our real work. We don't have to engage. We can choose no action or find another appropriate one to take.

Right Action

The second half of the "non-action" equation is allowing the "right" action to arise of its own accord.

> Therefore the sage activist
> acts without doing a thing
> and guides her colleagues without uttering a word
> Triumph and troubles present themselves and she
> lets them come
> They disappear and she lets go
> (*Tao*, 2)

Stephen Mitchell, in the notes to his translation of the *Tao te Ching*, says in response to this second verse: "Her actions are appropriate responses. Thus they are effortless." [5]

The *wu wei* of activism is to see conflicts and challenges as a river views a rock in its flow. Sometimes we can go around the obstacle, and sometimes we can go over it. Sometimes, as with the reviled Glen Canyon Dam on the Arizona/Utah border, we must simply wait. We step back and allow the right action to arise on its own and follow its course.

Constructed at the end of the big dam building era in the United States in the 1950s, the Glen Canyon Dam drowned what at the time was a nearly unknown stretch of the Colorado River. For nearly half a century, opponents of the Glen Canyon Dam have fought to have the floodgates opened and the wild Colorado River released from behind the imprisoning concrete. And while the public agitated, the river waited. And then in the spring of 2005, with the entire Colorado Plateau suffering through a five-year drought, the wild and free Colorado River emerged once again. Although it might be temporary, the Colorado River has shown that patience and persistence pays off.

---

5. Stephen Mitchell, *A New English Version of the Tao te Ching*, New York: HarperCollins, 1988, p. 87

> Our finest efforts will flow like a river
> Rocks, boulders, and even a dam, in time, will
>   succumb to the current
> We can learn to act with such patience and
>   perseverance
> In doing so, be like the Tao
> (*Tao*, 8)

Sceptics will say that this is yielding to opposition: it appears that way. But it is only temporary acquiescence. The river takes appropriate action. Its efforts to overcome obstacles are effortless, measured, and ultimately effective.

As an example, advocates for restoring the Colorado River through Glen Canyon and downstream through the Grand Canyon have seized on the natural events that led to the draw-down of the reservoir at Glen Canyon, and are using this opportunity to press their cause as never before. When the river emerged, its supporters responded with appropriate action: the application of pressure at the right time and the right place. They were demonstrating the *wu wei* of advocacy.

Lao Tzu reminds us again and again that the "soft shall overcome the hard." This takes time. In our impatience, born of our fear and our passion and our anger, we often rush in. We have to be gentle with ourselves at these times. We're driven to make change. That's why we are advocates. But we can learn to act *with* rather than *against*.

Think of *wu wei* as acting *with* something. Following Lao Tzu's teaching, we redirect an event to happen in a different way. The martial art of Aikido – and for those who have studied it long enough, Tai Chi – is about redirecting your opponent's energy to use it against them.

But there are other schools of martial arts. In Tai Kwon Do, for instance, when someone throws a punch, you use your hand or arm (or foot, as crazy as that sounds) to block it. Two forces meet and the greater force prevails. In Aikido, when someone throws a punch you step aside and sweep their arm around, redirecting their energy to bring them to the ground. Or you add to the energy of their punch and use just a few pounds of pressure to snap their elbow. Crack.

You use the force of the attack against you to defend yourself. After a session of Tai Kwon Do, I was often bruised and sore from trying to counter one force with another. I even ended up in the hospital once with cracked ribs after stepping into, rather than away from, an opponent's careless kick.

After Aikido, I was sometimes sore, but it was usually from being tossed to the ground like a rag doll too many times. I might use Aikido to defend myself from thugs in a dark alley. Then I'd ask myself what the hell I was doing in the dark alley in the first place.

Another way of thinking about the redirection of energy is this: if you were going to try to stop a boulder rolling downhill, would you step in front of it and act against it? Or would you run along beside it and try to redirect it to where it could do no harm?

In many ways, this is a mental shift, or a change in attitude. When we see ourselves in these struggles, what image comes to mind? Do we imagine ourselves in a clash of wills, or on a battlefield? Or do we see ourselves practicing Aikido, using a well-placed and well-timed piece of strategy to counter our opponent's energy and thus upend them?

As we'll see when we discuss the Tao of strategy in the chapter "Appear to Close Entrance," it is often the simple actions that have the greatest impact.

> Simplicity is the root of many things
> some of which, in the master's hands
> can be used to create monumental change
>
> Start by doing little
> to accomplish much
> (*Tao*, 28)

The ocean can be a particularly powerful teacher. Sometimes it rages, sometimes it is serene, but always it finds its balance point with the rise and fall of the tide.

I love to walk in the intertidal zone with my son Rio to see what the sea has offered up. Sometimes we find schools of jellyfish washed up on the beach, other times we discover a graveyard of Dungeness crabs, their bodies washed ashore and picked clean by gulls or ravens. Sometimes the shoreline is ankle-deep in seaweed, buzzing with flies and other insects attracted to this saltwater salad. Turning over rocks, we find tiny hermit crabs and larger porcelain and purple shore crabs, and many, many mysteries.

Rio always finds something to marvel at. The simple things astonish him. The way he hunches down and studies the universe inside the tide line in turn amazes me.

His attention to these microcosms reminds me to pay attention to the lessons learned at the seashore, or at the river's edge. This is the Tao speaking to me plainly and in the simplest terms it can find.

On many of the Vancouver Island beaches that I frequent with my family, tiny creeks cut across the sand and rocks. Sometimes we spend hours constructing dams of stones and logs and mud in these streams. The water backs up. It searches out the weak places in the construction and trickles through. It goes around. Or it pools and waits, patiently and gently pressing on the constriction, and then suddenly pushes through. In time, the water flows freely once again.

Or it finds a new path altogether, seeking out the lowest places. Construct a dam and the water simply changes course. Sometimes we give it a little help, digging with a stick to connect low-lying places on the beach – but most often the water simply finds its way to the ocean on its own.

That moment when the water finds the weak spot and pushes through the dam of sticks and mud to the sea is the moment we must try to find in our work. That is the moment we move from stillness to action. That is what the advocates for a wild and free Colorado River are doing in their fight against Glen Canyon Dam.

Maybe the only difference between our dams of sticks and mud on the beach and those constructed by the Bureau of Reclamation on the Colorado River is how long they will take to fall.

Lao Tzu says the way is like the ocean, because all streams flow downhill to the sea. That is why Alan Watts refers to the Tao as *The Watercourse Way*.

Action without acting is following the natural course – the flow; it is not about doing nothing.

Father Thomas Merton, in his book on Chuang Tzu, retells the story of Prince Wen Hui, who sees his cook carving up an ox and marvels at how easy the task appears. He asks the servant about his technique. There is no technique, replies the servant. He only follows the Tao.

The cook tells him that when he first began to cut up oxen, he saw the animal as one mass. But after three years, he no longer saw this mass; he saw the distinctions.

> But now, I see nothing
> With the eye. My whole being
> Apprehends
> My senses are idle. The spirit
> Free to work without plan
> Follows its own instinct
> Guided by natural line,
> By the secret opening, the hidden space,
> my cleaver finds its own way.
> I cut through no joint, chop no bone.
>
> True, there are sometimes tough joints. I feel them
>   coming,
> I slow down, I watch closely,
> Hold back, barely move the blade,
> And whump! The part falls away
> Landing like a clod of earth.[6]

Aside from horrifying the vegetarians and animal rights activists reading this book, this lesson from Chuang Tzu reveals some of the mastery of both taking no action and following the natural course of action – letting the right course of action arise of its own accord. If like so many others, the cook had just hacked away at the ox, he would have expended much more energy with a less satisfying result. His blade would have been dulled. He would not have had the

---

6. Thomas Merton, *The Way of Chuang Tzu*, New York: New Directions Press, 1965, p. 45

energy or tools to move onto his next task.

> The sage activist does nothing
> yet nothing remains undone
> The ordinary person is always doing
> and there is always more to do
> (*Tao*, 38)

The cook did next to nothing, but his task was accomplished with ease. (The story just wouldn't be the same if the cook was cutting up tofu, or bean sprouts, would it?)

The lesson of the ox is simple: follow the natural pattern of things. As the cook followed the natural pattern of bone and sinew, we activists must also find the natural pattern in our work. But while the lesson might be simple, developing the discipline is not. It is important to note here that the cook spent years training to reach a point where he could achieve this grace. To reach a place of *wu wei* – spontaneous ease of execution – is by no means an easy path.

Looking for and seeing this pattern in our work means spending time each day to map out its shape and form in our labours.

We have to ask questions. Who is really making the decision to dam this river? If a federal politician is responsible, will expending our organization's meagre resources on a political lobby campaign in Ottawa or Washington result in the decision we want? Or is the local politician driving the decision to dam the river because his constituents are complaining that they need water to irrigate their crops? Is he vulnerable at election time? Might the local reeve of the municipality or county commissioner be pressuring him? Or is it a combination of all of these?

Influence mapping is part of many organizations' campaign strategy. We can ask: "Where can we make a single cut, or as few cuts as necessary, in order to ensure the decision goes the way we want it to?"

Making as few cuts as necessary – taking the appropriate action – means that volunteers stay energized. It means there are resources left over to follow up with decision makers, ensuring that they don't stray from our desired outcome in the near future. It leaves resourc-

es available for important community development work so that we can address the root cause of the problem, such as drought conditions faced by farmers in the example of the dam.

Engaging in a campaign without first determining the appropriate action can really stir up a hornet's nest of controversy and acrimony. Sometimes this is necessary to get the results that we need, but not always.

Taking the appropriate action helps replace random aggressive energy with more thoughtful, focused effort. This helps keep our hearts from growing weary despite the struggles that we face.

"An important point to realize," says Cloudwalking Owl, "is that coming into a situation with a specific notion of what is going on and what needs to be done can be totally disastrous too. When practicing *toi sow* [push hands in Tai Chi Chuan], the point is to develop the ability to instantly feel a situation and flow with it unconsciously. This is an important skill for activists to learn. It is the exact opposite of creating a campaign and making big plans. Think of it as the difference between the way the Renaissance masters painted and the way a child fingerpaints. The former did a lot of planning and sketching, the latter just dumps some paint on the paper and goes for it."

He continues: "Saul Alinsky – the great community organizer – used to train new community organizers by having them do absolutely nothing except hang out in neighbourhoods, try to meet and talk to as many people of influence as possible (everyone from priests to gangsters), and then send him detailed reports every night by Dictaphone. He would force new people to do this for months before anything else. This process of connecting with and learning from the neighbourhood allowed his organization to connect directly with the real players in his community, accurately gauge support for proposed actions, and instantly react whenever a situation presented itself. It was the necessary *toi sow* training for the activists that allowed them to manifest *wu wei*."

Does this apply to direct action? Organizing protests? Logging blockades? Railing against globalization in the streets world-wide? What about taking confrontational legal action?

It is the nature of activism, not the type of action, that Lao Tzu seeks to inform when he says, "Do not force action, instead allow

action to arise on its own, and follow its course."

To apply the ideas of *wu wei* to any form of activism means stepping back, taking the time necessary to allow the *right* action to arise. It means thinking carefully about what the appropriate action is. It means questioning our motives. Are we acting now because this is the right time to apply pressure to achieve the outcome we want? Or are we responding to some artificial pressure like a deadline, or as retribution for a wrong we have suffered? Such thoughts ensure that we do not act out of anger or hatred which often results in deep divisions that lead to ever more disagreement, and ultimately the failure to implement our long-term objectives.

Applying *wu wei* to activism means leaving space to embrace the unforeseen.

> Sometimes the best action to take
> is to take no action
> and to embrace the unexpected as it occurs
> (*Tao*, 3)

Sometimes the appropriate action *is* to place ourselves between what we love and those we oppose. Sometimes direct action is necessary to buy some time for conditions to change that will allow us to sway public opinion, influence decision makers, or allow market forces dictate an outcome we are satisfied with.

The action that arises of its own accord is the action to take. A lifetime (long or short, but always carefully considered) of experience will help us know when that action is correct. Taking this action out of love, not anger or fear, and with compassion is the way to follow the Tao.

Possibly the most important thing about allowing the right action to arise of its own accord is to know when to step back. We can act from our passion and love, but often we fail to yield when it would be to our advantage.

I find it really tough to apply *wu wei* to my own activism. My inclination is to be in motion, always acting.

Like much about the *Tao te Ching*, *wu wei* is not an intellectual exercise: it is emotional. It is instinctual. When I stop thinking about

it and allow my heart to feel it, it becomes much more clear. If I take my eye off of it and look just to the side – like when I want to see the seventh star in the Pleiades – things become more lucid.

The *wu wei* of activism is about accepting things as they come. That includes our passionate – and yes, sometimes burning – desire to make change in the world. To fight this passion and the outrage it spawns would also be to go against the flow of things.

To understand this, to make it emotional, to make it something I feel in my heart, I always return to water.

All my life, I've turned to water as a source of strength and peace and to give me clarity. Sit by the side of a creek and watch how water moves around rocks and fallen logs. Stroll along the lakeshore and watch as the water moves back and forth against the shoreline.

"Thus the Tao is the course, the flow, the drift for the process of nature, and I call it the *Watercourse Way* because both Lao-Tzu and Chuang-Tzu use the flow of water as its principal metaphor," says Alan Watts.[7]

Water is a great teacher, and no form instructs better than the water within every cell in our own bodies. In the notes to Stephen Mitchell's translation of the *Tao*, Emilie Conrad-Da'oud says, "We are fundamentally water: muscled water."[8]

Matter, even at the most finite level, has memory. It's not the kind of memory that we call upon to recall our mother's birthday or where we left the damn car keys. It's an unconscious memory that we can't tap into mentally, but that we can perceive emotionally. We can feel it.

The matter that composes my skin, flesh, hair, eyes, bone, and blood was once plant or animal, and before that soil, and before that rock or hill or plains or mountain. We have been all of these things. We will be them again.

We are almost entirely composed of water. Thus we are the rivers and lakes that we drink. We are the underground aquifers – some nearly as large as the Great Lakes themselves – that we consume

7. Alan Watts, *Tao: The Watercourse Way,* New York, Pantheon Books, 1975, p. 41

8. Stephen Mitchell, *A New English Version of the Tao te Ching,* New York: Harper Collins Publishers, 1988, p. 89

through our food. That water has memory that lives in every cell of our body. We can remember the wisdom in that water if we are still and allow its wisdom to resurface.

"Hence the solution for the Sage who would transform the world lies in water," says the ancient statesman Kuan Chung. "Hence the Sage, when he rules the world, does not teach men one by one, or house by house, but takes water as his key."[9]

What does that water teach us? For each of us the lessons are different. A lifetime of dipping fishing lines and paddles and bare feet into sluggish creeks and raging rivers has taught me a few things about the action without acting, about stepping back and letting the right course of action arise of its own accord. Patience, persistence, timeliness, appropriate action, context, continuance, peace, and balance: these are some of the things that water teaches me.

Patience: In 1956, the Bureau of Reclamation began the process of damming Glen Canyon. Virtually unknown to the outside world at the time, Glen Canyon on the Colorado River – composed of hundreds of miles of sandstone cathedrals, temples, coves and arches, alluvial plains and sand bars with beaches and side canyons beyond counting. To the few who knew it, it was the living heart of the canyon country ecosystem in southeastern Utah. The dam changed all that: the Colorado River backed up, flooded places like Music Temple and Cathedral in the Desert, and buried the rich archeological history and diverse river ecology beneath hundreds of feet of water, silt, sand, and pleasure-boat detritus. I remember the spring day that I sat at dawn in Neon Canyon in the Golden Cathedral after wading the frigid Escalante River, upstream from where the fetid waters of Lake Powell reach. I was simultaneously in awe of its heart-stopping beauty and in mourning for similar places nearby lost to recent memory. But the river had patience.

The Colorado River region has suffered through several years of terrible drought, but that drought has had an unanticipated result. In the summer of 2005 Glen Canyon re-emerged from the stagnant waters of Lake Powell. Places such as Cathedral in the Desert have reappeared as the waters of the reservoir slowly dropped over the last few years. And though the dam still stands, the river cuts

---

9. Alan Watts, *Tao: The Watercourse Way*, New York: Pantheon Books, 1975, p. 49

through the Glen much as it did forty years ago before our delusions of grandeur manifested themselves in the desert.[10]

Will the Colorado River continue to run free? Many activists are working to keep it flowing through Glen Canyon, trying to preserve now what nature and the river has done of its own accord.

Persistence: Just downstream from Glen Canyon is the Grand Canyon. In the winter of 1993, I was blessed with the opportunity to live and work there as a volunteer through a fabulous organization called the Student Conservation Association.[11] The Grand Canyon is more than 400 miles long, a mile deep at its nadir, and sixteen miles across at its widest point. Over the last nine million years, two forces have been at work to create it: the Colorado River and its tributaries, and gravity. To stand on the rim of the Grand Canyon, the silence of early morning all around, and to hear, faintly, the voice of the Colorado River a mile below churning through Vishnu Schist, rocks from the basement of the earth, is to understand persistence.

Timeliness: The Colorado River is what river folks call a "pool and drop" river. During my time at Grand Canyon National Park, I experienced both the pools and the drops from the bow of a sixteen-foot raft. As a willing but not particularly helpful part of the Glen Canyon Environmental Studies team, I rafted the Colorado, assisting where I could (but mostly staying out of the way) the studies being conducted into the downstream impacts of the dam on the Grand Canyon environment.

The river understands that there is a time to be calm and a time to rage. There cannot be one without the other. Here, deep within the earth, the water is flat, tranquil, the boats drift lazily downstream, the canyon walls rise two, three, four thousand feet. From around the bend in the river comes a sound. Soft at first, then white noise, and as we drift closer, the furious sound of a train bearing down on us. The oars are plied, and downriver the water seems to drop off the edge of the earth.

---

10. To learn more about Glen Canyon and to stay abreast of changes to the free-flowing Colorado River, visit the Glen Canyon Institute's web page at *glencanyon.org*.

11. The Student Conservation Association is America's largest and oldest conservation service orientated organization. Each year it places interns and volunteers in 400 sites. Visit *thesca.org* for more info.

There is a moment before you enter the tongue of a big rapid when the water seems to stand still and you hang there for a millisecond – which seems an eternity – and then you plunge down into the gnashing teeth of white water.

There is a time for this wild ride of white water, as surely as there is a time for the peace of a long flat stretch of water where the world slips lazily by.

Appropriate Action: In December of 1966, a storm to end all storms battered the North Rim of the Grand Canyon, dumping fourteen inches of rain on the dry desert uplands in just three days. This amount of rain in an entire year would be considered a lot on the dry Colorado Plateau. The soils of the North Rim, and the Colorado Plateau in general, are unaccustomed to absorbing that much moisture, so the water was shed into the gorges that lead down to the Colorado River as churning, boulder-strewn, blood-coloured flash floods. To add to the fun, six inches of snow lay on the ground when the unseasonably warm rains fell.

In the Crystal Creek drainage where most of that storm's water was shed, it formed a wall of water forty-four feet high, carrying with it boulders as big as houses. This debris flow was estimated at 10,000 cubic feet per second. When I paddled it in the fall of 1993, the entire Colorado River held just 6,000 cubic feet per second. Think of one cubic foot as roughly the volume of a basketball. Imagine 10,000 basketballs thundering by you every single second to get a sense of what Crystal Creek must have been like that December day. That's a lot of game.

When this wall of water hit the river, it vomited a mass of rock and mud into the river that temporarily stopped its flow, creating a dam. But the river is patient and persistent, the call of gravity is loud, the beckoning of the sea is clear, and in a few moments the previously quiet Colorado forced its way through. It responded to the new obstacle with appropriate action by bursting the natural dam.

Boatmen camped upstream awoke to a new behemoth. Where the day before only a small riffle impeded a smooth stretch of water, a rapid without equal had been born. It was named Crystal, and today it stands among the most feared and respected rapids in North America.

Context: As magnificent as it is, the Grand Canyon is only a short stretch in the journey of two great rivers from their headwaters in the mountains on their way to sea. The Green River rises in the Wind River ranges of Wyoming and flows through other extraordinary landscapes – Dinosaur National Monument, the Gates of Ladore, Grey and Desolation Canyons, the San Rafael desert, Stillwater and Labyrinth Canyons – en route to the confluence with the Colorado, which rises in Rocky Mountain National Park and snakes through mountains down into the Colorado Plateau, cutting deeply into the earth and carving many extraordinary canyons. Where the rivers come together they chew through Cataract Canyon and into the newly resurrected Glen Canyon.

Sitting on the bank of the Colorado River at sundown, the November air temperature just above freezing, a fire blazing and illuminating the salmon-coloured cliffs, we are tiny points in the vastness of the landscape. Beside the surge of the river, flesh and bones, blood and sinew, seem insignificant. And the river itself is but a single vein in the earth's great circulatory system, pulsing with the lifeblood of the planet.

Continuance: Sometimes in our efforts to protect what we love, such as places like the Grand Canyon, Glen Canyon, and the Colorado Plateau, we forget that we are part of a continuum that stretches far back before our time and reaches far into a future we will not experience. For thousands of years, Native Americans travelled through and lived in these canyons. We can talk to our elders about the work that they have done before us and look to our children to glimpse the future, but all we can intellectually understand is the here and now.

The river is at once its past, present, and future. The water that slips by the sandy bank where our boats are beached is the same that rose in the Rocky Mountains of Colorado and the Wind River Range of Wyoming, and it is this same water that will meet its end far downstream. Alas the Colorado no longer reaches the sea, all of its sucked up for agriculture and human consumption, or evaporating along the way.

Balance: The essence of *wu wei* – of allowing the appropriate action to arise of its own accord – is balance. Camping on the banks of the Colorado River, watching the evening light play off the eddy line where the river turns back and tucks itself behind a giant boulder, it's hard to imagine that around the next bend in the river a massive rapid waits for us the next morning. There is a balance here between rest and rejoicing, between rushing forward and holding back.

Peace: The place where the river stands still before rushing over the tongue of the rapid is a place of tranquility. When we step back to let our hearts feel the pause before allowing the right action to rise, we find peace.

> The true Way is within us
> We must wait with patience
> for it to reveal itself
> for it is older than all the stars in the sky
> (*Tao*, 4)

5

APPEAR TO CLOSE ENTRANCE

The Tao of Strategy

This is the universal truth
The soft overcomes the hard
The slow overtakes the fast
(*Tao*, 36)

Late in the 1990s, Tzeporah Berman faced a strategic dilemma. Negotiations with the forestry industry on Canada's west coast were at an impasse, and the future of one of Canada's most important biological hotspots – the Great Bear Rainforest – hung in the balance. Berman was a veteran of a decade of acrimonious debate over the future of Canada's temperate rainforest. She had been among a group of influential and charismatic leaders who helped organize logging blockades in Clayoquot Sound on Vancouver Island in 1993, which brought the eyes of the world on Canada's savage treatment of its old-growth forests.[1] At the height of that summer of protest, she was arrested and charged with 800 counts of aiding and abetting civil disobedience. (That charge was later thrown out of court.

---

1. I first met Tzeporah Berman in the fall of 1993 when I was attending a conference of the Canadian Unified Student Environmental Network at activist Pat Potter's home on Lake Erie. Tzeporah gave a talk on Clayoquot Sound and was a powerful influence on me and many other young activists. I credit her with helping galvanize my passion for advocacy.

While she and partner Chris Hatch were on a rare two-week holiday, prompted by a near-nervous breakdown from stress and overwork, her Vancouver apartment burned to the ground. Arson was suspected, but never proven. Tzeporah worked in a hostile environment.

Up until this point, the strategy employed by Berman and her fellow activists had been to embarrass, out-muscle, out-spin, and out-manoeuvre the forestry giants in order to protect places like Clayoquot Sound and the Great Bear Rainforest. But the forestry industry had dug in its heels, and it appeared as though Berman and others would now have to turn up the heat of their market campaigns, a costly tactic that would almost certainly result in more venomous debate before coming to a settlement that would likely leave both sides deeply divided.

Tzeporah Berman, Jodie Holmes, Marran Smith, Karen Mahon, Catherine Stewart, and others made a strategic decision then that changed the course of the campaign for the Great Bear Rainforest. They decided to try something that Lao Tzu counselled 2,500 years ago: to try and capture their opponent whole. And they had something that Lao Tzu didn't: they had an Elton John concert (more on this later).

The *Tao te Ching*, whose intended audience included the rulers of feudal China during a highly volatile period of ancient Chinese history, offers key lessons on strategy. True to his own teachings, Lao Tzu kept his advice on strategy plain: make simple plans and keep them hidden; be prepared for the unexpected; know how to take advantage of opportunities as they arise; choose conflict as a last resort; know when to yield and when to stop. Of these, possibly the most important and most challenging is the notion of capturing your opponent whole.

Start With a Simple Plan

Beginning in late 1999, I spent much of my time working to help pass Canada's Species at Risk Act (SARA). It was an exciting opportunity to be a part of long-term change, and to work with some of Canada's best conservation activists. Although the United States passed a comprehensive law to protect species at risk of extinction and the places they needed to survive in the early 1970s, Canada had only piecemeal legislation to protect some endangered species, some of the time, in some parts of the country. With hundreds of plants, birds, fish, and animals at risk of extinction due to the loss of their homes, breeding grounds, and from over-hunting or fishing, Canada desperately needed a federal law to provide consistent protection for species like the beluga whale, monarch butterfly, and grizzly bear.

Other dedicated and talented campaigners such as Elizabeth May, Stewart Elgie, Sarah Dover, and Dr. Rick Smith had been fighting for this law for much of the 1990s and had seen their efforts repeatedly thwarted by Canada's sluggish federal government, recalcitrant provincial interests like those in Alberta, and powerful corporate and private property interests who profited from Canada's lack of protection for endangered species.[2]

In the effort to ensure SARA was passed, we conservationists pooled our abundant talent to create strategies for a campaign. But we soon found that creativity is no substitute for simplicity. The only indicator of a good strategy is one that is implemented and which succeeds in achieving the goals and objectives attached to it.

During the height of the fight for SARA, many strategies were crafted, including an elaborate plan for orchestrating both domestic and international pressure on the Canadian government. The plan seemed brilliant. It covered every conceivable avenue to apply pressure. It was many pages long, and had flow charts and multiple lines of attack. It was multi-layered and sophisticated. But it lacked the one thing that a strategy must have to be successful – the resources to implement it. It was a half-million-dollar plan for a campaign that could scarcely scrape together salaries for staff. Some potential funders were scared off by the plan's complexity, while others hedged on their commitments.[3]

The plan never saw the light of day.

It is said that we should dream no small dreams, for they do

---

2. Elizabeth May is the executive director of the Sierra Club of Canada, Stewart Elgie was then a senior lawyer for the Sierra Legal Defense Fund (no formal relationship with the Sierra Club), Sarah Dover was the director of the Endangered Species Campaign, and Dr. Rick Smith was then executive director of the International Fund for Animal Welfare Canada.

3. This story is complicated by the fact that one of our major funders continuously promised resources to implement such a plan, but didn't deliver the money in a timely way. Creating and implementing simple plans sometimes requires that we educate those who are funding them as to their value.

not inspire greatness. True. Activists have no shortage of grand dreams. What we have is a shortage of strategies that can effectively implement those dreams. But dreamers need to team up with those among us who can create the pathways that will lead to results.

With the Species at Risk Act, what got results was a simple strategy coupled with hard work and perseverance: grassroots political pressure; working with our allies in Canadian Parliament, such as Karen Kraft Sloan, Charles Caccia, Clifford Lincoln, and John Herron; finding common ground with the more progressive members of industry by addressing their fears and bringing them into the campaign so they could work for us; and having a great team that worked well together despite our differences. We succeeded in having SARA passed, and though it wasn't the law that we had imagined – now we protect a *few* more species, a *few* more times, and in a *few* more places across the country – it was a start.

Strategy is the trail map that we use to reach our goals. Tactics are the bicycles that we ride to get there. Strategy answers the question "what will you do to achieve results?" Tactics answer the question "how will you implement that strategy?" A simple strategy might involve just two or three key elements: dominate the media debate on this issue in major federal jurisdictions; rally support from grassroots activists in key federal politicians' ridings or districts; work with supporters in government to pressure decision makers. Those are strategic elements of the campaign plan.

Tactics are how we get things done: finding letter-to-the-editor writers who can respond to particular newspaper stories in an important geographical region; finding volunteers in key electoral ridings who can write letters and make phone calls to decision makers. The strategy is simple and clear. The tactics require considerable effort, expertise, and imagination.

Remember that while the elements of a campaign might be simple, organizing "grassroots political pressure" is anything but easy. Let's not assume that because we develop a simple plan that its execution will be undemanding. The work to put that plan in place might be painstaking and arduous. But having a straightforward map to follow makes that work much easier to achieve.

> Because the sage activist has a little sense
> she creates simple strategies that are easy to follow
> Her only fear is to be led astray by those
> who like to make things more complex than
>   necessary
>
> Know when you have strayed from the simple path
> and move slowly back to the centre
> (*Tao*, 53)

The world that we work in is complex, we argue, and so we need complex strategies to leverage resources and influence decision makers. We like complex plans because we can envision carrying them out, the wheels and cogs turning, engineering the necessary results, ensuring the final piece of strategy is put in place so that the campaign is won.

We like complex campaigns because they allow us also to demonstrate how much we know about the policy and legislative process and about the people who influence the decision makers.

This isn't to say that we should not create plans that have complex elements. I know of several examples of very elaborate plans being carried out for the protection of wildlands and wildlife that may well succeed. But we should *start* with simple plans. When we are able to put those plans in place and find that more is needed, then we can move on to the next level of complexity. We must also know our capacity to implement such plans, keeping in mind that challenges and opportunities arise on a daily basis. If we don't leave room to address them, such challenges can scuttle our plans and create crisis.

I was a board member of a new, ambitious, and exciting conservation effort. We hired a consultant to help us write a strategic plan. The planning process was expensive and time-consuming, and the result was broad and sweeping, appealing to the sense of urgency we felt about our conservation goals and to our vision for an ambitious and innovative organization. We approved the strategic plan and handed it to our paid staff co-ordinator to implement.

But, after some time, it became obvious that the co-ordinator was unable to do this. When the board assigned one of our directors to determine why, she reported that to implement the plan we would need *twenty-eight* full-time staff. At that time, the organization had eight or so full- and part-time employees and did not have the resources needed to hire twenty more people.

We had adopted the complex plan because it said all the things we wanted it to say. It covered every element of the work that we wanted to do. But it simply didn't match reality. It wasn't a plan; it was a list of our wildest and most inspired dreams.

So the complex plan was abandoned; we took its best ideas and created a much simpler plan and set about putting it into action. As an organization, we saw that we had "strayed from the simple path" and moved "slowly back to the centre." The centre in this case was a place of balance between the resources that were available and our ambitions to protect what we love.

The first step is starting with a simple plan grounded in reality that aspires to greatness but recognizes and respects constraints. Keeping that strategy hidden is the next.

Hold Your Cards Close

Once you have a good plan that matches the resources and abilities of those who are implementing it, guard that plan so that it remains a mystery to your opponents. "Keep your strategy and tactics hidden," says Lao Tzu. "Show only the results."

Elsewhere Lao Tzu cautions us against underestimating our opponents. Here we see that he advises the strategist to create the sense among those we oppose that *they* are clearly superior. We want them to underestimate our skills and abilities. We want them to think of us as incapable of winning.

> Sound planning leaves no evidence of a design
> Careful strategy makes people think they arrived
>   by chance
> Refined creativity allows for intuition
> Deliberate calculation appears random
> (*Tao*, 27)

As usual, Lao Tzu's recommendations on strategy are complete with head-scratching paradox. How can a "sound strategy leave no evidence of a design"? Why should we allow our deliberate calculation to appear random?

Lao Tzu is saying that we should make our opponents believe that we can win only by accident or luck. But luck only favours those who are prepared to seize it, and being open to capitalizing on opportunity is the sage activist's greatest strength.

When our opponents underestimate us, it gives us the room to use similar strategies a second or third time. If it's clear to our opponents that we have a winning strategy, they can move to defeat it when we try to use it again. But if they are led to believe we simply stumbled into a winning situation, then we are free to try that strategy again.

If strategy is a road map that we lay out for all to see, then those who oppose us can know where we're going. To follow the earlier metaphor, they can steal our bicycles. Our ability to execute our strategy depends on secrecy.

Often as we are engaged in a campaign, media will ask what our strategy is for winning. They will want to know "what's next?" Resist the urge to reveal more than necessary.

Some organizations use similar strategies again and again, like Amnesty International, as they work for the release of political prisoners world-wide, or the British Columbia-based Markets Initiative which convinced the Canadian publisher of the *Harry Potter* books to print them on 100% recycled paper. These organizations have clearly defined niches that require a similar strategy to be used each time they take on a campaign. But the *tactics* of how they execute that strategy can be kept confidential, and in doing so, keep those they are trying to influence them from knowing what might happen next in their campaign.

Daring Not to Be First

Allowing our opponent to make the first move is a very effective way of keeping our strategy hidden. This is counter-intuitive. Shouldn't we make the first move to catch our opponents off guard?

> The best strategists say:
> "It is better not to make the first move
> but to wait and see what your opponent does"
> (*Tao*, 69)

The translation of this phrase in the *Tao te Ching* varies widely. Brian Browne Walker says, "In conflict it is better to be receptive than aggressive." Stephen Mitchell says, "Rather than make the first move it is better to wait and see." "I dare not make the first move but would rather play the guest;" say Gia-Fu Feng and Jane English. Robert G. Henricks translates, "I don't presume to act like the host, and instead play the part of the guest."

The guest receives. The host offers. The sound strategist stays back to receive and allows the other to make the first move – to offer, to step forward.[4]

In doing so, we can understand better the general strategy of our opponents: do they intend to conduct a public media campaign, or play a quiet behind-the-scenes game using their position and influence to sway decision makers? By staying behind, we can determine their strengths and weaknesses. By waiting to see what they do and what they say, we can frame our response to effectively counter their arguments. This should not be taken to mean that we are following their lead; on the contrary, it allows us to read the terrain effectively before implementing our own campaign strategy.

But as with any strategy, the unexpected is often what is most effective. If we customarily let our opponents make the first move, from time to time we should be pre-emptive in order to throw them off guard. In doing so, their energy becomes focused inward, something that we can take advantage of.

And just as we can sometimes create the unexpected, we must also be prepared to take advantage of it as it "arises of its own accord."

---

4. The interpretation of verse sixty-nine, which is almost solely about strategy, is another example of where I've endeavoured to discern the spirit of the *Tao te Ching* while making the language applicable to our efforts as activists.

Expect the Unexpected

I've written enough campaign strategy documents to know that it's often what's not in them that leads to success: the spontaneous action that "arises of its own accord" that results in the successful culmination of your efforts. In debriefing such a campaign, those involved will ask, "Why did that campaign succeed?" We have all the usual answers – good teamwork, the right match of ambition and resources, good political timing, favourable media coverage, perseverance, etc. But inevitably, someone will say, "Things just seemed to fall together," or "We were at the right place at the right time," or "Everything seemed to go our way after so-and-so said / did this...."

Then we wonder, can we duplicate that success? The answer to this is a little harder. We can always replicate the basic elements of the campaign – the media strategy, the outreach work, the public events – but what we can't duplicate are the coincidentals.

We simply have to be open to them. We need to give them space and time and be prepared to act when they do arise. We need to learn to recognize them and trust them and ourselves so that when a colleague comes into the office one morning and says, "Hear me out on this; I think we might consider giving this a try," we should give that person our full attention and be open to the unexpected, the unorthodox, and ultimately, the beautiful.

That's how I think of a well-conceived, well-executed piece of strategy. Beautiful.

Appear to Close Entrance

In Tai Chi, there is a set of movements called "Appear to Close Entrance." I practice these movements when struggling with the idea of advance and retreat. First push your hands forward, hips squared, left leg forward and bent at the knee and your right leg back, forming a straight line with your back. Here you are fending off some invisible opponent or using your energy to advance your cause. First we push forward, then we fall back. Pivot your hips and transfer your weight from your front leg to your back leg. Move your hands to protect your chest, arms up, palms in. We appear to close the entrance.

We pivot back and forth, never overextending, never pulling all the way back. In our motion we see that the way is blocked. What do we do? Do we push forward with all our strength hoping to dislodge that which blocks our way? No. We pivot on our hips, pulling our hands up before us and pulling back, to pause. We are patient. And when we see an indication of an opening ahead, we pivot again and push. We wait until the moment is right. We wait until our effort won't be in vain.

Making It Soft

There is a practical application from "Appear to Close Entrance" for developing strategies. The successful path honours *wu wei*, the soft, the naturally arising.

> This is the universal truth
> The soft overcomes the hard
> The slow overtakes the fast
> (*Tao*, 36)

When developing our strategies, we can be mindful of this in two ways. First, we might consider strategies that help us win without entering into open conflict. What can we do to win our campaign without having to get into a public fight with our opponents? Developing a strategy that first examines these options can save us resources and energy for other stages of our campaign. Being mindful of the risks of these campaigns is critical. What do we lose if we *don't* engage the public on an issue, building their awareness and long-term support? What do we lose if parties to an agreement are replaced by others who don't share the same views? According to Charles Wilkinson, author of the *Eagle Bird* and other books, "Developers need win only once, conservationists must win always." The same can be said for human rights and child labour activists.

Second, we need to think long-term. Many campaigns take a decade to be won, others can go on for a *generation*. Many of Alberta's eastern slope landscapes – such as a magnificent Castle Wilderness in the province's south-western corner, adjacent to Waterton Lakes

National Park – that are today threatened by oil and gas development, logging, mining, and off-highway vehicle use, were first proposed for protection in the early 1970s. That's around the time that I
and many others who now struggle to protect them were born.

Nobody in their right mind would enter into a campaign and
proclaim, "Let's develop a thirty-year strategy," but that kind of
thinking is exactly what is needed not only in order to succeed, but
to protect our success as well. "The slow overtakes the fast," says
Lao Tzu, advising us to think long term.

In the United States, advocates for endangered species have been
fighting to uphold and enforce the Endangered Species Act for more
than thirty years. The law, introduced by President Richard Nixon,
has survived Ronald Reagan, George H.W. Bush, Newt Gingrich,
George W. Bush, and countless other detractors. Even Republican
Congressman Richard Pombo's attacks, which are the most threatening yet, are being tempered by the effective work of the Endangered
Species Coalition. The coalition and others and other defenders of
the law have successfully thwarted repeated attempts to undermine
its effectiveness. Those labouring to safeguard the nation's endangered plants and animals recognize that simply passing a law isn't
good enough. They need to be vigilant, and to keep in place the
resources to uphold it. In short, they have a long-term strategy to
protect the nation's endangered species.

Taking Whole

Following the principle of *wu wei*, or not forcing, means expending time, energy, and thoughtfulness to find the path of least resis-
tance. I think our tendency as activists is to charge in. "Attack and the
rest will follow," said Napoleon Bonaparte. That credo has been the
mantra of more than one activist.

Instead, we should try to find a strategy that does not pose a risk
to the possibility of a lasting victory. Lao Tzu – and incidentally, Sun
Tzu, author of the Taoist text *The Art of War* – both advise that it is
best not to attack at all, but to capture your enemy whole.

"Taking whole is both a way of being and a way of seeing," says
the Denma Translation Group in the introduction to their transla-

tion of *The Art of War*. "Because our actions arise naturally out of it, it is also a way of acting. It does not preclude the use of force, but in using force, it seeks to preserve the possibilities – to keep the options open and include the welfare of the other. It leads ultimately to victory."[5]

Sun Tzu's thinking is the topic for another book, but the idea of capturing your enemy whole is very much in line with the concept of not forcing, or *wu wei*.

How can we put these sages' thinking into practice? It's about an Elton John concert, remember?

It's September and I'm sitting with Tzeporah Berman, who is now the program director for Forest Ethics, Darcy Riddell, program director for the Hollyhock Leadership Institute, and Andrea Reimer, executive director of the Western Canada Wilderness Committee. It's lunch time during a conference for social entrepreneurs at Hollyhock, on Cortes Island. I ask them about the nebulous concept of "capturing your enemy whole."

Our conversation turns to the ongoing effort to preserve British Columbia's Great Bear Rainforest, one of the world's last temperate rainforests. For a decade, Tzeporah has been at the forefront of the effort to protect it from logging. The campaign, often times acrimonious, took a turn in 2000 when both sides of the debate began to address the barriers that kept them from finding a solution to the stand-off.

Environmentalists led by Forest Ethics and the Rainforest Action Network had steadfastly demanded an end to old-growth logging in the region and the protection of much of the Great Bear Rainforest from further development. Logging companies dismissed the demands as unreasonable and continued to push forward with plans for large scale clear-cut logging. Forest Ethics turned to consumer action campaigns to reduce the market for old-growth timber.

The group had done its homework. "Power mapping is a critical component of any campaign," says Tzeporah. "Inevitably it leads you back to the public, but in the case of a markets-based campaign, the public is being directed to take action with industry rather than

---

5. Sun Tzu, *The Art of War, A New Translation*, trans. The Denma Translation Group, Boston and London: Shambhala, 2001, p. xvii.

with government." That action could be a boycott of Home Depot until it stops selling products produced from old-growth timber, or demonstrations in front of Staples stores until the company gives in to consumer demand for more sustainable paper products. "It's a way of identifying the power base and influencing it," she says.

So successful was the work of Forest Ethics and the Rainforest Action Network that the logging companies soon called the environmental groups to negotiations.

Darcy Riddell says, "We're never going to win if we think that people need to come closer to our personal value set. Instead we must take an evolved approach to activism that includes the ability to engage people where they are – to motivate the whole person."

That is exactly what Forest Ethics did in 2000, but it wasn't easy. With negotiations at an impasse, and an escalating consumer boycott looming, the facilitator for the negotiations between environmentalists and industry asked both groups to attend an Elton John concert in Vancouver, and to use his private box to enjoy the show.

"You want us to do what?" was Tzeporah's initial reaction. But the facilitator insisted, and so forest activists and chief foresters came together to watch the show. "At first we sat on opposite sides of the box," says Tzeporah. "But after a few drinks, and listening to this rocking music, we were on our feet and dancing." Enviros were on one side of the box and forestry execs on the other. "But it was a small box," laughs Tzeporah, "and soon I was dancing with a chief forester."

"There was a break in the music," Tzeporah continues, "and one of the forestry negotiators asked Jodie Holmes, a negotiator for the environmental groups, to dance. Jodie scoffed and said, 'You've got to be kidding!' The forester grinned and said, 'I'll give you a valley,' and without missing a beat Jodie asked, 'Which one?'"

The next morning's negotiations were very different. Foresters and environmentalists were laughing about the previous night's entertainment and casually mingling over coffee. The tone of the meetings had changed. People on the opposing sides of the debate over the future of the Great Bear Rainforest now shared a common experience; they had shown each other that they too were human beings, not so unlike the other. The experience meant that Tzeporah could now appeal to the foresters as human beings, and that the industry negotiating team regarded her and her colleagues in the same way.

In doing this, both industry and environmentalist were able to let go of their preconceived notions of each other. "I was able to accept that my counterpart from industry didn't wake up each morning and say to himself, 'I want to log all the old-growth forest in the Great Bear Rainforest,'" says Tzeporah. "And he was able to say, 'the environmentalists don't want to ruin my company.'" Instead, they were able to work together to find solutions to each other's problems.

The result was a ground-breaking agreement between industry, First Nations, public interest organizations, and government to legally protect portions of the Great Bear Rainforest from logging. Four million acres of rainforest would be permanently protected. As important, says Tzeporah, "First Nations will have increased control over decision making and support for conservation-based economic development in the region. And logging practices will be dramatically changed in the rest of The Great Bear Rainforest."

The agreement has its vocal detractors, in particular those who argued for even more protection for a greater number of watersheds in this last refuge of coastal rainforest. A recent analysis of the agreement states that as much as seventy-seven percent of the fragile and ecologically unique region could be logged, and that since the agreement was signed thirty-seven percent of the logging in the Great Bear Rainforest region has been of rare, old-growth cedar forests.[6]

The end result isn't always as was intended. Long negotiations often don't yield results unless backed up by a "credible threat," and a willingness to take action. Tzeporah points out that the negotiated agreement only came to fruition after an acrimonious period during which the environmental groups had demonstrated their power over the marketplace.

But what is now part of history is the way that a group of activists came together to try to capture their enemy whole: to achieve success in protecting the Great Bear Rainforest without destroying those who opposed them.

---

6. The David Suzuki Foundation, Clearcutting Canada Rainforests, 2005 Status Report, Vancouver, *canadianrainforests.org*, 2005

"Of course," says Tzeporah, "MacMillan Bloedel thought that they were capturing us whole too." That win-win approach is one of the clearest ways of using the Tao in our efforts to protect what we love while honouring those we oppose with respect and compassion.

Recipe for Change: Add Yogurt, Agitate

Here's another way of looking at the idea of capturing your opponent whole.

In 1982, Gary Hirshberg was a grassroots environmental and social justice advocate and back-to-the-land radical who had been recruited to the board of directors of the Rural Education Center in Wilton, New Hampshire, which was dedicated to educating people about organic foods, natural living, and environmental protection. One of its founders, a man named Samuel Kaymen, had recently perfected a yogurt recipe that they made on site for the organization's volunteers and board members to enjoy. It was good yogurt. Really good yogurt, and Hirshberg, a serial entrepreneur, thought that it was good enough that the centre could make a little money for its operations by selling the yogurt commercially.

With seven cows and a draughty barn perched atop a New Hampshire hill where the winter winds blew frigid and the roads iced up and the lights went out, Hirshberg and Kaymen started Stonyfield Farm. For much of their first nine years, they flirted with disaster. (Some might say that things went way beyond flirting.) Equipment broke down regularly, entire batches of yogurt were ruined, delivery trucks got stuck in the mud and on the ice of the winding farm road, cash was always in short supply, and if not for the grace of the Sisters of Mercy, one of Stonyfield's early investors, all would have been lost.

But Hirshberg and Kaymen persevered. Their vision was that by creating a successful business they might also create a tool for effective advocacy.

By 2003, Stonyfield Farm had become the fourth largest producer and distributor of yogurt in the United States, with sales surpassing $200 million.

Like many ethically-driven businesses, Stonyfield gives away a percentage of its profits to non-governmental organizations. But

Stonyfield surpasses nearly every expectation of corporate generosity by giving away ten percent of its profits every year. It is an advocate for its farmers who supply organic milk for the production of its yogurt, and for its suppliers of organic fruit, a key ingredient in its success.

Stonyfield exceeds the standard elements of good Corporate Social Responsibility (CSR). It actively encourages its yogurt-loving customers to become advocates for a wide range of causes, from women's health to the environment. It does this through a successful and creative "lid" program, where every two months a message printed on the lid of each cup of Stonyfield yogurt encourages consumers to get involved in issues dear to Hirshberg and Kaymen's hearts. The company's website is a portal for civic action, and it has partnered with other advocates from within civil society to work on environmental, health, food security, and social justice issues.

Corporations have often been advocates. They often advocate for lower taxes and less government regulation, and against regulations that would protect endangered species or the rights of non-smokers. But Hirshberg and Stonyfield Farm and a handful of other ethically-driven businesses such as Ben and Jerry's, Aveda, Salt Spring Coffee, and the Co-operative Bank of the UK are changing the model. They are helping to turn the voice of the consumer into the voice of an advocate.

I believe that this is a powerful example of what Lao Tzu and Sun Tzu would call capturing your opponent whole. These businesses are harnessing the power of commerce for social and environmental good, and as they do, have used the tools of corporations, often used against the causes that we champion, to instead advocate for them.

Working to capture whole is not a strategy that will work in every situation. Considerable manoeuvring must occur to create the opportunity to capture your opponent whole. During that time you will no doubt end up in conflicts that may become bitter and divisive. You may find yourself in crisis as your organization, your support, and your movement teeter on the brink of disaster. Conflict and crisis are part of our daily jobs; how we can manage them is of paramount importance.

6

STEP UP TO SEVEN STARS

Flowing through Conflict and Crisis

> Therefore, the sage
>> cuts without wounding
>>> strikes without bruising
>>>> carves without leaving a mark
>
> (*Tao*, 58)

Think for a moment about the nature of our work. Think about the words we use to describe what we do: struggle, fight, overcome, surmount. We clash with those whose agenda we oppose, wrestle with those in power, butt heads with whom we disagree. On top of all that, we struggle internally within our families, our organizations, and our cultures to maintain the structures that allow us to wake up the next morning and do it all over again.

We occasionally experience great success. New laws to protect our children are passed, a new treaty is signed to ban indiscriminate weapons such as land mines, or a place we care deeply about is spared from development and ruin. But the process of achieving these gains is often a long and tiring struggle, and the costs can be high. The work can bring us together with our family, friends, and community, but it can also tear us apart.

We can manage the natural by-products of our activism – conflict and crisis – in a way that not only allows us to achieve greater, more lasting success, but also ameliorates the impact that these destructive energies have on our personal lives, our organizations, and our chances at future achievement.

"Love your enemies," advised Jesus of Nazareth, "so that you may be children of your father in heaven: for he makes his sun rise on the evil and on the good, and sends his rain on the just and on the unjust."

> Remember this: winning and losing both have costs
> By always attacking, you will always be attacked
> (*Tao*, 42)

"The violent will not die a natural death," is how Stephen Mitchell translates verse forty-two. What Lao Tzu is saying is simple: live by the sword, die by the sword. The harder you push, the harder others will push back.

There are ways to ameliorate this, the most important being to consider Jesus's advice. We can love our enemies by treating them with compassion and respect. As I noted earlier, thinking of others as our enemies is the first step down a short road to confrontation.

> All living things are soft and flexible
> All things in death are hard and brittle
>
> The hard and the brittle will be broken
> the soft and flexible will endure
>
> In conflict, bend and flow
> and you will endure and triumph
> (*Tao*, 76)

It is unrealistic to think that we won't need to engage in some form of conflict to see an effective strategy come to resolution. As we push forward, someone will likely push back.

"I think that conflict is a natural result of being in a position of weakness. If two men get into a fight, the weaker guy will be the first to pull a knife – simply because he is over-awed by the other," says Cloudwalking Owl.

Lao Tzu cautions against entering into conflict in the first place, and advises that all other means be exhausted before we engage this way. If we must enter into conflict, Lao Tzu suggests doing so with a "humble heart" because, he says, we cannot truly win any battle. Someone, he says, always loses, with long-term consequences for both sides. Bitterness and resentment on the part of the loser often results in the desire to re-stage these battles again and again.

But conflict is sometimes inevitable, even with a strategy that purposely seeks to avoid it. Given that a victory achieved through these means will not be clean or absolute, what can we do to incorporate Lao Tzu's teachings into our efforts? Bend and flow. Do not use force. Win lasting victories by not denigrating or shaming your opponent. Remember that the soft shall overcome the hard.

> Prevent conflict before it arises
> Start by putting in place simple plans
> The greatest flood
> started as a single drop of rain
> The hardest journey of many miles
> can only be completed after taking the first step
> (*Tao*, 64)

Though it seems simple enough, avoiding conflict by intervening before it arises is no simple task. It takes a great deal of experience and good judgment to foresee conflict, and this only comes after a significant investment in our own emotional and spiritual health.

The conflict I write about here is not only external to our organizations, but internal as well. Sometimes we can see it coming – a divergence between members on a board of directors, a breakdown of consensus in dispute resolution, a difference of opinion among staff or volunteers. It's always easier to cross the river at its headwaters, but sometimes the headwaters are hard to find.

Because we can't always – and some would say, often – avoid conflict in our work, having some tools to navigate through conflict is essential.

Here Lao Tzu offers three important reminders. First, before entering into any conflict, be certain that an honest and open effort has been made to avoid it. Second, when entering into a conflict, act with humility, restraint, and love towards our opponent. Finally, when emerging from a conflict, regard winning and losing in a similar light.

Lasting victories are not born from acrimonious conflict.

Collision Course

In late 2000, Wildcanada.net was asked to provide some assistance to the Raincoast Conservation Society in their effort to stop the hunting of grizzly bears in British Columbia. Wildcanada.net had just been publicly launched in September, and we were excited to be approached to help with this high profile and very important campaign.

Raincoast is an aggressive, uncompromising, and highly principled organization, and I was attracted to its "take no prisoners" approach to the issue. It hammered on the British Columbia government of Premier Ujjal Dosanjh, and it wasn't alone. Dosanjh's party, the New Democrats, had lost two sitting premiers to scandal in the last ten years, and so the bloodthirsty BC media and the official opposition were both snapping at its heels. Though Premier Dosanjh was personally popular, his party was tanking in the polls and was expected to be soundly trounced in an election expected the following spring.

Raincoast was trying to extract a three-year moratorium on hunting from Dosanjh before he and the NDP were banished to opposition, or oblivion, by the right-of-centre and ironically named British Columbia Liberal Party. Raincoast's campaign was a no-holds-barred event. It took out graphic advertisements in daily newspapers across BC and ran similar ads in bus shelters and on billboards. It co-ordinated editorials, recruited scientists to speak to the issue, targeted overseas markets such as the European Union for grizzly bear trophies, and used the fax technology that Wildcanada.net had just developed to help thousands of people from around the world pepper the government with angry letters. Early that spring, just before the election was called, the NDP announced the establishment of a hunting moratorium.

The Guide Outfitters Association of British Columbia and the BC Wildlife Federation – a pro-hunting lobby group – opposed the moratorium, as did the presumed future government, the Liberals. Backed by the powerful pro-grizzly hunting groups, the Liberals made it an election issue, vowing to reverse the decision should they come to power. When the Liberals won, they did so with one of the largest majority governments in Canadian political history. I don't think the ink was dry on new Premier Gordon Campbell's inauguration speech when he re-opened the hunt.

As this book goes to press, the hunt continues. Thanks to the tireless efforts of Raincoast, fewer bears are killed each year in British Columbia, owing to closures in areas where grizzlies are worst off. But the fact remains that under the Liberal – and likely even a future NDP – government, ending the barbaric hunting of the endangered grizzly bear will take many, many years, and exact a huge cost in both human and financial resources.

On December 13, 2005, Raincoast, with the support of the Wuikinuxv and Heiltsuk First Nations, purchased one of the largest commercial sport hunting licenses in North America along the rugged coast of British Columbia, in the heart of the Great Bear Rainforest. The $1.35 million license covers nearly 20,000 square kilometres of grizzly bear habitat, and according to Raincoast spokesperson Ian McAllister, is the first step toward eliminating hunting grizzly bears and wolves in the region. Instead, the focus will be on wildlife viewing, photo-safaris, and eco-tourism as economic drivers for tourism in the region. This is an unprecedented move by a conservation group in Canada, and will further advance Raincoast's efforts to protect grizzly bears in BC from hunters.

I played a very small part in that campaign, and I hasten to add that hindsight is twenty-twenty. But if I knew then what I know now, I would have argued against delivering the *coup de grâce* – the last round of intensive lobbying coupled with aggressive, NDP-focused advertisements. While the campaign was well underway when I joined it, I should have advised letting up just enough on the NDP government so as not to extract the commitment of the moratorium.

I would have turned *down* the heat, so the incoming Liberal government could avoid taking an unretractable position on the hunt. Instead, I would have dedicated all of my energy and resources to ensuring that the incoming Liberals were neutral on the issue, so that when they did come to power, which was inevitable, we could then begin a new campaign to quietly compel them to end the hunt.

This would have avoided the open and rancorous conflict that led to the taking of sides which resulted in the quick reversal of the moratorium. Would it have taken another three or four years to stop the grizzly hunt using this strategy? Yes. Maybe longer. But grizzly bears are still being hunted anyway, and the Liberals will be in power in British Columbia for some time to come.

This sort of perspective comes easily in retrospect, and from an outside observer. When we are in the thick of things, it's much more difficult to think in these terms.

Lao Tzu himself recognized how difficult it is to accept this.

Bend and Flow

> Water is as soft as anything on earth
> yet mountains and canyons have been sculpted by
>   its force
>
> Thus the soft overcomes the hard
> the yielding overpowers the rigid
> Though a fact of nature
> this truth is difficult to put into day-to-day practice
> (*Tao*, 78)

In strategy and conflict, the principle of not forcing is among the *Tao te Ching's* most important concepts. "*Wu wei* is thus the lifestyle of one who follows the Tao, and must be understood primarily as a form of intelligence – that is, of knowing the principles, structures, and trends of human and natural affairs so well that one uses the least amount of energy in dealing with them," says Alan Watts.[1]

"The practical message," says Watts, "seems to be that the only

---

1. Alan Watts, *Tao: The Watercourse Way*, New York: Pantheon Books, 1975, pp. 78, 81

trouble is made by those who strive to improve themselves and the world by forceful means."[2] The practical message for those of us – activists with non-governmental organizations and business leaders alike – whose self-appointed task is to improve the world, is to resist the use of force whenever possible. Our opponents use force – political, economic, military, and that of the industrial machine. My friend and mentor Brock Evans reminds me that those we oppose often seem to be acting out of anger or even hatred towards us. They act out of anger, and they are winning.

If we use the tools of our opponents to defeat them, are we any better? Does it matter so long as we win and they don't? I believe that Lao Tzu would argue that it's not enough to win. We have to win without becoming what we struggle against. In doing so, we might overcome the odds that are often stacked against us, where our opponent has more money and more access to power. To win by perpetuating conflict will almost certainly mean that our victory is short-lived.

"Understanding [*wu wei*] is a matter of getting the point intuitively, not a result of some discipline," continues Watts. It is a matter of trusting ourselves and what Lao Tzu describes as the natural order of the universe to see us through to success.

Much of the perspective that I bring to this book is from the standpoint of public policy advocacy, specifically around the protection of nature in Canada and across North America. As conservationists, we've got a certain bag of tricks at our disposal. Those who work in other fields – such as social justice or anti-poverty advocacy – have their own set of skills and techniques. Leaders of ethically driven business bring their own set of talents.

When evaluating this, it might be easy to see why some readers might believe that one type of activism is more "Taoist" than others. Activism involving consensus-based, community-led discussions, working from within industry or government, and non-violent civil disobedience are examples, as is running a successful business that uses market forces to create powerful change.

"When we look at things in the light of Tao," says Chuang Tzu,

---

2. Ibid, p. 81

"nothing is best, nothing is worst." [3]

Simply put, nearly every form of activism that we might engage in can follow the teachings of the *Tao te Ching*. Rather than focusing on the specific kind of activism, we might turn our attention to the how. And the how of the Tao is to "bend and flow." The key to managing conflict and crisis is to trust your instincts and what Taoists call *tzu-jan*, or "by itself so." This is the process of letting go of outcomes and trusting that opportunity will arise of its own accord. Our job is to recognize opportunity as it emerges and seize it.

We can also help it along. After all, we are part of the Tao – the Way of the universe – and our role as activists is to aid in the process of helping goodness prevail in the world. But there does come a point where we simply have to trust that good things will happen.

The key is in the idea of *wu wei* – not forcing. Guiding, yes. Assisting, yes. Forcing, not so much.

As activists we face a myriad of crises every week. Crisis compels us to do our work; our activism is about responding to it. Some of us aren't happy unless we are in crisis. But crisis doesn't necessarily bring out the best in everyone.

Chuang Tzu tells the story of an archer competing for a prize of gold. He says that when there is no prize, the archer retains all of his skill, shooting one true arrow after another. But as the stakes rise, the archer becomes increasingly desperate, and as a result, "loses his skill" and is "drained of his power." [4]

We've all seen this on the sports field. Athletes at the top of their game stumble during competition, as Canadian hurdler Perdita Felicien did in the 2004 Summer Olympics, or US figure skater Michelle Kwan at the 2002 Winter Olympics. In a way it's a part of the drama: the pressure of competition brings out both the best and worst in us. There are of course extraordinary examples of sports figures who are able to overcome this pressure: people like Wayne Gretzky and Lance Armstrong. What they possess is the ability to block out distractions of the mind and the body in order to focus on the task at hand. I can't say that they block out thoughts of reward or satisfaction of the ego – that might be taking things a little far – but for at

---

3. Thomas Merton, *The Way of Chuang Tzu*, New York: New Directions Press, 1965, p. 87

4. Ibid, p. 107

least critical moments of competition, they are able to be fully present to the task at hand. They are able to harness and channel the Tao in a way that few people can. They let the Tao flow through them.

There are no stakes higher than those we compete for as activists. We're not shooting for a prize of gold; we're trying to save lives, species, ecosystems, the future. This is not a game, but real life, with real consequences if we fail. It's no wonder the pressure sometimes trips us up and causes us to stumble along the way.

What can we learn from Chuang Tzu? He says of the archer, "He thinks more of winning than of shooting...."

We're like that too. Our minds are fixed firmly on the outcome. We're *desperate* to win. The reasons are complex. At our core, we are driven by our desire to be of service, to help, to make a difference.

The most important mental shift we can make that will allow us to accept crisis and respond appropriately is to view crisis with detached amusement, or at least detached horror. Only then will we be like the archer who has let go of her need for financial reward, who has set aside her ego, who has cleared her mind of desperation and can simply focus on aiming and releasing one true arrow after another.

When I was starting out in activism, I read this quote by Leo Rosten: "The purpose of life is to matter; to count; to stand for something; to have it make some difference that we lived at all."[5] That line has been my mantra for all of my life as an activist. But that desire can drive us to distraction. And our egos, and the stories that we tell ourselves about our own worth and how others will regard us if we win or lose, further blind us.

There are times that I wish hadn't read that line by Rosten, hadn't printed it on out an old dot-matrix printer and pinned it above my desk and looked at it every day. But I think about it almost every day, and as a result strive to use my life to make some difference.

Taking our ego out of the equation would be one way to lessen our desperation. We could more easily let go of the outcome of our efforts if we weren't so concerned about how our careers will be af-

---

5. Here I'm mostly quoting from memory, but have found numerous references to this quote online and in the public domain. Try *quoteland.com* or *quotegarden.com* for quotes by Leo Rosten.

fected or how we think others will regard us. Remember: "The sage activist remains unattached to desired outcomes; that is why she is never disappointed."

In the chapter on fundraising, "White Stork Cools Wings," I explore the idea of desperation a little more. Desperation is one of the most destructive emotions we can bring to our work. When we are desperate, we claw and scratch at ourselves and our opponents in order to merely survive. Our focus narrows, and we stop seeing the big picture. Think about some of the decisions you've made from a position of desperation. How do we treat other people when we are desperate?

But time and time again, we find ourselves facing one crisis or another.

How we respond to crisis is another matter. Somehow we must come to a place where we honestly believe that the world will not end if we don't win. Only then will we be free enough to realize our full potential as advocates, as leaders, and as business people trying to create positive change in the world. If this seems like a paradox, it is. The *Tao te Ching* is a book of paradoxes.

Dusting Ourselves Off

It can be that the conflict we are struggling with isn't with our opponents, and it might now even be within our organizations. Sometimes our greatest struggle is with ourselves.

"I wage a battle every day," says Maia Gibb, owner of the Victoria, BC-based business Dusting Divas. "Sometimes my vision for my business wins, and sometimes it doesn't."

The business is a natural cleaning products and services enterprise that Gibb started in 2003, following what amounted to a spiritual journey to Cape Breton, Nova Scotia, where Gibb became the custodian of a set of natural cleaning product recipes.

"I was standing in a grocery store line-up and just said out loud, 'If I could fine a job, I'd stay here.' The woman behind me said, 'OK, you can come and take care of my father.'"

She did. Lockey MacLellan was a ninety-three-year-old widower whose wife Mary had died five years earlier. When Gibb showed up to take care of him, she says "he was pissed." He was all alone, and really didn't want to live anymore. Gibb says she had grown up hating cleaning, but was suddenly charged with the care of Lockey and his rambling farm house. She soon fell into a pattern of rhythm and ritual that gave her "a soulful connection to my living space." But it wasn't without its setbacks.

"I was completely incompetent," smiles Gibb. "I knew nothing about taking care of a house or a ninety-three-year-old." She turned to Mary's cookbooks which she says were like diaries, full of notes and stories written neatly in the margins for inspiration. She learned that Lockey enjoyed cod cakes, and she set to preparing them for dinner one night. "I didn't realize that it was salt cod, so I didn't soak it before preparing it. When I served it to Lockey, I was pretty proud. He took one bite and spat it out on the table. Then he looked and me and said, 'At least I know now why you're not married!'"

Among Mary's many recipes were those for cleaning products. The MacLellans didn't have money to buy fancy cleaners, so they made their own from simple ingredients. But those simple, natural cleaners had another benefit. "I didn't realize that the reason I hated cleaning so much was because I was poisoning myself," says Gibb.

She returned to the west coast where she refined the recipes with her own research on aromatherapy and essential oils to create a product line that many of its users agree change the way they feel about cleaning. In addition, self-styled Head Diva Maia has hired a team of women, many from disadvantaged situations, to offer cleaning services, *feng shui* consultations, and insight into the connection between health and home. The Divas see themselves not as maids, but as activists helping people rid their homes of toxins while providing people with a soulful connection with their residence.

But as any entrepreneur will tell you, starting a business is fraught with peril. Gibb is the first to admit that her strong point is her vision for a company that makes people less dependent on toxic products in their homes and helps women find self-worth through the work that they do, and not on the day-to-day business management.

"When I form a picture of myself in my head," she says, "it's of a woman who doesn't have the skill to pull this off. But then I also have this picture of what this business could be."

That's where the daily battle is waged. Like any social entrepreneur, whether they are leading an ethically driven business or a human rights organization, Gibb experiences conflict – internal and external – and crisis on a near daily basis.

It was amid this inner battle that Maia received a call from, of all places, Cape Breton, asking if she was interested in franchising Dusting Divas. It seems that a local co-operative was being formed by women who wanted to follow the model that Maia Gibb had established on the opposite coast of the country. Could she fly out to Cape Breton and teach them how to do it?

"What was I going to show them?" laughs Gibb. "How not to make money? I still had all these unanswered questions. How could I teach these folks anything?"

Gibb says, "The moment that I let go of the idea that I had to have all the answers, I was able to see that I did have something worth teaching these women. Failure and mistakes were just part of the process of what I needed to learn. Each stumble seemed like an absolute failure, but it wasn't!" Gibb flew back to Cape Breton and helped establish Dusting Divas there. She's now actively engaged in setting up Dusting Divas co-operatives elsewhere across North America.

"I don't feel so afraid to make a mistake anymore," she says. "When I started, I expected myself to be perfect right from the start." But she has learned that conflict and crisis are just a part of the struggle to make the world a better place, and that how we respond to them determines whether or not we succeed.[6]

Yielding, Stopping

Part of responding to conflict and crisis is knowing when to stop.

Chuang Tzu says:

> To know when to stop
> To know when you can get no further
> By your own action,

---

6. To learn more about Dusting Divas, visit *dustingdivas.com*.

This is the right beginning![7]

It was the late 1990s and Rob Sinclair was the only card-carrying member of the Progressive Conservative Party of Ontario who worked for the International Fund for Animal Welfare (IFAW). Early in Conservative Premier Mike Harris's first term in office, Sinclair had been an assistant to a cabinet minister. Now he was working with other conservation-minded Conservatives to force Premier Harris to end the inhumane hunting of the province's black bears each spring. As an insider with an acute sense of the political strengths and weaknesses of the Harris government, Sinclair understood that convincing them to abandon the spring bear hunt would not be a matter of traditional campaign strategies. They needed a plan that would take the campaign to a place where every politician pays attention – at the polling booth.

Working with the Schad Foundation's David Cotter and Peter Kendall, Sinclair exploited the weaknesses of the Harris government in order to force a ban on the spring bear hunt. "We weren't afraid to do whatever we had to do to get people's attention," says Sinclair. They put the issue of hunting on the map during a by-election in the traditionally pro-hunting Nickel Belt riding around Sudbury, Ontario, by focusing on the province's recent decision to lower the hunting age in the province from sixteen to twelve. "Guns for kids" became the biggest story during the by-election.

What did that have to do with the spring bear hunt? Except that guns were involved in both issues, very little. But Rob knew that the spring bear hunt was popular in northern Ontario, so he and his colleagues chose an issue that would resonate instead. They made this clear to the provincial government.

"That brought the province to the table," says Sinclair. The Ministry of Natural Resources convened a secret meeting at Toronto's Regal Constellation Hotel in October of 1998. "In that meeting the province offered us a ban on hunting with dogs and a ban on using bait to hunt," remembers Sinclair. But the campaigners wanted a complete ban on all spring black bear hunting. Hunting with dogs only accounted for 150 black bear deaths each year, while the spring

---

7. Thomas Merton, *The Way of Chuang Tzu*, New York: New Directions Press, 1965, p. 133

hunt accounted for an average of 4,000 kills each spring alone. "We asked ourselves: does this look like a win?" The answer was no. "We walked away from that meeting and turned up the heat."

The next step of the campaign was to target eight politically sensitive ridings coveted by Harris's Conservative government around the Niagara Peninsula in the south of the province. In these largely suburban ridings, the spring bear hunt issue did resonate, so they led with it. Using money from Robert Schad, himself a high-profile Conservative donor, Sinclair and Cotter orchestrated intense political pressure in the swing ridings, using newspaper ads, video drops, and billboards in a hard-hitting campaign that boiled for months. Election day grew closer.

"That's when the phone rang," says Sinclair. Premier Harris asked Robert Schad for a meeting, and there offered an end to the black bear hunt. Schad asked about baiting and dogs and the Premier refused to put them on the table. (The goal of the campaign was to ban spring hunting, baiting, and dogs.) "We knew that getting the banning of the spring bear hunt was huge," Sinclair says. Robert Schad told Premier Harris that his "war" was over.

To know when a win is a win is a key element in achieving success.

How is this campaign to end the spring bear hunt in Ontario different from the example about grizzly bear hunting discussed earlier? Strategically, the grizzly bear hunt lacked several key elements that made the spring bear hunt campaign in Ontario a success. In Ontario, IFAW demonstrated that it was willing to speak to any similar or related issue in order to demonstrate its ability to threaten politicians at the polls. And in Ontario, the electoral math wasn't so hopelessly lopsided towards a rout. In British Columbia, Raincoast's campaign placed all of its eggs in the NDP government's basket and failed to secure a commitment from the BC Liberals so that when they came to power, there was no foundation for support.

To know when to stop, we must first know our own strengths and weaknesses. When in 1999 I helped create Wildcanada.net I told my board of directors that I would dedicate five to seven years to the endeavour. I knew that I would be able to take the organization just so far, and no further. I did my best, and then I stepped aside. I knew that its success or failure must not depend on me. There are times when you have to be able to admit that your skills are not the ones needed to carry a campaign or an organization to the next place, the next step in its evolution, or to completion.

Another element of knowing when to stop is to know when to yield.

"Know when to yield to opposition, and you will overcome challenge," says Lao Tzu. We can think through the myriad ways in which our opponents will act against us, and we believe that we have a clear sense of how we will define a victory when it occurs.

But even with this forethought, it's hard to know when to yield. It's also difficult to see yielding as a strategic withdrawal rather than acceptance of defeat. We have to know in our hearts when it is time to fight or to walk away, which is no easy task. It's hard to accept defeat graciously and understand that something you love might be lost. It helps me sometimes to think of this as a tactical retreat. We step back to regroup and revise our strategy and then step forward again to re-engage.

> It is better to take a step back in confidence
> than to creep forward in doubt
>
> This is said to be moving forward without
>   advancing
> pushing your opponent back without aggression
> (*Tao*, 69)

The business community is filled with stories of entrepreneurs who failed in their first, second, or third attempts to start a business, but who found success in their next effort. These leaders knew when to yield (sometimes called bankruptcy) and then step forward again.

To be strategic, our campaigns must ebb and flow. There is a continual advance and retreat.

> The sage activist realizes that all things are in flux
> and so she does not try to hold too long to one
>   tactic

If she is not afraid of failure
there is nothing that she won't try in order to
succeed
(*Tao*, 74)

Finding Grace in the Flow

Chuang Tzu tells another story that illustrates how we can strive for a response to challenge and opportunity with grace. Khing, the master woodcarver, is summoned by the Prince of Lu to carve a bell stand. When Khing has completed his task, all who see the bell stand believe it must have been the work of spirits, it is that lovely. But Khing explains that he is only a simple workman.

Khing says that the way to make the perfect carving is to first set your heart to rest by avoiding distractions. He fasts, which we might take to mean a mental fasting as much as a physical one. He then sets aside any hope of gain or success, praise or criticism, and in doing so abandons his own ego. Only then does he go into the forest to seek the piece of wood wherein the monument lies concealed. He says:

My own collected thought
Encountered the hidden potential in the wood;
From this live encounter came the work
Which you ascribe to the spirits.[8]

Khing simply allowed his own natural talents to reveal what was already there. But to "allow" it to occur, a deep and profound spiritual journey had to take place first, one that was the result of years of discipline.

We've all experienced that which the woodcarver talks about: a campaign of graceful simplicity that seems to come together with little effort and whose outcome seems assured from the start. What we are experiencing here is the power of following the Tao. We should not be tricked into believing that these campaigns are easy. They are not. But rather than acting out a sense of crisis, we

---

8. Thomas Merton, *The Way of Chuang Tzu*, New York: New Directions Press, 1965, p. 111

should allow our natural talents, experience, and inherent wisdom to rise and guide us. Instead of resisting, accept the natural flow of events and our actions will arise of their own accord. Like the wood-carver, we seek out the natural forms where our plans already exist and, with a lifetime of experience embodied in our every word and thought and gesture, allow substance to emerge naturally.

Calming the desperation in our hearts will allow us to see the world as it really is, rather than through the blinders imposed by our ego, our fear, and our anger.

> Strive for emptiness and openness
> Practice being still
> Be at ease
> When turmoil swirls around you
> be as the stone in the river's flow
> Allow the waters to come and go
>   come and go
> Be still
> Wait for the right moment to act
> ...
> Knowing that the Tao is the source of our efforts
> we can have faith that we will not fail
> (*Tao*, 16)

Practice being still. Be as the stone in the river, letting the course of events flow around you, sometimes over you, shaping you, slowly moulding you with its softness. Wait for the right moment to act: let stillness give rise to the appropriate action. Have faith: we who struggle against injustice in the world are the Tao's means of finding balance and harmony in the universe. With such noble purpose, how could we possibly fail?

7

WHITE STORK COOLS WINGS

Hot Taoist Tips for Fundraising

> When an organization is in harmony with the Tao
> it shares openly with others, prizing above all the
>   others' successes
> When an organization is out of harmony with the
>   Tao
> it hoards and competes and tries to stifle friends
>   and foe alike
> (*Tao*, 46)

If you've been reading this book from the start, you can probably guess that there are no hot Taoist tips for fundraising, at least not the type that will give you means to generate quick cash for your business or not-for-profit. If you want hot tips for raising money for your non-profit, read Kim Klein, Andy Robinson, Harvey McKinnon, Madeline Stanionis, or Mike Johnston.[1] In the Warring States period of ancient China, fundraising was likely done the old-fashioned way – taxes, taking your goods to market, or highway robbery.

---

1. For resources go to *harveymckinnon.com, grassrootsfundraising.org/howto/,* or *donordigital.com.* Visit *hjcnewmedia.com* to find information on Mike Johnston's books.

Instead of instructions on writing a good fundraising letter, theories on direct mail response rates, or securing venture capital, what you'll get here are some riddles and paradox, a short lecture on scarcity and organizational theory, and just possibly the secret to eternal happiness.

And really, doesn't that sound better than fundraising?

As activists and as business owners we have to raise money to do our work. Even the smallest organization or ethically driven business incurs expenses, and as such, must raise money. For a number of years, I was on the board of directors of the Bow Valley Naturalists, a Banff, Alberta-based organization that conducted bird counts and nature hikes while being one of the staunchest and most vocal defenders of Banff National Park and the Bow Valley from exploitation. We had a whopping budget of $500 a year. When I worked for Wildcanada.net, we spent that in the first two or three hours of each day. And for a short period of time, I worked for a large American conservation organization that spent $500 every five minutes!

This challenge isn't confined to the non-profit sector, as any business owner will tell you. I have friends who run small businesses with the goal of creating social or environmental change who struggle with the same challenges as executive directors of small non-profits: the never-ending challenge of raising money. What can we learn from each other to help make this necessary task easier?

Since the late 1980s, I've been raising money for various causes and organizations, and I will confess that it's the hardest thing I do. And since it's true confession time, I'll admit that though the concepts behind each chapter in this book challenge me in different ways, writing a chapter on fundraising actually raises my blood pressure.

As activists and small business owners focused on change, we often have this response to raising money. There are many reasons. We have a complex relationship with money. We associate it with power, and sometimes with the opponents with whom we struggle. Many people in civil society view money as the cause of society's woes, though I believe it's more complex than that.

Some of us have personal challenges that are associated with money, wealth, abundance, or success. Money is a taboo subject in some families, and a constant source of stress and friction. And many people believe that money is a personal matter that shouldn't be discussed even among friends.

For some, money is tied to our own sense of worth and value. "As we walk in the world we say 'This is my money, my world, my house, my things,'" says Carol Newell of Renewal Partners.[2] "Once we come into possession of something, it's hard to let go. For many, business is about building up possessions, and about making profits at all cost. But we are all part of a bigger picture that we sometimes lose sight of." Newell is a leading advocate for placing substantial personal wealth into the service of social change-making. Since 1989, she has increasingly directed her financial assets to support and stimulate economic development and civil society that complement natural systems and the local economy in British Columbia, Canada.

Newell inherited money at the age of twenty-one, and chose to invest it in the efforts of others who wanted to make the world a better place. Such selflessness is uncommon. Many of us come from backgrounds where wealth is fiercely guarded, owing to our belief that it alone can make us happy.

For these many reasons, we sometimes have a visceral reaction to the idea of asking for money. Some people view fundraising as a type of begging. We picture ourselves stooped over, cap in hand. Sometimes we think that asking for money is beneath us. Recently, when discussing my departure as executive director of Wildcanada. net, someone close to me said, "I bet you're happy not to be *begging* for money any more."

It was an interesting comment. More interesting was that in my mind I briefly thought, "Isn't that the bloody truth."

But instead of begging there is supplication, which means "to ask for humbly or earnestly." The difference is whether we bring a scarcity mentality to our efforts to raise money, believing that there will never be enough and always waiting for the next shoe to drop, or an abundance mentality, believing, as Lao Tzu says, to "know that there is enough and there will be."

---

2. Visit *renewalpartners.com* for more information on Renewal Partners and Carol Newell's vision.

The *Tao te Ching* offers insight into our relationship with money by speaking to our attitudes about abundance, scarcity, resourcefulness, and humility. It has suggestions for how to match the size of an organization to the availability of resources. It addresses an ideal vision for philanthropy. And it offers some sage advice for those of us who are willing to look in the mirror and examine ourselves first, seeking to understand our own attitudes and responses to the challenges we face as activists before going to others seeking support. That's where we'll begin.

> The Tao is easy to understand
> and to apply to your efforts
> Yet try to grasp it with your intellect
> or recite it as rules
> and you will be confounded
>
> These teachings are simply part of the world
> and nobody can fully know them
>
> To start, understand yourself
> and keep your heart wide open
> (*Tao*, 70)

When it comes to money, it's easy to close our hearts.

Virtue and the White Stork

Many of us operate within a scarcity belief system, which drives us to respond out of fear and clouds our judgment and decision-making. It also causes us to act out of desperation.

When we practice White Stork Cools Wings in Tai Chi, we open our hearts. This can help us let go of the fear and the attitude of scarcity that we have concerning money. With your right foot, step sideways and press your left hand across your body while cupping your right hand at your left hip. Then stand up, switching your hands so that your right hand presses on the dome of heaven, while your left hand presses toward the earth. Feel your chest open wide.

When I do this posture in Tai Chi, I always take a big breath, filling my lungs with oxygen, and in doing so, opening my heart to the world.

Fundamental to the Taoist belief system is the concept of te, or virtue. Alan Watts says of te, "The chances of survival are best when there is no anxiety to survive, and that the greatest power (te) is available to those who do not seek power and who do not use force."[3]

Lao Tzu's hot tips for fundraisers are about the attitudes we have toward money and the scale of the organization that we fundraise for. How we approach fundraising has as much to do with our belief systems as it does the cause we represent.

Te means virtue or power and factors into how we seek what we need from the world. For it is with virtue that we can address our attitudes toward the difficult task of raising money.

Watts references the *Bhagavad Gita's* principle of "action without concern for results" in his discussion about virtue. In the *Bhagavad Gita*, Krishna says, "You have a right to your actions, But never to your actions' fruits."[4]

There are two ideas for fundraisers here. The first is that the greatest barrier to finding sources of money for our work is our anxiety about finding money at all. The second is to not be attached to outcomes. Our ability to raise money is inversely proportionate to our anxiety level around finding it!

Madeline Stanionis is one of the best online fundraisers in North America. She and her colleagues at San Francisco- and Washington, DC-based Donordigital have helped dozens of organizations as diverse as Amnesty International, the Humane Society of the United States, and UNICEF raise $15 million each year for their causes. Though she might not call it the Tao, Madeline employs the teaching of Lao Tzu in her work with her clients. She says that "having faith in your cause" is the most important aspect of raising money. But she admits that, "I often waiver between sheer panic and knowing that we will have enough to do our work."

---

3. Alan Watts, *Tao: The Watercourse Way*, New York: Pantheon Books, 1975, p. 113

4. *Bhagavad Gita: A New Translation*, trans. Stephen Mitchell, New York: Three Rivers Press, 2000, p. 54

Stanionis says that the art of fundraising is "knowing when you have enough to accomplish your goals." It comes down to approaching whatever problem we are trying to solve with honesty. "We have to know that the work we are doing is true and is good and is helping the world." She says that when we know these things in our hearts, we can then honestly approach others to ask for their support.

We also have to accept that the return on our hard work and our investment in a fundraising program may not happen on the day we expect, or in the way we want it to. But if we trust ourselves and our commitment to our good work, "the money will find us," says Stanionis.

"If you are pushing hard on something, but that issue and the public are not ready," says Stanionis, "people will see that. But if you do the activism first, tell a true story and prepare people, and are prepared yourself to take advantage of events as they occur," then you will be successful. "If there is a match, then the art is to simply be ready." Be ready to accept the generosity of others; be ready to welcome their gifts with an open heart.

What does it mean to be ready to take advantage of events as they occur? "You must have the ability to sense that something is in the air, and that it's more than just a one-day story, but instead is a stirring of the hearts and souls of people around an important issue," says Stanionis. This means being able to stand back and understand when the public and an issue have aligned.

If people aren't ready to give and you approach them out of anxiety and fear, they will sense that and won't give. But if your timing is right and if you are in touch with something that "captures the deep stirring of the soul of people," then you can have great success. "You have to have trust in people, and have faith in your cause," says Stanionis.

Letting Go of Outcomes

The *Bhagavad Gita*'s principle of "action without concern for results" also suggests that sage fundraisers not concern themselves with the outcome of their labours. This is "doing our work, and stepping aside."

As fundraisers, we expend our energy on the front end, using our skill and intuition to craft a message or a program or organization that stirs something in the public's souls. Then, when we have done our work to the best of our abilities we need to step back and not tie our egos or self-esteem to the outcome of the effort.

Easy? Not. Neither the outcome nor the lessons to be learned are unimportant. The trick is learning not to fixate on the results.

In 2004, I undertook a direct mail program for Wildcanada. net. We borrowed money to develop the campaign, hired a talented fundraising consultant to help put the package together, and mailed to 20,000 households. And then we waited. The week that passed between when we dropped the mail-out (that's fancy fundraiser talk for put the envelopes in the mail) and when the first cheque arrived at our office was one of the longest weeks of my life. Then, when the mail trickled rather than gushed in, I became first anxious, then annoyed.

I tracked the results using an Excel spreadsheet, adding new figures each day for the number of donations, number of return-to-sender replies, amount of donations. I auto-calculated each day the percentage of responses and created ratios of donor to donation size. I had a fancy line graph that wiggled up and down the page to show the spikes in donor activity and the deep valley that came afterwards. For the better part of two months I was fixated on that chart and the results of the campaign. While it was a modest success for a first-time mailing, my scrutiny after the fact was just a waste of energy.

In short, I was struggling: I could not give up my interest in the fruits of my work.

I believe that fundraising is the hardest job that we do as activists. Whether we are holding a bake sale to raise money for a small community association, or undertaking a multi-million-dollar capital campaign to purchase a headquarters for our international organization, fundraising is both stressful and rewarding – and almost always difficult.

It's stressful because the consequences of failure are high. Without money, we can't employ staff to do the good work that they do. Without money, serving our cause becomes much more difficult.

But it's also rewarding because it provides us with the opportunity for direct contact with people who support our work. One of my most enjoyable tasks as an executive director was to contact those who sent our organization money to thank them. Donors would be so surprised to get a call! It was often the highlight of my day.

Lao Tzu's fundamental message for today's fundraisers is to not see raising money as a struggle, and to approach the task calmly, not out of desperation.

Scale, Scope, and Pace

Moderating the size and scale of our organizations can have a profound effect on the resources needed to operate those organizations and accomplish our goals within civil society.

Lao Tzu advised that the ideal size of a state is about that of "a village." A village also suggests a place/size wherein everything necessary is available, but not in triplicate. It's just big enough to be efficient. What can we learn from this about our organizations?

If he were writing today, he might say that the ideal size of an organization or company is modest in scope. Too big and it strays from its mission, becomes obsessed with growth and self-preservation, struggles with bureaucracy and succumbs to competition with other large organizations or businesses for power, customers, and resources. Too small and it isn't able to leverage the power and resources needed to accomplish its tasks or develop its market potential.

Knowing how to determine the ideal size of an organization and how to develop a strategy to achieve it is another matter altogether. We need to ask questions: What is the scale of the problem we are addressing? Who else is working toward a solution? What is our unique role?

For example, Gideon Rosenblatt, the executive director of ONE/Northwest – a Seattle-based non-profit that provides technology assistance to environmental groups throughout the Pacific Northwest of Canada and the United States – and a former Microsoft manager, suggests that there are three primary types of organizations within a social movement: people organizations, solution organizations, and resource organizations.

"People organizations define themselves by serving distinct audiences," says Rosenblatt in his paper *Movement as Network*.[5] "These organizations come in two varieties: small grassroots organizers and large environmental brands. Their role in the network is to reach out to various segments of society and help them build appropriate connections with environmental causes. The keys to success for these organizations are carefully defining audiences and listening closely to their needs.

"Solution Organizations define themselves not only by the issue they focus on, but also by their particular approach to solving it. Solution Organizations house the movement's issue-related technical and policy expertise. They also play a critical role in ensuring that ecologically important issues receive focus even if they lack the kind of mass appeal to draw large constituent bases.

"Resource Organizations define themselves by the particular expertise or resources that they bring to the rest of the network. These organizations specialize in developing unique resources and expertise and in deploying these resources throughout the network to raise its collective effectiveness. Examples of expertise include fundraising, technology, campaign strategy, legal strategy, or marketing and communications."

Rosenblatt says that for organizations to be effective they need to specialize in only one of these niches, and no more. "Specialization and a focus on core competencies open the door to new strategies and new types of relationships between organizations. Complexity theory suggests that for the environmental movement to evolve to its next stage this kind of specialization of institutions is half the problem," she says. "The other half is weaving these very different individual nodes together into an integrated, harmonious whole."

In Rosenblatt's model, we see three types of organizations working together in symbiosis. These organizations maintained their own unique identity, purpose, mission, and mode of operations, while collaborating together on aspects of their work. I would suggest that

---

5. Gideon Rosenblatt, *Movement as Network*, published online by ONE/Northwest at *movementasnetwork.org*.

the next step is to begin to dissolve the membranes that separate us as organizations so that we function more as a collaborative, as a *movement*. In this way, we can avoid the duplication of basic functions that are needed to serve our organizations – human resources, clerical services, administration – and create a pool of leaders that can serve the entire movement.

Rosenblatt's paper is an important read for anybody wanting to define their organization's niche. Once we've discovered it, there is another set of questions that are equally important. How big do we need to be to properly address our niche, and what resources are needed to achieve such a size? How will we know when we're there? What mechanisms do we have in place to manage such growth?

Here we also need to separate growth and size from appropriate scale.

There is tremendous momentum in civil society to grow. We equate growth with effectiveness, success, and sustainability. This is the corporate paradigm of growth.

We grow because we believe that stagnation sends a signal of imminent decline to our funders; because bigger budgets, more staff, and additional programs make us believe we can accomplish more. We grow because it gives the illusion of power, and in the case of civil society organizations, the power to affect positive change, and because it satisfies in us a desire for that power, and the belief that we can control it.

Growing larger isn't necessarily bad. It's not how large you grow that matters as much as how you grow. Top-heavy organizations now dominate the environmental movement, leading many in our ranks to question what happened to the grassroots movement that led to the first Earth Day in 1970 and subsequent passage of the Endangered Species Act, the Clean Air Act, and the Clean Water Act in the United States. If bigger means expanding our base of support to include more culturally diverse communities and average citizens working in their own backyards on issues that are complementary to our own, then grow we should. But adding another office for another vice-president runs contrary to what many are coming to accept is needed to make our movements more effective. Bigger isn't necessarily better.

Reaching that optimal scale to be effective is a matter of planning, taking care to develop the strengths of the people we work with. Lao Tzu says to "focus on your organization's people, not its capital." Develop the skills, leadership, and effectiveness of the people we work with, rather than invest in fancy offices, expensive equipment, and capital-intensive projects.

Organizations that have found the appropriate scale are more efficient with their resources, more creative in their approach to advocacy, and frequently more in touch with the issues they are working on.

Of course, large organizations aren't simply going to pack up shop on the advice of a 2,500-year-old sage. And they shouldn't. But large organizations have a special responsibility in civil society given their resources and the number of people they can reach with their message. Lao Tzu would also advise another tactic: "Focus on improving, not growing."

One of the things that I struggled with while working with Wildcanada.net was the pace of growth. I know that many other organizations struggle with this as well. Lao Tzu says:

> To grow too fast is to hasten your demise
> Be as careful with your success as with your failure
> (*Tao*, 31)

In our early days, Wildcanada.net grew much too quickly. We set up our online resources to serve one campaign at a time. But we quickly learned that we could not wait for one campaign to end before starting the next, so we had to modify our software on the fly in order to accommodate multiple campaigns. And then a crisis would occur and we'd have to add yet another campaign before we finished jury-rigging the last one. Programmers Paul Novitski, and later Mike James, worked in a frenzy to duct tape our campaign software together with each new initiative. But you can only hold things together so long with this method of approach, and the result was that from time to time, things fell apart.

Often, though certainly not always, civil society's preoccupation with growth creates rifts between organizations as they compete for finite resources, struggle to carve out a niche for themselves, and argue over petty differences rather than focusing on solving problems.

> If you seek to build an empire of your organization
> others will compete with you for power and
>> resources
>
> (*Tao*, 3)

There are examples of organizations that, faced with declining resources, have chosen to down-size or merge with other organizations with similar mandates.

There are also examples, such as the Sage Centre, associated with the Tides Canada Foundation, of organizations who offer shared administrative services for groups, thus eliminating overlap and duplication, and letting them focus on their core mandates. With resources so scarce for our program work, organizations could eliminate many unnecessary costs by availing themselves of such services.[6]

There needs to be a balance between individual organizational interests and the long-term goals of the alliance when working together. Organizations come to exist because they feel they have a unique approach to solving a problem. There is strength in the diversity of ideas that emerge as a result of different organizations taking different angles and offering new perspectives. The development of these new perspectives must be balanced against the saturation that can come with the proliferation of new charities and non-profits in civil society, but in general, diversity breeds strength. Guarding that unique perspective is crucial, but more important is loyalty to our cause above almost all other considerations.

I say almost all, because as I discuss in the final chapter of this book, some considerations like our own personal health and well-being must take priority so that we can make our contributions are long-lasting.

---

6. Visit *sagecentre.org* for more information.

Know when you have enough to accomplish your
    goals
and you will succeed
Know when to stop
and you will always move forward
Seek nothing
and you will find everything you need
(*Tao*, 44)

Cloudwalking Owl says that finding support that also strengthens our ties to our grassroots community is critical to our long-term
success. "I am not the first person to make this point," he says. "Mo-
handas Gandhi referred to similar points in his book *My Experiments
With Truth*. He felt that the only sort of organization that would
keep its connection with the grassroots was one in which the entire budget came from funds directly from the membership. In this
way, if the group disconnected with the grassroots, the funding base
would evaporate. In other words, Gandhi argued that the group
should never accept government or NGO grants, donations from
wealthy individuals or trusts, and should never acquire a trust fund
of its own to ensure stable funding."

Some would argue that this is not realistic in the twenty-first
century. Others might point out that there are many causes and mis-
sions being undertaken today that defy explanation and involvement
at the grassroots level. But Gandhi's point has strength: our greatest
virtue as activists is our connection with everyday people. Growth
that outstrips that connection is not sustainable.

Growing because you have resources available today, but have
no plan to sustain those resources in the future, is an almost certain path to failure. At Wildcanada.net, we grew very quickly in our
first couple of years when our success was dependent on short-term
grants from philanthropic foundations. As we made the uncomfortable shift away from these grants to longer-term forms of funding
such as direct mail, online fundraising, and earned revenue, we had
difficultly maintaining our level of income.

Many organizations experience this. In part, poor long-term
planning is to blame. We focus on the problem we are trying to

solve rather than building sustainable organizations to address the long-term consequences of that problem. As I've said elsewhere, this is understandable: it's the reason we become activists in the first place!

But the consequence is that we run short-term plans instead of looking ten, fifteen, or twenty years ahead, knowing full well that we'll need that sort of time scale to address the issues we are tackling. The opposite of this approach is our refusal to let our organizations die once they have served their purpose, an instinct that is discussed in coming chapters.

The Gift of Not Being Dependant

Part of the reason we don't address long-term organizational stability is that funding from philanthropic foundations rarely covers these organizational development challenges. Such funding is most often earmarked for particular causes, not the structures needed to face them successfully over the long-term. Knowing this, we must find a way to work together with those who support us to ensure our organizations achieve their optimal size and carve out their appropriate niche.

We must also remember that organizations, like individuals, must know when to step back.

Lao Tzu might suggest how philanthropists approach the causes they support. "[The sage] knows when to stop and becomes a true help," he says. "A true philanthropist, like a good parent, brings people to the point where they can help themselves," says Stephen Mitchell.[7]

But usually the nature of how organizations are funded doesn't encourage this sort of independence. Financial support from granting agencies and donors comes sporadically, or in waves, even though any given campaign might take five, ten years, or even longer.

And as organizations dependent on outside support, we become addicted to short-term grants and annual donation drives. When a philanthropic foundation shifts its focus, as many do every five or ten

---

7. Lao Tzu, *The Tao te Ching: A New English Translation*, Stephen Mitchell, trans., New York: Harper Perennial, 1988, p. 110

years, we act surprised. Instead, we should be prepared. That means developing revenue diversification programs for our organizations that take advantage of many types and sources of support.

Virtue in this case is about finding a balance between the effective size an organization must be to carry out its mission, and the resources available to it. This is where our power comes in, virtue being the natural arising power available to us through the Tao.

Finding the optimal size of our organization isn't easy. Only because of its massive clout backed by tens of thousands of letter writers can Amnesty International successfully advocate for the freedom of political prisoners. MoveOn.org, an Internet-based organization in the United States, has well over three million members, and depends on those numbers in its efforts to shift the balance of power in the US from conservative to progressive.

Finding the appropriate scale of our organization for the resources available will ease our fundraising challenges. "Let go," advises Lao Tzu. "Avoid excess, extremes, and complacency."

The single greatest barrier to successfully raising money is our fear. We fear our failure and we cling to our hope for success. But Lao Tzu argues that both hope and fear are phantoms.

> What does this mean that hope and fear are
>   phantoms
> of the organizations we lead?
> We think of ourselves as the organizations we lead
> But these bodies are merely the vehicle to
>   accomplish our work
> When we stop clinging to them, we can abandon
>   many fears
> (*Tao*, 13)

Organization as Identity

As activists, we have become very attached to our organizations. The proliferation of charitable and non-profit organizations in the United States – with 40,000 new groups being created each year – illustrates this point.

But we also have failed to respect the life-cycle of our organizations. Like anything, they have a birth, a life, and a death. But we have a hard time letting go of our organizations when they have served their purpose and run their course. We don't like to let go. We fail to heed Lao Tzu's advice to do our work and then step aside.

> Understand attachment
> yet remain unattached
> Accept things as they are
> and the Tao will well up inside you
> and you will return to the origin of the Way
> (*Tao*, 28)

When organizations stop serving a purpose, or when that purpose has been met, we should recognize this and think carefully about how best to serve the movement. We need to acknowledge what we have accomplished and learned through the organization, and then, if necessary or appropriate, move on to the next challenge or opportunity.

In evaluating our organizations, we might ask: Are there others who can address the issue better? Are there those who can watch over the outcome of our work after we're gone? Does keeping this organization functioning, even nominally, provide us with options for the future that we would lose if the organization ceases to exist? Are there other more pressing issues that we now need to turn our attention to?

All of this is to suggest that organizations can function like a genuine *movement* within civil society, or even simply within the environmental community of organizations, rather than as the largely unrelated groups that we currently are. To achieve this would require a degree of co-operation that is currently not present.

But organizations have an energy of their own – part of the "whole being greater than the sum of its parts" equation. When we do choose to let an organization end, seeing that its own unique energy is transferred within the movement is very important.

And because we grow so attached to the organizations that we build and serve, letting go of them can be painful and difficult. Let's not forget that we serve a cause, and that servitude to our organizations is merely a means to an end. (I talk more about this in the chapter "Wave Hands like Clouds," which is about moving through challenge and change.)

Learning to Live with Abundance

As fundraisers, we are leaders within our movement. We don't hold the purse strings, we create them, and as a result our voices carry sway within our organizations. With that power comes responsibility. We have to be on the lookout for the matters that might poison our virtue, our te, and hamper our ability to do good work, serve our cause, and help us raise money.

> Fear drives us to make mistakes
> and creates a culture of scarcity
> Do not be afraid
> and you will flourish
>
> Know that there is enough
> and there will be
> (*Tao*, 46)

Lao Tzu advocates for this throughout the *Tao te Ching*. He talks about developing an abundance mentality. "Whether we live in resource-poor circumstances or resource-rich ones, even if we're loaded with more money or goods or everything you could possibly dream of wanting or needing, we live with scarcity as an underlying assumption," says Lynne Twist in her groundbreaking book, *The Soul of Money*. "It is an unquestioned, sometimes even unspoken, defining condition of life.

"In the mind-set of scarcity," continues Twist, "our relationship with money is an expression of fear; a fear that drives us in an endless and unfulfilling chase for more, or into compromises that promise a way out of the chase or discomfort around money."

Twist speaks from direct experience as a fundraiser for the Hunger Project, born from experiences serving the most desperate people in some of the world's poorest countries. Twist's examination of our relationship with money is a must-read for anyone who hopes to make a lasting difference in the world.

"Scarcity is a lie," she says. "Independent of any actual amount of resources, it is an unexamined and false system of assumptions, options, and beliefs from which we view the world a place where we are in constant danger of having our needs unmet."[8]

The belief that if you "know there is enough then there will be" as Lao Tzu advises is a tough message for fundraisers to hear, as we are constantly seeking more. It's made easier knowing that the organizations that we serve are the appropriate size and continue to operate with a vibrant and timely mission.

> If our leaders were to keep the Tao at their centre
> the world and its creatures would be at peace
> Nature would be in balance
> People would be content with simplicity
>
> ...
>
> With freedom from desire
> would come tranquility
> (*Tao*, 37)

Our jobs as fundraisers are made all the more difficult by the complex human emotions that accompany any discussion of money.

Lao Tzu – like so many other sages – advises simplicity. With simplicity, the need for large amounts of capital is eliminated, and we gain freedom from desire. Simplicity need not mean living in a cave and communicating by smoke signals while we dry animal pelts over a fire to prepare for a winter without heat or light (though that does sound like good clean fun). Instead, it might mean omitting the etched glass logo on the wall-to-wall windows at the entrance to our high-rise office tower.

Simplicity of needs and freedom from desire both speak to the Taoist principle of making use of emptiness, expressed best in this passage from the *Tao te Ching*:

---

8. Lynn Twist, *The Soul of Money: Transforming Your Relationship with Money and Life*. New York, London: Norton, 2003, pp. 45, 47

The bicycle glides on two wheels
but it is the hole at each wheel's centre
that makes it move

We fashion a cup from clay
but it is the space inside the cup
that we drink from
(*Tao*, 11)

If we can begin to see that having less allows us to top up our coffers with creativity and passion, we might go a longer way to achieving our goals.

One of the most effective organizations working to protect Canada's national parks is a tiny grassroots one called the Bow Valley Naturalists. For thirty years, this group was led by the likes of Gerry Wilkie, Jon Whyte, and most predominantly, Mike and Diane McIvor, volunteers all. As mentioned earlier, they ran this feisty organization for around $500 a year, which they used to mail newsletters and rent a hall for monthly meetings.

While other organizations professionalized, hiring staff and developing advocacy programs that required fundraising, the Bow Valley Naturalists got by on sheer passion and determination. Over the years they fought countless battles in defence of Banff National Park in Alberta, and leveraged that park's pre-eminence to advocate for stronger laws protecting all of Canada's parks.

They did it as part of a team of organizations, some of which had paid staff, and some of which had budgets for travel, lobbying, advertising, and the like. But those partnerships didn't form until the late 1980s. The Bow Valley Naturalists were working to protect Banff and other national parks for two decades before that.

I'm not suggesting that we abandon the professionalization of our organizations or movement. But it's true that with professionalization comes many challenges, not the least of which is the need to raise large sums of money to maintain organizational infrastructure. For some groups, it could be argued that keeping that infrastructure in place *appears* to be their mission. Daily bureaucratic activities often outweigh actual on-the-ground efforts. We build very large organizations, believing that we need them in order to successfully leverage the kind of decisions we are seeking to protect what we love, but in the end, we often spend far more time keeping the organizations afloat than we do working on the issues at hand.

"The sage activist focuses on the fruit and not the flower," says Lao Tzu. The flower is pretty, but it is a distraction. It is the fruit that bears the seeds. It is the fruit that we eat. And while the flower is necessary for pollination, it is the fruit that yields a harvest.

In fundraising, we should focus on the fruit and not the flower. Do not be distracted by colour and flash: focus on substance. In the end, our values and our virtue will attract the people to provide us with the resources we need to do our work. And while it might run contrary to conventional fundraising advice, keeping the message simple, without a lot of flowery distractions, might be the one hot fundraising tip provided by Lao Tzu.

I promised paradox and riddle in this chapter, and there you have it. It may be that none of the *Tao te Ching's* ancient wisdom will find its way onto the pages of your fundraising strategy. That is not its intention. It's for your heart. Lao Tzu's message is intended not so much to provide tips and techniques as to gently guide us to a place where we can find some peace around that most difficult task of sustaining the organizations that allow us to do together what we cannot do alone.

> Know when you have enough to accomplish your
> goals
> and you will succeed
> Know when to stop
> and you will always move forward
> Seek nothing
> and you will find everything you need
> (*Tao*, 44)

8

SWEEP THE LOTUS FLOWER

Leadership: Stepping Aside, Trusting, Acting with Conviction

> Following the Tao we should
> create without holding on
> work without expectation
> lead without controlling
>
> To guide without directing
> is to follow the Way and its Virtue
> (*Tao*, 51)

I first joined the conservation movement when I was in high school. My outrage at the loss of my forest sanctuary spurred me on to become aware of the threats to the earth's precious life support systems. Acid rain, ozone depletion, CFC pollution, the loss of forests to logging, and the great mountains of garbage (some apparently visible from space) were part of a laundry list of problems suddenly thrust upon my teenage consciousness around the age of sixteen.

I remember compiling a stack of fact sheets from environmental groups and Canada's federal government on these issues and others. After my first satisfying but unsuccessful attempt to impede the passage of a superhighway through my green refuge, I looked for a task appropriate in scale to a disgruntled teenager, one that wouldn't land me in a juvi-detention centre if I were to be caught. It was the late 1980s and Greater Toronto's overflowing landfills seemed like an issue that a high school student could tackle at a grassroots level. I decided that my school of more than 1,000 students needed a recycling program. I found others who thought so too, and together we appealed to the high school's administration.

I guess I was hoping that they would proclaim what a brilliant idea it was and set to work implementing a program to recycle all of the school's paper *tout de suite*. Instead they said simply, "Go ahead and do it." Besides introducing us to the school's surly janitorial staff (you'd be surly too if you had to pick up after 1,000 teenagers every day), they made no other overt contribution. I was troubled by their lack of willingness to run with our idea. They wanted *us* to do it *ourselves*? Left with no other option, a bunch of us organized the high school's first environmental club, and for the better part of a year we collected and recycled paper from each classroom several times a week.

To fund our efforts we organized a plant sale, launching me at the age of sixteen down the dark and shadowy road of fundraising. We struggled with those in the maintenance department who seemed ideologically opposed to recycling. We asked the same agonizing question as we ask ourselves today: Are we making a difference?

But what I perceived at the time as a lack of guidance from the school's administration might actually have been an example of *real* leadership. They recognized our determination, and we cannot know what barriers, hidden from us as idealistic teenagers, were swept aside by the administration's invisible hand. The obstacles we encountered were overcome with our perseverance; thus the administrators taught us to become leaders ourselves.

Many times in my work as an activist, I have looked to others for leadership and, not finding it, or not recognizing it, I stepped forward myself, ready or not for the challenges in store. I know people – like John Keating of Calgary-based green power producer Canadian Hydro – who have looked to their peers in business for leadership on issues such as greenhouse gas emissions, and finding none, started their own businesses as a way to champion these issues.

Leadership is often *the* critical element in any public interest campaign or successful business venture. Good leadership can galvanize the efforts of people to work together toward a common cause. A failure of leadership can often result in long-term setbacks.

Lao Tzu had a great deal to say about leadership. It is a central theme of the *Tao te Ching's* eighty-one verses, and in particular in verses thirty-eight through eighty-one, which have more of a socio-political bent. The *Tao te Ching* has three central messages for leaders – step aside, trust, and act with conviction. Ultimately, these three ideas are part of the same premise – that leadership is about service, to others and to our cause. Leaders, like the lotus flower, emerge, blossom, and then fade away, allowing others the opportunity to blossom.

Stepping Aside

Stepping aside as leaders has many elements: it means allowing others to find their own path; allowing those we lead to make mistakes and to serve those people as they correct them; taking appropriate time with decisions; letting go of desired outcomes; and learning to master oneself before trying to lead others.

Struggling to protect what we love, we often find ourselves in positions of leadership without any formal training for the task, sometimes without even wanting to be in such a role.

Despite our best efforts, we can fail to provide inspirational leadership that promises real guidance to the people we are working with. This happens because we haven't learned that being a leader requires more than telling people what to do, when to do it, and how to do it. Leadership is more than doing things ourselves because we think that we can do them better, in less time, and with better results. Leadership means more than exerting power over others because we have been entrusted to a position of authority.

The *Tao* says:

> The mark of a good leader
> is that his colleagues do not require his attention
> Next best is a leader who is loved
> After that, one who is feared

203

And worst of all, one who is hated

Trust that the people you work with
are able and worthy of your confidence
and they will exceed your expectations

Lead by example
Do your work and be humble about your
    accomplishments
When you have finished, and your colleagues say
"Look at what we accomplished all by ourselves"
Then you will be a leader
(*Tao*, 17)

The *wu wei* of leadership is to step aside at the appropriate time and let others find their way. The sage leader knows that her colleagues have the skill and wisdom to accomplish the tasks that they have accepted for themselves.

The sage leader also knows that mistakes will be made; the trick is allowing others to make mistakes and to learn from these missteps. Leaders step back and encourage all involved to press on with their efforts.

Lao Tzu advises:

The sage leader
doesn't try to teach his colleagues
but helps them only to follow the Tao on their own
...
To learn how to lead
avoid having all the answers
...
The sage leader
simply lets others find their way
on their own
(*Tao*, 65)

Of course, the sage leader doesn't sit back in her office with her feet up on the desk reading the paper before heading out for an early lunch. A balance must be found between directing and guiding, between holding on and letting go.

The sage leader must know when to step back and when to step in. Despite our natural tendency to step forward, to direct, to provide what we believe to be leadership, we must learn restraint. There will always be a natural tension between knowing when to let go and when to hold on. But the strength to hold on wanes over time, and as leaders we must learn to let go before we simply lose our grip.

> Lead with tolerance
> and your colleagues will perform well
> Lead with rigidity
> and they will flee
>
> If you try to exert too much control
> things slip through your grasp
> (*Tao*, 58)

My friends who ride call this giving the horse its head, which means that as the rider, we need to let up on the reins and let the horse pick its own footing through rough ground. This might feel a little risky at first, but with practice it becomes more natural.

Chuang Tzu tells this simple story to explain:

> Kui [the one-legged dragon] said to the centipede:
> "I manage my one leg with difficulty:
> How can you manage a hundred?"
> The centipede replied:
> "I do not manage them."[1]

The sage leader learns to guide her colleagues gently and with compassion through the challenges that they encounter. This guidance is best when it's nearly invisible. Gentle approaches like coach-

---

1. Thomas Merton, *The Way of Chaung Tzu*, New York: New Directions Press, 1975, p. 89

ing, mentoring, and supporting our colleagues' development are the best forms of guidance.

Listening to others means taking a little more time to make decisions. We usually have more time than we realize. Instead of telling staff exactly what we want and how we want it, we can teach them their responsibilities and then listen and learn how they want to proceed. By doing this, we give them ownership of their work.

But that is a routine situation. What happens when we must respond to a crisis?

We rarely need to decide how to proceed the moment a challenge arises, but so often we charge ahead, disregarding the input of our colleagues, not allowing ourselves enough time to sort through the options.

It is better to make a good decision than a quick one.

When faced with a challenge, I feel a strong impetus to act quickly and decisively. Sometimes the action I choose makes things worse. As I noted in the chapter "Retreat to Ride Tiger," I am learning that instead of acting too swiftly, I can step back for a moment and let my mind be at ease. I try to remove the pressure to make a decision.

Following Thich Nhat Hanh's advice, I might go for a walk around the block, through a patch of woods, or down by the river. When I lived in the mountains, I spent many lunch hours cross-country skiing to create some space for myself, to be at ease with whatever big decision I had to make that day. Now that I live on the coast, I regularly run in the hills around Victoria. I do my best to focus on my movement, on the woods, on the people that I pass by. During these times of quiet, when I work hard *not* to engage my mind on the dilemma at hand, the right course of action arises suddenly in my mind, as if lit by a neon sign. When I get back to my office, I can act with confidence.

There are times when we need to make a split-second decision. Leaders who embrace the Tao will be able to respond to these challenges with confidence. Like someone who has practiced a martial art for many years, the instinct to respond to a threat becomes second nature.

Letting Go of Desired Outcomes

Activists want victory. We feel a need to win, to make a difference. It is why we struggle day after day. The stakes are high in our work. We are fighting for the lives of impoverished and hungry children, for the rights of workers, for the freedom of people imprisoned for their political convictions, for the fate of plants or animals on the verge of extinction. The pressure to succeed creates inordinate demands on leadership and on everyone who serves these causes. It would be helpful to mind the words of Lao Tzu on this matter:

> The sage activist leads
> by freeing people of expectations
> and opening their hearts
> by dissolving their personal ambition
> and strengthening their passion
> He helps his colleagues let go of prospects for
>   victory and success
> and casts doubt over the best-laid plans
> so that what is not seen and not spoken
> can be revealed of its own accord
> (*Tao*, 3)

It's worth noting here that some people interpret verse three of the *Tao te Ching* differently than I have. In Robert Henricks' translation based on the Ma-want-tui texts, he says that the sage "empties their minds, and fills their bellies. Weakens their ambition, and strengthens their bones."[2]

At the core of this verse is the assertion that the leader must help those that she leads overcome the obstacles that the mind and its ambitions create.

To let go of desired outcomes, the sage leader must abandon her ego. Sometimes we cling to a process, a plan, or a strategy long after it has proven ineffective simply because we have invested so much of ourselves in it. It has come to represent our reputation. If we avoid

2. Lao Tzu, *Te-Tao Ching, A New Translations Based on the Recently Discovered Ma-Want-tui Texts*, trans. Robert G. Hendricks, New York: Ballantine Books, 1989.

becoming attached to a single outcome or a single way of doing things but instead keep focused on our goal, we can lead in a way that seizes opportunities as they arise.

In the chapter on strategy, "Appear to Close Entrance," I wrote about the passage of the Species at Risk Act (SARA) in Canada, and alluded to some tough sledding that occurred over the years before the act was passed. One of the rockiest times for the effort to protect Species at Risk came late in the fall of 1999 when then federal Environment Minister David Anderson travelled to Calgary to announce what he hoped would become Canada's legislation to protect endangered species. This event was rockier still because of how attached many of us, the minister included, were to the expectation that the legislation would be comprehensive and effective.

In the months before Minister Anderson's announcement of the proposed legislation, conservationists had been working behind the scenes in Ottawa, meeting with government officials to ensure that Canada's approach to protecting endangered species and their habitats would be effective. After a succession of federal Environment Ministers that left much to be desired, we thought we had found a friend in Minister Anderson. He had, after all, been responsible for placing a moratorium on off-shore oil and gas drilling in British Columbia some years before. His credentials suggested to many of us that he would deliver on the species file.

On the day before the release of the proposed framework for the Species at Risk Act, I got a call at around 5 p.m. from a colleague who was very close to the government and who had been privy to an advanced copy of the proposal. He was very disappointed with what he saw. Many of the key elements of the legislation that would ensure mandatory protection for Canada's growing list of endangered species and the places they needed to survive were absent from the draft. My colleague had arranged for national media to break this story, and ten minutes later I had an interview with the CBC, Canada's national radio network. It was the beginning of a very long twenty-four hours.

After my interview, which effectively let the cat out of the bag that Minister Anderson couldn't count on the environmental community's support for his proposed bill, I collected my colleague Kevin Scott from the airport and we began to strategize. Calls went back and forth between my home in Canmore, Alberta to Ottawa until very late in the night. Media releases that had been drafted to give the Minister support were rewritten. Early morning meetings between local representatives of national conservation groups in Calgary were arranged. It was 2 a.m. before we were done. My phone started ringing two hours later with colleagues from eastern Canada chiming in on the expected events of the day.

Prior to the media announcement for the proposed legislation, Minister Anderson met with members of the conservation community, ranchers, and representatives of the mining, oil and gas, and logging industries. Before then, I spoke with his assistant, whom I had met on several occasions, and gave him the heads up that we would not be supporting the Minister that day. It was obvious from his reaction that we weren't the only ones with expectations. Without saying a word, he left the room. I learned later that he was calling my colleagues in Ottawa to try and get them to reel in what he considered to be the Calgary fringe of the environmental movement.

It seemed difficult to believe that just a few days earlier I had been discussing with this same aide the recruiting of likely supporters from the ranching community to appear at the Minister's media event to speak in favour of a tough federal endangered species law. I had gone so far as to call my acquaintance Ian Tyson to ask for his support. I was deeply relieved when Ian didn't appear at the event that day.

Things only got worse. The media conference was held at the Calgary Zoo, which has one of the country's most successful captive breeding programs. Anderson was caught largely off-guard by our lack of support, so in addition to deflecting criticism from some landowner associations and industry groups that the Species at Risk Act would harm their livelihoods, he had to swim solo, without the support of the environmental movement.

The event culminated in a heated debate between leaders of four major conservations groups and the Minister. It was the beginning of a long period of bad blood between him and the environmental community which was never successfully resolved. It was put to bed when Commons Environment Committee Vice-Chair Karen Kraft

Sloan negotiated a settlement between the Prime Minister's Office and the environmental community three years later, but the disappointment felt on both sides of the debate at that early betrayal was never really resolved.

There are several key lessons to learn from this example that speak to Lao Tzu's caution against attachment to outcome and ego.

We in the environmental community had made the strategic error of believing that because Minister Anderson talked like one of us, he *was* one of us. In his heart the Minister – now retired from federal politics – was, and still is, an environmentalist. He still fights for the moratorium on off-shore oil and gas drilling in British Columbia, and for tougher standards to slow or reverse climate change. But on species at risk, the Prime Minister's office called the shots and the Minister had to toe the line.

On a more personal level, the environmental community had become very attached to an expected outcome that day. When it became obvious that our expectations would be dashed, we let our disappointment cloud our judgment. On something as complex as a law to protect endangered species, there are bound to be widely disparate opinions on how to proceed. But when faced with the crisis of that day, many who had invested their personal reputations and those of their organizations in the process were deeply threatened. Our fragmented response was not our finest hour.

Many of us had our egos bruised that day. What we hoped would be a victory for endangered species and for ourselves was a dismal setback.

To the lasting credit of Canada's environmental movement, those divisions didn't surface publicly, and nobody ever called and asked Kevin or me to back down from our hard-line stance with the media that day. I know from subsequent conversations some wanted to, but they held their tongues.

Better not to attach our ego to the outcome. Harder still to gently guide people who have become attached to an outcome see beyond it. As leaders these are among our greatest challenges.

By abandoning her own ego, the sage leader can also give herself more fully to the people she serves. By letting go of expectations, she becomes more open to the unexpected. Both of these acts of letting go are an acceptance of humility, of stooping low to reach high.

> To be a sage leader of people
> bend down before them
> honour them
> follow their advice
>
> The sage leads
> but his colleagues do not feel exploited
> He strides ahead of them
> but they do not feel left behind
>
> He competes with no one
> so no one feels threatened by his leadership
> (*Tao*, 66)

Get a Hold of Yourself

As leaders, we sometimes focus on our own accomplishments and abilities, hoping to inspire others to emulate our aptitude for activism. We talk about the battles we've waged and won, the legislation we've crafted, and the power we wield with decision-makers. However, to lead effectively, our focus must not be on our own accomplishments, but on the potential of our peers. If we shine a light on ourselves, we cast long shadows over others.

> [The sage leader] does not make a spectacle of
>   himself
> so that others can see his example
> He doesn't try to prove himself
> so then people can trust him
> He does not boast or exhibit pride
> so others can give him credit due
>
> He does not overuse his influence
> and so it will last forever

211

> He does not compete with others
> so people feel comfortable sharing with him
> He abandons who he is
> so others see themselves in his actions
> (*Tao*, 22)

Leaders in any movement rise to the top because of charisma, intelligence, organizational skill, political savvy, and sheer bull-headed determination. Many of us are alpha wolves with a natural urge to "direct" others. The Tao turns this lesson about leadership back upon ourselves. It teaches us that:

> Controlling others is force
> Controlling yourself is real power
> (*Tao*, 33)

If we want to lead, we must first be able to master our own wills, our own egos, and our own challenges. We must learn to serve others first, ourselves second.

What does it mean to master ourselves first?

Attending an annual gathering of activists who use the Internet for social and environmental causes, I've had the invaluable opportunity to do just that. For five years, I've participated in Web of Change at Hollyhock on Cortes Island, the first time just ten days after September 11, 2001.[3]

We were an emotionally damaged group coming together after the horrifying events of that September day. One participant had witnessed the collapse of the Twin Towers from his office window. But over the course of four days, we came together and I began what has been for me a transformational experience in leadership.

At first I was guarded and a little defensive in the sessions, threatened by the accomplishments of others. I struggled, at times successfully, to give myself wholly to the group.

But there is something in the power of the place and the intent of the community at Hollyhock that guides even hard cases such as myself towards an openness of spirit and service. On the eve of

---

3. Visit *webofchange.com* for information on future events.

my fifth Web of Change conference, I had a marvellous flash of insight. As I was reviewing the biographies of the attendees, I noticed something very liberating. Rather than trying to figure out how my interests might compete or intersect with participants at the event, I wondered how my own experience and expertise could serve them.

It was a moment of clarity for me around my own personal leadership qualities. I am beginning to come to grips with the restrictions that keep me from being a better leader.

Leading by Stepping Aside

I'm often frustrated in my effort to live the *Tao te Ching*. More often than not I feel as though I'm veering wildly off or away from The One Way. After spending years working on this book, I feel that my understanding of the Way and its Virtue is less clear now than when I started! In my moments of clarity, though, I remember that a path is not a destination but a process, and that I must be gentle with myself. I'm learning too.

Much of our jobs as activists, as leaders, as humans is to simply get out of the way.

One of the mistakes I made during my time at Wildcanada.net – and that list of mistakes is long – was to not get out of the way early enough, or often enough. There were reasons – some of them good – but regardless, when I did finally step aside, I think my colleagues felt some sense of abandonment.

Leadership takes practice, and one of the ways we can inspire a depth of leadership within our organizations is to provide our colleagues with opportunities to practice leadership routinely as part of their day-to-day efforts.

I believe that my colleagues at Wildcanada.net would have found their new roles as leaders much easier had I spent more time and energy helping them find their footing earlier in the process of leadership transition. I should have much sooner "offered them the gift of not being dependent" on me, as Stephen Mitchell puts it.[4] In the end, that's not what happened, and maybe it's only hindsight

---

4. Lao Tzu, *Tao te Ching, a New English Version*, trans. Stephen Mitchell, New York: Harper Collins Publishers, 1989, p. 109

that can provide this kind of clarity.

Our true work as leaders and activists is to live in what Alan Watts calls skilful harmony with the course of nature. I take that to mean both the natural world and human nature. The word skilful implies a certain level of active involvement. This is not guidance or leadership by absenteeism. Don't mistake all the talk of "not-doing" and "no-action" for permission to check out physically and mentally while your colleagues soldier on. Skilful harmony means using our creativity, compassion, and love to find innovative ways to solve problems. It means finding the pattern of the grain before applying the saw. It means listening carefully to what is actually happening – not just with your ears, but with your heart – before you speak, or take any action at all. As with the story of carving up the ox, it means finding the way to make the fewest cuts.

As leaders, we must encourage our colleagues to develop the skills, confidence, and courage to act on their own and to be leaders themselves. To do this we must provide a solid framework and clear guidelines for them to work within, but once we've established the parameters, our role should be to guide them gently to a place where they no longer need direction. We can and must be available for advice, to act as a sounding board for ideas, and to provide suggestions, but this is a different approach than telling someone what to do and how to do it. Instead, we step aside and let them discover how to do it themselves. Our guidance should be invisible to them. Frequently we discover that their way is not the way we might have done it ourselves, but often we will be pleasantly surprised to learn that their way is actually better. So we learn from those we lead.

> The sage leader stands back
> and lets others take the lead
> They look at her with wonder
> but she only smiles and stands aside
> (*Tao*, 49)

Every person we work with – from the volunteer who stuffs envelopes on weekends, to the canvasser who goes door to door, to the chief financial officer of the largest non-profit organization – can and should be leaders. Every one of us sitting around the kitchen table to discuss the latest threat to our rights, our health, or our environment can be a leader. Each of us has something to teach others. Each of us has something to contribute to how we accomplish our goals. Whether we are the recognized leader of an organization or not, we can assume a leadership role and encourage others to do so.

Don't confuse this with a "too many cooks in the kitchen" syndrome. Once people have found their appropriate roles within a community group or a national organization, the leadership role will be assumed by the person who is best suited to the situation. If she is in tune with the Tao, the person who carries the formal title of "leader" of that group or organization will not feel threatened by this.

Trust Each Other

The concept of stepping aside is bound to the notion of trust. If we trust those we work with, stepping aside will not be a frightening idea. It is critical that in all our efforts we trust each other. Nothing destroys morale, nothing dissolves passion, like mistrust.

> When leading
> act for the benefit of others
> Trust them, let them follow their own course
> (*Tao*, 75)

Trusting and stepping aside are two parts of the same thing. But as leaders we must relearn, and teach by relearning again and again, that letting go is critical to our efforts.

Letting go of expectations, we've learned, is important in order to be open to the unexpected. Letting go of our concept of how things should get done is important for colleagues to feel free to accomplish their goals in a new, innovative, and creative manner. Letting go of our fear, anxiety, and mistrust is critical for a healthy working relationship with our colleagues.

Often we are fearful that others will make mistakes that will reflect badly on our efforts, on our organization, or on us as leaders.

But part of leading is allowing mistakes. We cannot move forward without making errors. Making mistakes means we are continuing to try, experiment, and reach out.

I've had to ask myself, what is a mistake? It's a decision that doesn't stand the test of time. Sometimes – like when we decide to touch something really hot – the feedback is immediate. But often it's slow in coming.

When we make a mistake, we should admit it and look carefully to discover why it was made, and to set it right. We must then work to incorporate any lesson learned into our lives. It is not the mistakes that we make but how we address them that is the measure of our success in leadership, and in life.

The sage leader does not want to surround herself with people who always agree with her. She wants as confidants those who are willing to gently but firmly point out her mistakes and weaknesses, and suggest ways to improve and grow. The sage leader wants as peers and colleagues people who think for themselves, who help her mature and learn by being part of the process of gently guiding her through her own challenges. That way, we learn together.

It would be naïve to think that all the people we work with will reward our trust with outstanding performance. It would be foolish to believe that the people we step aside for won't trip, stumble, or even fall. Just as we must admit our mistakes, correct them, and learn from them, we should be willing to help others do the same. While we must be eager to lead with courage and accept that sometimes that means making mistakes, we must be equally willing to forgive others when an error is made, knowing that for all involved, important lessons can be learned.

At times, we discover that some people are not well-suited for the work that they've been asked to do. It is rarely that they are inherently bad. Sometimes, the fit isn't right. Other times, circumstances interfere with their ability to accept another person's trust.

We must remember that the three virtues of the *Tao* are restraint, compassion, and love. In our dealings with each other, we must demonstrate the restraint that comes from patience. If after standing back and watching, listening, learning, and gently guiding, the action that arises of its own accord is to find more suitable work for a colleague within the organization or even dismiss an employee, then we do it with confidence, and with compassion.

Even in those rare circumstances when our trust has been betrayed, it is better to respond with compassion than anger or spite. In these cases, our actions might be swift, but they needn't be blind to the humanity that exists in every person.

Leading from the Centre of the Circle

The hierarchical view of leadership, which is in place in most activist organizations or businesses, is that there is one leader at the head of the organization, a few lesser leaders managing programs or departments, then staff, contractors, and volunteers filling in the ranks. Leading with the Tao does not necessarily mean abandoning this form of organization, but rather that its function changes.

I once asked a gifted leader with a history in both business and non-profit management about his vision of leadership. If you were walking along a sidewalk with those you were leading, I asked him, how would you situate yourself? Without hesitation, he said that he would surround himself with those he was leading, neither going before them or trailing behind them. This is how leaders in a traditional, hierarchical organization can embrace the teaching of Lao Tzu.

When I draw organizational charts, I create concentric circles rather than the standard flow charts, with the board of directors at the centre, and the staff and volunteers radiating out from there. There are arrows indicating energy and ideas flowing from outside the circles – from peer groups, the public, decision-makers, etc., toward the centre – and there are dash lines that indicate permeability between positions and responsibilities. When I was on the board of directors of the Alberta Wilderness Association, we created such a chart and called it an organizational *mandala*.

But we must also respect that there are myriad forms of organizing and decision-making, and that one is no better than another. A consensus-based model might work in one case, while a more hierarchical system might be better suited for another.

Frying a Small Fish

Petty matters can sometimes tear us apart. We agree that we need a strong law to protect endangered species, but we can't agree on a policy to determine who takes their vacations and when. Remember that trust in one another is key to solving these problems, and that the sage leader steps back and watches carefully before acting, allowing the right action to arise on its own accord. Then the sage leader can speak with confidence, if at all, on the matter. Lao Tzu advises:

> Running a complex organization
> is like frying a small fish
> Turn it too many times and it will fall apart
>
> Start by centering your organization in the Tao
> and preoccupation with petty things and infighting
>   will not take hold
> Not that they won't be present
> but you will be able to sweep them aside when
>   they appear
>
> Give pettiness nothing to take root in
> and it will not find energy to grow
> (*Tao*, 60)

What does it mean that running a complex organization is like frying a small fish? (And how come it's never frying a small block of tofu?)

When you are cooking a fish, if you are always poking it, it is going to fall apart (same as tofu...). When you are leading an organization, if you keep interfering with its day-to-day operations, it's not going to function. Most leaders know this. We know not to hover over the shoulders of people we have entrusted to complete a task.

What interests me most about this verse of the *Tao te Ching* is its reference to pettiness. Pettiness is born of insecurity. It is a result of a lack of trust, fear, and low self-esteem.

Nothing dissolves otherwise productive and positive relationships like pettiness, and as leaders, we must prevent it from taking root. This means addressing trust issues between staff, volunteers, and board members early and often as our relationships develop. I've seen pettiness harm otherwise productive relationships and grow into full-scale disputes. Crossing the river at its headwaters means identifying these challenges early, and working to resolve them before they flood over.

Acting with Conviction

The third element of leading by following the Tao is acting with confidence.

> Do you have the patience to wait for the clouds to
>   clear
> and for the sun to cast its light on things to make
>   them seen?
> Can you wait for the right action to present itself
> and then know what must be done?
> (*Tao*, 15)

The natural outcome of our patience and trust is the confidence to act with assurance. There is no way to be certain that we will avoid mistakes when we act, but because we have abandoned our ego and are no longer attached to the outcome, and because we have the humility to stoop low and admit our mistakes when we make them, action no longer becomes something to be hesitant about or frightened of. It is a natural part of the Way and its Virtue. It is the yang of non-action's yin:

> A great weight gives birth to lightness
> Stillness is the source of action
> (*Tao*, 26)

Part of the balance we will find by following the Tao is the equilibrium between stillness and action.

219

When we do act, we do so with humility and quiet confidence. And when we have done our work, we step back again into the shadows and allow those whom we serve – our colleagues, peers, volunteers – to enjoy the light of their own accomplishments.

> When your colleagues regard you as an equal
> you can be a leader
> When they no longer need you to lead
> you will have done your work well
>
> If your opponents and friends fear your power
> you have no power to wield
>
> The sage leader knows himself
> but does not boast
> The sage leader loves himself
> but is not vain
>
> Lead by following, teach by learning
> and you will find heaven in your heart
> (*Tao*, 72)

Service

The *Tao te Ching* is ultimately a book about service. As leaders, we serve many people and causes, but our primary service is to those we lead. Through our service to others, and our successful leadership, we can most effectively advocate for our cause. As effective leaders, we can multiply our impact on society one hundred fold through our service to others.

Sometimes we fail to do this because we are too busy dealing with seemingly important, but ultimately trivial matters.[5] But in focusing our service to others, we can pass on our passion and our belief in a better world to those around us.

---

5. If this is something that you fall prey to, consider reading Stephen Covey's book *First Things First*, New York: Simon & Schuster, 1994

The sage leader is available to all people
and turns none away
For him, all situations are opportunities
to learn, grow, and guide people towards the Tao
When no opportunity is wasted
you are following the true path
(*Tao*, 27)

So what is service?

Dr. Rachel Naomi Remen, a medical doctor, says, "Serving is different from helping. Helping is based on inequality: it is not a relationship between equals. When you help you use your own strength to help those of lesser strength. If I'm attentive to what's going on inside of me when I'm helping, I find that I'm always helping someone who's not as strong as I am, who is needier than I am. People feel this inequality. When we help we may inadvertently take away from people more than we could ever give them: we may diminish their self-esteem, their sense of worth, integrity and wholeness. When I help I am very aware of my own strength. But we don't serve with our strength, we serve with ourselves. We draw from all of our experiences. Our limitations serve, our wounds serve, even our darkness can serve. The wholeness in us serves the wholeness in others and the wholeness in life. The wholeness in you is the same as the wholeness in me. Service is a relationship between equals."[6]

That sounds a little like the sentiment behind *Namaste* described elsewhere, doesn't it?

It is a fundamental point for us as leaders. Service is a relationship between *equals*.

Leadership is so much more than simply helping someone develop a campaign strategy or write a fundraising appeal. It is honouring each person's unique qualities, and the extraordinary contribution that he or she brings to the work we do together.

"Service rests on the basic premise that the nature of life is sacred, that life is a holy mystery which has an unknown purpose,"

---

6. Rachel Naomi Remen. M.D. "In the Service of Life," adapted from a talk given at a conference of the Institute for Noetic Sciences in July, 1995, and reprinted in the *Noetic Sciences Review*, Spring 1996

continues Dr. Remen. "When we serve, we know that we belong to life and to that purpose. Fundamentally, helping, fixing, and service are ways of seeing life. When you help, you see life as weak, when you fix, you see life as broken. When you serve, you see life as whole. From the perspective of service, we are all connected: All suffering is like my suffering and all joy is like my joy. The impulse to serve emerges naturally and inevitably from this way of seeing."

When we serve as leaders, I believe that we are saying to those we work with: I love you, I share your caring and compassion for this world, and I will exercise restraint in how I interact with you.

That is the embodiment of the *Tao te Ching's* three treasures. As leaders who follow the Tao, we can teach it, and the best and really the only way to teach the Tao, is to live it. We cannot tell people what the Tao is. But by making our lives an example of it, we can inspire others to discover its strength and value. This is one of the greatest gifts we can give the people we serve.

Sweep the Lotus Flower

Ancient Egyptians believed the world emerged from the first lotus flower. In the Hindu religion, Brahma, said to represent God's intelligence, stepped out of such a flower. The *Lotus Sutra* is one of the most famous scriptures of Mahayana Buddhism, whose principal belief is that all beings can attain enlightenment and Buddhahood.

Each night, the lotus flower – in North America the water lily – closes and sinks beneath the waters, only to re-emerge with the morning's first light.

To sweep the lotus flower, take several steps to the side twisting to the right and coil your body around your spine, hand up and pressing outward, taking in each perspective and point of view.

We're at the end of the Taoist Tai Chi set and we're now prepared for release. With a deep exhalation, unlock your posture and bring your hand up to connect with a kick and step forward.

Our bodies release like a coiled spring. We are action with conviction, balancing the trust and restraint that characterizes our movement to this point. This is the harmony of the Tai Chi Tu in action.

Leadership is like this too. Stepping aside and stepping forward can be a preposterous act of balancing; of trusting when we think there is nothing left to trust in; of acting with conviction when our convictions have been shattered. But leadership is our calling as activists – if not us, then who? If not now, then when? With restraint, compassion, and love, we can find the strength and courage to continue to forge ahead with the work we do to protect and restore what we love.

Sometimes we too can sink beneath the waters as leaders, but we must re-emerge with the morning's first light.

9

CREEPING LOW LIKE A SNAKE

Working with Others with Humility

When an organization grows and gains power
it should become like the ocean
so that all streams will run downhill to it
The larger the organization grows
the lower it should stoop in humility
Trusting the Tao
it will never need to be defensive
(*Tao*, 61)

Think back to the first time you worked with others to accomplish something that you couldn't accomplish on your own. Maybe banding together with other neighbourhood kids, you built a snow fort. Maybe you teamed up with your siblings to petition your parents for a later bedtime. For me, my first memory of real teamwork was when my friends and I conspired up to build a "cabin" in the backyard of my northern Ontario home.

Having watched with fascination the construction of my family house, I had grand ideas about building my own play space from the construction debris. But at five years of age, I wasn't very handy with a saw. Powertools were off limits, so it took me an hour to cut through a two-by-four. I recruited other neighbourhood kids to help with some of the cutting and hammering while I smoothed the way with the landowner on whose property we were squatting (a.k.a. Dad). The cabin came together quickly as different kids worked together to accomplish the task. While one kid framed a window, another put down carpet. While one kid roughed in the door, another installed the roof.

It was my first experience where kids of different ages and skills came together to work smoothly towards a common goal. Though short-lived – things fell apart when we tried to add a second floor – it remains an important reminder of the value of groups. Together we share our strengths, compensate for our weaknesses, celebrate our successes, and recover from our setbacks.

As activists, we cannot accomplish our goals alone. We work with others to form alliances – which could be two or three people around the kitchen table, a small family-run business, or a large multinational organization – because like kids building a cabin, we can accomplish together what we can't do by ourselves. We leverage each other's strengths and ameliorate each other's weaknesses through successful collaboration.

The *Tao te Ching* does not counsel people to work together, but rather assumes that people will collaborate, whether in organizations, governments, armies, and businesses. Lao Tzu focuses on *how* we might successfully work together to accomplish our goals. In this chapter, I extrapolate on the advice offered to political and military leaders of ancient China so that it might be applicable to our work together in civil society, and in ethically driven business relationships. Lao Tzu has some practical advice for us as advocates: learn the true source of our power and invest in it; abandon our ego so we can effectively serve others – work with humility, not conceit or excessive pride.

This chapter focuses on how we can take Lao Tzu's counsel for our own personal and interpersonal use to strengthen the organizations we work with and the relationship between the organizations and businesses that we collaborate with. These lessons are transferable, however, to many other situations where we find ourselves working together with others.

Organizations are the tools we use to accomplish our work, to pursue our values, to create the world we want to pass on to our children. Various organizations work together because through our common voice we are able to leverage more power and influence over those who make decisions, be they corporations or government, and because each organization has individuals with unique skills that can be applied to different situations. It's an efficient way for us in civil society to share the talents of many.

Often our organizations form coalitions to work together on issues of great importance, where our common voice will carry more weight with decision-makers than if we worked on the issue separately, or worse, in competition with each other. Working together in this way further emphasizes our strengths and helps us eclipse our limitations.

Given some of my comments in this book, you might gather that I think that organizations are a part of what ails our society rather than being an important part of the cure. I believe that organizations can be both. The complex human dramas that get played out through our organizations make them ripe for the abuse of power and other human foibles. But it is through these bodies that we are often able to achieve our greatest good. These same maladies and opportunities have existed for thousands of years. Seeing the pitfalls of organizations, Lao Tzu helps us steer them in such a way that we can work together more effectively and achieve much greater success.

The Power of Many

In the chapter "White Stork Cools Wings," we talked about organizational size from the perspective of fundraising. We sought to answer the question, "How big is big enough to accomplish our goals?" Now ask yourself this: Why do organizations need to be big? As in the Amnesty International example, big can mean greater political power. One thousand voices can be more effective than one hundred when demanding, say, the release of a political prisoner.

But as often as not, the largest organizations within civil society fail to leverage the full weight of their political power.

Lao Tzu says that "though you might have power, you should never display it openly." This is called the judicious use of power. It is akin to his advice that a country should never "openly display its sharpest weapons."

Power, according to Lao Tzu, is not something to seek or use carelessly. It is to be used with restraint or else you risk losing it. Openly displaying your power encourages those you oppose to seek more power to counter yours. But if not through the accumulation and use of power, how can we create change in the world?

In the *Tao te Ching*, power is associated with virtue. Our power as activists arises naturally as a result of our virtue, the by-product of the change we hope to create in the world. Our challenge is to use that power with care. As people are attracted to our work, we can invest in them the skills and confidence to become advocates for what *they* love. Giving our power away, then, is the true source of our power. In large organizations, we might have the power to enact a law in Congress and the Senate, but unless we've instilled in our grassroots members across the country their own sense of empowerment, defending and enforcing that law will be next to impossible.

This is what Lao Tzu refers to when he says that all streams run downhill toward the ocean. We can be like that ocean, pooling the collective waters as so many streams and rivers flow into us. This is the power of many working together towards a common cause.

But sometimes as organizations grow larger, gaining resources, staff, and larger and larger memberships and supporter networks, they begin to wield their power less and less. While this may be because they are using their power more thoughtfully, it can also be the case that they fear losing it.

I believe that is one of the greatest risks associated with organizational growth.

As I wrote in the chapter on fundraising, civil society's sometime preoccupation with growth can seriously hamper our ability to work together effectively. It should come as no surprise that we struggle with these dilemmas. We're only human, after all.

Forging Unusual Alliances

One of the things that working together can do is provide different parties with access to ideas, skills, and social capital – the power of relationships and social networks – that they could not access on their own. "There's a huge amount of social capital that simply wasn't there before," says David LePage, executive director of Vancouver's Fast Track to Employment. He's referring to the powerful relationships being developed between businesses that are providing goods and services, employees who are being hired as a result of increasing sales, and purchasers looking for products that are ethically made and good for both the environment and society through Vancouver's Social Purchasing Portal. LePage serves as the portal's director of business development.

"The Social Purchasing Portal is a website that directs socially responsible purchasing of goods and services," says LePage. "There is a database that allows companies who want to blend their social conscience with purchasing to locate suppliers who have taken an ethical stance in the development of their products."

Social Purchasing Portals have appeared across Canada in the last few years. In the United States, the Interra Project, whose principal advisor is Visa founder and former CEO Dee Hock, aims to create a network of Social Purchasing Portals across the country in the coming few years.

The Vancouver Social Purchasing Portal is a result of a partnership between Fast Track to Employment and the BC Technology Social Venture Partners, themselves a unique endeavour – a charitable foundation created by individuals in British Columbia's technology industries that support innovative non-profit groups serving children, women at risk, and people living in Vancouver's downtown eastside and inner city.

The Social Purchasing Portal's goal is to build healthier communities by creating employment opportunities for the hard-to-employ – folks recovering from addictions, people without a permanent address, people with a physical or learning disability – and creating targeted business growth.

Thirty-five non-profit employment groups work together to prepare hard-to-employ people to fill the needs of the various businesses using the purchasing portal. To date, fifty-four job openings have been created and filled as a result of the unique partnership, twenty-seven in the private sector. The rest of the jobs have been created with non-profit organizations that are engaged in social enterprise.

LePage points to the Potluck Café – a full service catering and event planning company in the heart of downtown Vancouver – as an example of the portal's success. In addition to high-quality, premium foods, Potluck Café is a charitably licensed organization, with 100% of its proceeds funding employment training and meal programs for residents of Vancouver's poverty-stricken downtown eastside. It takes advantage of the Social Purchasing Portal's referral system to build its business.

LePage says for such a disparate group of people to work together they had to set aside their cultural differences. "We had to get people to understand each other's point of view. Employment service providers had to understand the needs of business people," while business people had to recognize values other than profit.

Another example, he says, is Mills Basics, an office supply store that is part of the Basics office supply purchasing group. A hallmark of stationary and business services in Vancouver since 1949, Mills has hired people from the downtown eastside community as a result of the Social Purchasing Portal. It now has seven hard-to-employ people on staff, working in the company's warehouse. "There has been a ripple effect across the company," adds LePage. "As a result of the Purchasing Portal, Mills Basics examined their corporate social responsibility program, and from that came the introduction of a green line of products."

He says that by working together through the portal, the relationship between the various NGOs has changed. "The various employment service non-profits used to see each other as competition, but now the basis of our relationship is co-operation. And the suppliers of goods and services didn't know each other existed, and today they buy and sell to one another. Larger corporations now have a relationship with the inner city that didn't exist before. This program has really changed the way they relate to one another," adds LePage.

He says that the unique alliance of business, social-enterprise, employment service NGOs, and consumers has led to synergies that benefit all, but most importantly those plagued by the vicious cycle of poverty, homelessness, and joblessness in one of Canada's poorest neighbourhoods.

Three Sins to Guard Against

Organizations are simply groups of people. The principle that the whole is greater than the sum of its parts certainly holds true, but not unless each of those parts is acting in a way that allows for synergy to occur. However, human behaviour often trips us up in our efforts to find that synergistic moment when we become more than just individuals working next to each other, and instead become a collective entity.

What keeps us from reaching that point? Lao Tzu warns against "our greatest sins: desire, greed, selfishness."

What do we desire? Our wish for peace or for a cure for cancer are not the obstacles that we must watch for. Instead, more base desires for things such as promotion, monetary reward, or control are what Lao Tzu cautions against. In putting aside such desires, we can open our hearts to helping each other achieve real greatness, regardless of our organizational affiliation. We know that we need to work together to achieve our vision of a peaceful, safe, and sane world. Petty desire is a hindrance to that.

Greed has no place in our work together as activists, but let's not be fooled into thinking that greed is always intentional. As discussed in the chapter on fundraising, many of us operate with a mentality of scarcity. In this case it's difficult not to want just a little bit more for ourselves and our organizations to buffer us against what might be tough times ahead. Letting go of this paradigm and acting with temperance will help us find ways of working more effectively together, not just within our movements, but across sectors in civil society.

Selfishness is born from a lack of compassion. Compassion is one of the activist's greatest treasures; it lets us see the world from the perspective of others. Selfishness banishes us to see the world

231

only from our own narrow point of view. To work effectively and humbly with others, we must forsake this in favour of compassion.

In shunning these three traits and embracing the three treasures – restraint, compassion, and love – we can find a way to lower ourselves before others, and to be like the ocean, accepting the flow of many great rivers as they make their way to join our waters.

Competition and Service

Fundamental to the *Tao te Ching's* teaching is that the more power you gain, the less readily it should be displayed; the more power you gain, the lower you should place yourself before those you work with. In the chapter on leadership we saw how the sage leader should step aside and allow colleagues the opportunity to lead the way. In working with others, whether it is inside our own organizations or when working in coalitions or alliances, the same principles apply.

> When working with others
> resist the urge to compete, and focus instead on
> co-operation
> and you will win the greatest respect
> (*Tao*, 8)

Intellectually this might be an easy argument to make, but emotionally and on a purely practical level, it's anything but simple to implement. Even with foreknowledge of its pitfalls, it's hard not to compete when working with other organizations.

For two years during the lead-up to the May 2005 provincial election in British Columbia, I worked with a collaboration of non-governmental organizations who were interested in influencing the agenda of the various political parties contesting the writ. The groups worked together in a loosely affiliated manner, sharing what they knew about each political party's position on issues such as health care, education, and the environment, and where they perceived the various parties to be strong or weak in terms of their chances at the polls.

This sort of collaboration is unusual. Relations between groups in different regions are often so acrimonious that it's rare for them to work together effectively, even within a single movement. But in this instance, the coming together of labour unions, public interest groups, youth organizations, health care advocates, cultural advocates, anti-poverty advocates, ethically driven businesses, and others was very unusual and very rewarding.

There were many lessons learned through this collaboration. For me, one of the most powerful lessons was also deeply personal. The greatest challenges working with this large group was my fierce loyalty to the goals and interests of my own organization. At times, these interests intersected with others in the collaboration; at times, they did not. In reviewing the experience now, it's interesting to consider my personal reaction when there was a divergence of opinion. There were times when I felt threatened or left out, and times when I struggled to control my own ego, or place my own ideas in perspective. I did this in part of out fear that the needs of my organization would not be met.

How did I respond in those circumstances?

In short, I found it very difficult to serve the greater cause when I was primarily concerned with my own organization's interests. This happened despite my sincere commitment to strengthening the leadership of our movement as a whole.

I've led coalitions in the past. I've learned that we've got to put our own ideas and agenda into the proper perspective when working with others in a coalition or loose collaboration. We've got to accept that our way is just one of many, and our true work is to find a way that works for all.

> When you see your way as the only way
> other ways of doing things go unobserved
> When you see your cause as the only just cause
> the efforts of others become unjust
> (*Tao*, 2)

What interested me about my response to the collaboration was my gradual realization of it. Shortly after the election, I met with Jodie Tonita of ONE/Northwest, one of the leaders of the collaboration, and I found it much easier to focus on results rather than organizational self-interest. I had just stepped down as executive director of Wildcanada.net, and now was able to listen better, to really hear what was needed to move the public interest agenda forward, and not fixate on what role my organization could or could not play.

This time my heart didn't ache with fear or shut down because of my deeply ingrained scarcity mentality. I could leave it open to possibilities.

I explained all this to Jodie after our meeting. When you're on a journey to become better at what you are doing to protect the planet and its creatures, it's good to have some company.

In thinking about this experience, I know that I'll need to learn from this lesson so that when next I assume a formal leadership role I maintain this inclusive view instead of my old myopia. My goal is to serve. Competition only hinders that goal.

Remember that this is hard work, even for those of us engaged in the conscious process of embracing these concepts and ideas in our labours. Go easy on yourself.

Setting Aside Ego

My anxiety about advancing my organization's interests is tied to my ego. When we identify with our organizations and focus on advancing them, we're also focused on advancing our own personal benefits.

Some part of my activism is related to my ego. Yes, I was called at a young age to work in defence of nature. And I do now see the thread that is woven through issues like poverty and the way society treats children. This thread keeps me searching for a common cause to our human malfeasance. But a small part (maybe much bigger than I'm willing to admit to) of me does this work to satisfy my self-worth.

Ego is not necessarily a bad thing. One definition is "appropriate pride in oneself; self-esteem." These can serve a purpose. It is good to take pride in the work we do and derive self-esteem from our accomplishments. But Lao Tzu suggests that we need to set disproportionate pride aside when he says, "Exercise excessive pride and you will be shunned."

> By following the Way the sage activist
> becomes a leader for others to follow
>
> But he does not make a spectacle of himself
> so that others can see his example
> He doesn't try to prove himself
> so then people can trust him
> He does not boast or exhibit pride
> so others can give him credit due
> (*Tao*, 22)

Ego can also mean "an exaggerated sense of self-importance; conceit."

So what? As long as the work gets done, who cares if people exaggerate their self-importance?

Well, our egos can and do get in the way of getting our work done. Yes, our egos propel us forward in our work, and as long as we are conscious and our egos are limited to appropriate pride in ourselves then they can be powerful fuel for our efforts. But when our egos turn to self-importance and conceit, they begin to obscure our work.

Excessive pride can keep us from making appropriate decisions about the direction of our campaigns. It can keep us from working effectively with other people.

> The sage activist doesn't seek fulfillment
> and because she is not distracted by her ego
> she can seize opportunities as they arise
> (*Tao*, 15)

We've all been in a crowded room when one of our colleagues talks at length about the great things he or she has done. How do we feel when that happens?

If we want to work harmoniously with others, it is best not to call attention to our own strengths, but rather to emphasize the strengths of others. Doing this in a way that doesn't belittle others is the way of the Tao.

I believe that more than one campaign has been lost because as activists we've let our egos get in the way. We've lost opportunities because we were distracted by concern for our own future, rather than the issue we were fighting for. In some cases, in order to secure a win, we rush to accept the terms of a compromise that in the end fails to protect something important; in other cases, we hold out for an all-or-nothing result. In both of these situations, we must examine what is driving the decision. Are we acting in the best interest of what we are advocating for? Or are our egos involved too?

It would be extraordinarily rare for an activist to consciously make a decision based on satisfying his own ego. But because our egos continue to drive our decision-making at the subconscious level, it is all the more important to address.

> The sage activist never strives for grandeur
> thus his accomplishments are all grand
> When he is confronted with a challenge
> he stops and gives himself to it
> He forgets his own ego and pride
> He never underestimates the contest
> and so his challenges seem easy to overcome
> (*Tao*, 63)

Pride and ego make decision-making tricky. As I was in the process of leaving Wildcanada.net, and challenges arose that called into question the organization's path forward, I was asked to help find a solution to those problems. At first my ego was deeply threatened: I had worked so hard as part of a talented team to build the organization to where it was, and I was proud of my accomplishments. This made me worry about what would happen to it if we couldn't find a new path forward. At first I was as much worried about how it would reflect on me if things went wrong for the organization, as I was about the organization's future.

When I realized that my own ego was deeply intertwined with

the organization's future – even after I had left it – I struggled to set my pride aside. Doing so, even to a small extent, made it easier to find solutions to the challenges that the organization faced.[1]

This is why dispassionate observers can often be helpful to our work. Their egos aren't tied to the organization's success, nor is their pride dependent on the success of the work that the organization does. "I am often struck by how different – and often less effective – my engagement will be in initiatives where I am not impartial," says Julian Griggs of Vancouver-based Dovetail Consulting. Julian speaks from the perspective of someone whose job it is to help organizations, coalitions, and often disparate interests find common ground.

I know that I have benefited greatly from the guidance and coaching of David Thomson, a senior associate at Training Resources for the Environmental Community, and his insightful question, "What's *that* all about?" asked many, many times over the last few years. There have been days when I don't know what I would have done without him.

Conceit can also keep us from looking for help from allies and from other like-minded people. Conceit is "a favourable and especially unduly high opinion of one's own abilities or worth." It can alienate those we need to reach out to the most – the general public. At least in the environmental movement – and this may hold true for other causes within civil society – we've been accused of being elitist. I don't know if that's true, but I think sometimes excessive pride is mistaken for elitism, and to a lesser extent, conceit.

How many times have we thought to ourselves, "I'll just do it myself, it will get done right that way"?

> If you think that you have all the answers
> you are in fact the most ignorant of all
> When you realize how much more you have to
>   learn

---

1. Though the story of Wildcanada.net and ActionWorks.ca isn't over as this book goes to print, I am proud of how the team worked together to wrap up the organization's affairs. Wildcanada.net's principal asset, its 35,000 network participants, now support the Canadian Parks and Wilderness Society's online campaign efforts. ActionWorks.ca was sold to UK-based Advocacy Online to support their expansion into Canada.

> you can finally start to see the Way
> (*Tao*, 65)

And who can we learn from? From each other, and from those we serve: members, colleagues, and the public.

Reaching Out to Others

One of the reasons that some of our movements are lagging badly at present is because we've failed to connect with the general public in a way that empowers them to fight our fight as their own. We've failed to recognize that the things that matter to them might be the same things that matter to us. Abandoning our ego, and the superstition that we know best, is critical to encouraging others to share our vision.

Though it doesn't get a chapter of its own in this book, finding more effective ways to work with the general public is very much on my mind as I pen this section. In my experience, working effectively with networks of concerned individuals and volunteers is about building a sense of worth and creating a powerful relationship between the volunteer and the cause.

One of the things that has made the online organization MoveOn.org such a wild success has been its ability to create opportunities for people to get involved in a meaningful way. While it has some of the standard online gizmos and whiz-bang that allow people to send messages to elected decision-makers, MoveOn.org has its online advocacy off-line as well, inspiring individuals to get involved at the community level: house parties and vigils, canvassing and phone calls. MoveOn.org regularly seeks feedback from its many supporters about the direction the organization is taking. The result: MoveOn.org can raise millions of dollars in a matter of days for the campaigns it champions, and has become one of the most powerful voices in American civil society.

In a sense, MoveOn.org has replicated online what the best grassroots community organizers have been doing for decades: giving its power away to make its power more effective. Instead of directing, it guides action. Instead of dictating to its members, it serves them.

One of the things that keeps us from doing this is self-importance, which can cause us to forget the context in which we work: suddenly we see ourselves as the only thing standing between disaster and those responsible for that catastrophe. Exaggerated self-importance can keep otherwise good activists from working well with others who they perceive as less competent.

One of the things that has caused the environmental movement in both Canada and the United States to lose touch with its grassroots aspects is the misguided belief that we can accomplish our goals without engaging those people we count among our supporters. Gradually over the last decade or more, our focus has shifted to high stakes power politics in our nations' capitals, and at the state and provincial levels. Being outgunned and outspent in the lobby of the House of Commons and the Rotunda of the Capitol Building, some groups are now turning back to our true source of power – the average citizen. To do this, we must put aside any notion that we have all the answers and embrace a broader range of ideas and input.

Our members don't serve us, we serve them.

Working to serve others out of humility is a powerful goal to set for oneself. It's not easy to achieve. It is a life's work. But we don't necessarily have to achieve the goal to experience the rewards of trying. In the effort, we will discover that others will follow our leadership, and our efforts at working together will become much more effective and rewarding.

The purpose of our work together is to find ways to accomplish our goals that we could not achieve single-handedly. It's about creating the right conditions to seize new opportunities, leverage new resources, and build a base for future successes.

> The sage leader lets go
> of his own concept of how things should be done
> He is accepting of others' ideas
> and saturated with compassion
> stands solid like a rock wall
> yields like a field of grass

239

> He sets no hard and fast rules
> so he can take advantage
> of every opportunity that comes his way
> (*Tao*, 59)

This verse is another example of the paradox that infuses the *Tao te Ching* and often leaves readers scratching their heads. In many translations of the *Tao te Ching*, this is called the "mother principle of ruling."[2] Standing like a rock wall establishes a firm foundation for the sage activist. Yielding like a field of grass lets her bend and flow with each opportunity. Combining these, the sage activist can take advantage of the strengths and ideas of others while holding fast to her own foundation.

An exaggerated sense of self-importance has another downside: it can lead us to accept far too much responsibility within our organizations and communities. This must certainly be among the top reasons for burnout. Ironically, when we fall by the wayside of our movements, we often – though not always – see others step up and carry the flag for our cause. (The issue of burnout and renewal is examined in the chapter "Step Back to Ward off Monkey.")

If we could keep our egos in check from the start, we might find those standard bearers long before we suffer from a critical case of self-importance and burn to a crisp.

So what keeps us from embracing these concepts in our work with others?

Know the White, Follow the Black

Our work together is hampered by many obstacles. The desire for power obscures our path forward. Ego clouds our judgment. Humility often eludes us. Sometimes we fail to trust those who can help advance our cause and work towards a common objective.

Given these challenges, so deeply ingrained in human nature, how does Lao Tzu counsel us to move forward? He says:

2. Lao Tzu, *Tao te Ching*, trans. Gia-Fu Feng and Jane English, New York: Vintage Books Edition, 1972

> Know the white
> yet follow the black
> Follow the simple patterns of the world
> and follow unerringly the path of the Tao
> to surpass all that you dreamed was possible
> (*Tao*, 28)

To work well together, we might follow some of the simple patterns of the *Tao te Ching*. The Tai Chi Tu, which I introduced at the beginning of the book, is the common yin-yang symbol that is associated with the complete, whole, and balanced universe. The white is yang, the dry side of the mountain, the masculine, the dominant. Black is yin, the cool, wet side of the mountain. It is the feminine. It is yielding.

The Tao makes no judgment between each side of the Tai Chi, but instead says that each has a role to play in our efforts. How can we use this to help us work with others?

Yang, the white, is the more dominant, obstinate force that pushes against, rather than with. Yang actions are more ego-motivated, and are generally influenced by desire for personal gain or advancement. We are aware that in the white, the yang, the inflexible, people sometimes come to the coalition table seeking power, or with the increase of their own power in mind. Lao Tzu counsels us to know the white, but follow the black.

How do we do that? The black sits back, and is aware. The dark side of the mountain is free from judgment.

> If you allow yourself to judge others
> and let yourself be caught up in wanting more
> you will never achieve your goals
> If you cast off judgments
> and accept that there is enough
> you will move beyond winning to true success
> (*Tao*, 52)

Without judgments, we have the capacity to find a way to make use of everyone's talents and gifts, increasing the effectiveness of our coalition or organization. Judgment creates two sides, if only in our own minds, with one side being right and the other side being wrong. When working together for a common cause, there can be no absolute right or wrong.

The dark side of the mountain shuns power.

> The sage activist shuns power
> and thus is powerful
> (*Tao*, 38)

If you come to work with others simply to gain power and influence, you are doing a great disservice both to your colleagues and to your cause. There are certainly cases where coalitions are formed and alliances built to demonstrate leadership to funders or to illustrate collective strength to decision-makers. While these can be advantages of working in alliance with others, they are not the reason to come together.

The sage activist shuns power, and in doing so, is beyond the influence of the powerful, and in his own way, becomes self-empowered. When we seek power and influence to further our cause, we are forced to keep amassing more in order to stay influential.

Therefore, in all matters, and especially when working with others, we should be wary of the accumulation of power. If we refuse to recognize power and instead replace it with compassion, effective grassroots advocacy, and genuine concern for the interests of others, we'll enjoy much greater success when we work in conjunction with others, be it inside or outside our own organizations.

In doing so, we will learn that real power is not derived from influence over others, but from mastering ourselves. We become powerful when we can check our egos and judgments at the door, and focus on making our work together effective and rewarding.

This is contrary to my traditional way of thinking. For years, I've counselled to build power to leverage influence with decision-makers. But examples of where this has led to positive decisions are few and far between. When we give our power to others – notably to average citizens through grassroots mobilization – we find that power dispersed among many yields far greater results.

The dark side of the mountain also shuns desire for personal gain or advancement.

> Relinquish the desire for gain and advancement
> and people will stop pushing each other out of the
>   way
> (*Tao*, 19)

The most effective players in civil society are those who have put aside personal ambition and are willing instead to focus steadfastly on the task at hand.

One of the most compelling examples I've seen of this occurred during the Banff Bow Valley Study in the mid-1990s. The federal government called together people representing disparate points of view to talk about the future of Canada's most popular national park. The study convened a round table, with different sectors sitting together, to hash out concepts such as the appropriate use of a national park. Each sector was a loosely affiliated coalition, and selected a chairperson to participate.

The chair of the local/regional environmental sector was Mike McIvor. For more than two years, Mike steered our sector through very challenging waters with poise and humility. One of the many traits that characterized Mike's success as sector chair – and has come to characterize his thirty-year career as a volunteer activist – was his utter lack of personal desire for gain.

This is not to say that he lacks hopes and dreams. But Mike's ambitions are focused unwaveringly on protecting Banff National Park. He and Diane McIvor, partners in life and conservation for more than three decades, have no ambition to lead a large conservation organization – they have been serving the tiny volunteer-based organization, the Bow Valley Naturalists, for most of their adult lives. Mike has also volunteered for the Federation of Alberta Naturalists and the Alberta Wilderness Association. In fact, they are not seeking any financial remuneration for their efforts – they both had careers elsewhere. They have not sought advancement of any kind – they have been content to be dedicated and humble servants of the Bow Valley and its surrounding mountains and the wild things that live there. In doing so, they have consistently been the most effective voices for conservation in the region for more than thirty years.

The dark side of the mountain acts with humility

> Act with humility
> Take care of your colleagues and volunteers
> Avoid meddling in the affairs of others
> and you will be a light to guide the way
> (*Tao*, 61)

The dark side of the mountain seeks only to serve

> Those who act of out service
> leave nothing undone
> Those who act out of kindness
> always leave something undone
> Those who act out of a sense of justice
> leave many things undone
> Those who act out of moral righteousness
> turn to brute force when they do not get their way
> (*Tao*, 38)

Creeping Low Like a Snake

Humility is about bending low. Creeping Low like a Snake lowers the body: Push out with your left foot and bend your right leg at the knee to support your weight. Sink down into the earth. Extend your left hand, palm out, over your left leg, and bend your right arm at the elbow, hand cocked and fingers pointing down as if you were gingerly holding a wet cloth in your fingers. In bending low like this, we humble ourselves.

Following Our Mentors

I've told you a little about two of my mentors, Mike and Diane McIvor. Lao Tzu does something similar in the *Tao te Ching*. As we think about how to work with others more effectively, there is value in seeing how he characterized the sage leaders that inspired him.

Our mentors were wise and insightful advocates
We cannot describe their ways
we can only describe how they appeared

They were as careful as a person crossing a river in
    flood
They were as alert as if surrounded by their
    opponents
They were as courteous as one who is seeking
    support
They could flow like a melting glacier
They could be shaped like a mound of clay
They were empty as a starless sky
They were like the sun on a cloudy day
(*Tao*, 15)

In the translations that I have studied, Lao Tzu of course does not use the word mentor. That's my interpretation to make the *Tao te Ching* speak to us as advocates. Variously, what I call mentor is referred to as "one who was skilled at practicing the Way in antiquity," according to Robert G. Henricks,[3] or "Ancient Masters" according to Stephen Mitchell.[4] The point is clear: Lao Tzu was referring to role models for following the Way and its Virtue.

Think about the people you count among your mentors. What traits do they display that inspire you?

Lao Tzu's mentors have exemplified care, taking their time to find the proper footing, aware that to slip when fording a river in flood is to be washed away. When working with others – with staff or volunteers – we should exercise care in our work. Care in what we do and what we say will ensure that our work with others is as effective at serving our cause as it can be.

Lao Tzu's mentors were alert as if surrounded by their oppo-

---

3. Lao Tzu, *Te-Tao Ching: A New Translation Based on the Recently Discovered Ma-want-tui Texts*, trans. Robert G. Henricks, New York: Ballantine Books, 1989

4. Lao Tzu, *Tao te Ching: A New English Version*, trans. Stephen Mitchell, New York: Harper Perennial, 1988

nents. In the traditional translations of the *Tao te Ching*, the ancient masters acted as if "surrounded by danger on all sides."[5] When in enemy territory, you've got to be on alert for danger. When working with compatriots, you've got to be alert to their needs, their wants and desires, their motivations.

Remember, Lao Tzu counsels to know the white but follow the black: knowing the white means being alert to what others might be thinking and feeling, and working to ensure that they are addressed so that real progress can be made. This is not to suggest that every board of directors meeting should be a group therapy session (though I've been in a few board meetings that could have used a relationship counsellor). But when you are sensitive to other participants' motivations and underlying assumptions, you can craft agreements, decisions, and strategies that will serve your cause better.

Lao Tzu's mentors were courteous as one who is seeking support: decency and decorum go a long way when working together.

They could flow like a melting glacier – as ice calves from the toe of a glacier and tumbles into a lake or into the ocean, it eventually melts into the water. When we sit together to find a common way forward, our ideas can come together like this. They are separate and individual, but all moving in the same direction with ease.

They could be shaped like a mound of clay. The sage activist is pliable. While holding her own values close, she is shaped by the hands and hearts of those around her. She does not allow them to change her basic properties, but she does allow them to shape her ideas.

They were empty as a starless sky: one of the fundamental lessons of the *Tao te Ching* is that "being has form but non-being has usefulness." This is expressed elsewhere as "Only nothing fills a void: That is the value of non-being." Non-being is the space in the cup we fill with hot tea or coffee in the morning, it is the space in the room that we occupy to work, it is the silence and stillness from which we allow the right action to arise. The sage activist, working with others, is that empty space. He is the starless sky that allows others to become the pinpoints of light that shine bright.

We can be so much more together than we can be on our own.

5. Lao Tzu, *Tao te Ching: The Definitive Edition*, trans. Jonathan Star, New York: Penguin, 2001

When we work together toward a common cause with respect and love for those we stand shoulder to shoulder with, we find a deeper sense of purpose. At their very best, that's what our organizations, unions, alliances, and coalitions can be.

Together: It can mean, "in harmony or accord." *Together* is the tool that we can use to achieve as activists our most important goal: to protect and restore what we love.

10

WAVE HANDS LIKE CLOUDS

Moving through Challenge and Change

Be humble and bend
Be watchful and flow
(*Tao*, 76)

In this chapter I'll share with you some of the things that I have learned from the *Tao te Ching* about moving through challenge and change. The practice and art of movement has been my most important teacher in my inquiry into the *Tao te Ching*. Movement has allowed me to access the wisdom of the Tao. Movement has enabled me to use this wisdom to face life's challenges.

The *Tao te Ching* teaches that each of us has what we need to meet the daily tests of our lives, our work, and our choices as activists.

First, the Tao teaches us to accept all things. "Accept things as they come to you/ Do not try to control them," advises Lao Tzu.

By doing so, we must also accept that we will face challenges in our lives and in our work as activists. Just as a mountain has a rain-soaked slope and a rain shadow, so too is there darkness and light in the world; and as we are part of the natural world, there is darkness and light within each of us as well. The Tai Chi Tu teaches that yang, lightness, gives rise to passion, fear, and anger. Darkness, or yin, gives birth to our love and compassion. These qualities are inseparable. We cannot have one without the other. It is through their harmony that our challenges arise and are confronted.

When we accept that there are things in the world and within us that are challenging and sometimes frightening, we can begin to address them.

Lurking at the base of many of our challenges as activists is our fear of failure and defeat. In order to address the challenges in our life we must accept, even embrace, these things. The sage activist:

> does not fear the piercing horns of failure
> or the sharp claws of defeat
> Because he has embraced them
> they can find no place to wound him
>
> He holds nothing back
> and therefore, come success or failure
> he has done his best
> and then can step aside
> (Tao, 50)

In all the translations of the Tao te Ching that I have read, verse fifty is about accepting the inevitability of death. Here I have changed its literal meaning and interpreted it for us as activists to suggest that we must accept the inevitability of failure.[1] We all fail, and when we do, we die a small death. But failure is part of our work. It helps us learn in order to achieve success. Failure is not to be feared, but em-

---

1. In Jonathan Star's *Definitive Edition* this verse says "One in three are followers of life, one in three are followers of death, and those just passing from life to death also number one in three. But they all die in the end. Why is this so? Because they clutch to life and cling to this passing world. I hear that one who lives by his own truth is not like this…. Going about, he does not fear the rhinoceros or tiger. Entering a battlefield he does not fear sharp weapons. For him the rhino can find no place to pitch its horn. The tiger no place to fix its claw…. Because he dwells in that place where death cannot enter." Some readers might think it a stretch to interpret this in a way that speaks to our fear of defeat as activists, but I do not. Defeat is as inevitable as death in our work. The one who lives by his own truth does not fear death, just as an activist who lives by his or her own truth embraces defeat so that its tiger's claw can find no place to pierce. Verse fifty is one of the reasons why I chose to provide my own interpretation of the *Tao te Ching* for activists rather than referring to another's translation.

braced as part of the inevitable balance contained within our work, part of the yin and yang of our efforts. When we learn from our failures, we move through them and beyond them.

At Wildcanada.net, I always said that my greatest indication of success would be to look back two years after leaving the organization and see it thriving. I wanted to pass the organization into the hands of another capable leader after I had taken it as far as I could, who would then craft it and mould it according to his own vision. It's not an easy thing to accept that you are not necessarily the best person to take the organization you helped found to the next level, but for me it was part of my maturation as a leader and as a person.

After about four-and-a-half years as executive director, the board of directors and I developed a transition plan for the organization's leadership. It was an eighteen-month strategy that involved strengthening the role of the board so that they would be knowledgeable about the organization, enabling them to work independently of my advice, as well as recruiting staff who themselves were leaders. The plan also had designs for giving the organization greater financial stability. It laid out a time-line for an executive director search, and set an approximate date for my departure.

But things went sideways at the eleventh hour, and the leadership transition didn't happen as we had hoped. There were two factors that hobbled us: our lack of financial resilience – we were never able to find more than a few months of operating cash at any one time – and our inability to create internal leadership.

The organization did not survive the transition, at least not as it had been envisioned. I knew even before my last day that the likelihood of being able to "look over my shoulder" a year or two down the road and see Wildcanada.net thriving was anything but certain.

I was surprised by my reaction to this turn of events. When things started to deteriorate, my first response was to realize that my ego was bruised. I wanted to be able to point to Wildcanada.net later in life to say, "Look at what I helped to create," not just because it was an important component of the environmental movement in Canada, but because of the pride of creation that I felt in it.

My second response was, okay, let's accept the very real possibility of defeat and move on. During the attempted transition, I thought carefully about the decisions I had made as leader and wondered if I could have done things differently. Of course, looking back provides a certain clarity that the present moment rarely provides. But even in that context, I felt there were only a few small things that I would have done differently. The biggest omission I made in my planning, though, was to fail to accept that defeat was possible, thus protecting myself from the piercing of those particular horns.

What intrigues me now was my initial response. After eighteen months of planning, when I was suddenly faced with the possibility that the organization I was consciously letting go of might not succeed, my response was fear for my own reputation. I'd been talking about "doing my work and then stepping aside" for a while, but when faced with the possibility that stepping aside might mean failure, I felt very differently about the prospect. I felt fear. I felt depression and anger. I questioned my ability and my motivation as a leader.

The lessons learned from that experience in leadership transition could fill a book on their own. Suffice to say, the biggest lesson for *this* book is that as activists, we sometimes fail, and our real challenge is to use that failure to propel ourselves and our work forward. Contextualizing any failure as a learning opportunity takes the sting out of it.[2]

And as others have reminded me, there is no such thing as a complete failure. In any defeat, there are victories (though God help us if all we can claim are moral ones). What we take from those victories defines our future success.

Aside from being an interesting exercise in self-examination, this transition also highlighted an important element of leadership for me: I don't make very good decisions when I am letting my ego drive me. Before I could be of service to my staff and my board of directors, I had to wrestle my ego into place. If I was making decisions about the organization by thinking what might look best on

---

2. I first realized that Wildcanada.net might not survive the leadership transition when I was at the B-Bar Ranch on the Montana/Wyoming border taking part in a leadership retreat with my colleagues from the Training Resources for the Environmental Community (TREC) Strategic Leadership program. These colleagues (whom I name in the acknowledgments to this book), along with David Thomson and Brock Evans, our invited guest at the session, helped me in ways beyond counting. They continue to. I am in their debt.

my resumé afterwards, then I wasn't serving Wildcanada.net, and more importantly, our mission.

> Abandon your ambitions
> surrender personal motives
> and you will succeed beyond your imagination
> (*Tao*, 48)

I can't say that I have succeeded beyond my wildest imagination in this case. I have a pretty untamed imagination, after all. But I've learned a great deal that I can use to help avoid similar pitfalls in the future.

During this time of transition and turmoil at Wildcanada.net, one of my directors, who is also a close friend, suggested that maybe I should have left six months sooner. In hindsight this seems like a good idea. I knew even when I helped start Wildcanada.net that my strengths lay in establishing programs and building ideas, not necessarily maintaining the organization for the long-term.

> The sage activist abandons possession
> of the projects, programs, and organizations he
>   builds
> He knows that they will all run their course
> and he has no stake in the outcome of his efforts
> He has nothing to hold onto
> and therefore has nothing to hold him back from
>   success
> Every moment he can give what is needed to
>   succeed
> (*Tao*, 50)

I planned to abandon my claim on the projects, programs, and organization I had helped to build, but I didn't succeed in creating the internal structures needed to ensure they would last after I stepped away. That was not for lack of trying. Had I been successful in that final task as a leader, this chapter might have been very different. In the end, I just heeded Lao Tzu's advice: "When you have come to the end, leave with grace and your efforts will be remembered forever."

As I will discuss in the final chapter, "Step Back to Ward Off Monkey," stepping away from this highly stressful job was an extraordinary relief to me. And I am also relieved to know that I do have what I need to move through challenges with some small degree of grace.

Changing Course Along the Cumberland River

Not all change is driven by such difficult circumstances. In business and in many non-governmental organizations, evaluating progress and then making mid-course corrections is standard operating procedure.

Village Real Estate of Nashville, Tennessee, has changed its course to better reflect both market opportunities and the values that founder Mark Deutschmann wanted to express through his business practices.

Village Real Estate, says Deutschmann, is "selling, marketing, and redeveloping urban Nashville." But while making a profit is part of the company's motive, making Nashville a more livable, green, and community-oriented city is what drove the change in Deutschmann's business. Long interested in how business could contribute to bettering society, Deutschmann has been associated with the Social Venture Network (SVN) for many years, and found himself asking, "What am I going to do with my life to make a difference in the world?"

He decided that existing businesses needed to shift the way that they operated if they were going to create positive change, so in October of 1996 Village Real Estate was born, founded on the idea that the real estate transaction – the act of buying and selling homes – could be used to create community.

The first thing Deutschmann did was place a portion of the company into the Village Fund, to be managed by the Tides Foundation, a San Francisco-based philanthropic organization that helps individuals and companies manage charitable giving. The Village Fund would be used to support what Deutschmann calls "social profit" organizations – charities and other non-profits – that were doing good work to build community in Nashville. As Village Real Estate's profitability grew, the Village Fund started to support organizations working to clean up toxic waste in Nashville and preserve greenways along the Cumberland River.

Nashville's urban communities were in transition at that time, and they needed support, says Deutschmann. "Essentially, there was no residential living downtown," he says. In fact, Nashville prohibited residential development there. "We had a city that was sprawling endlessly, but we weren't taking care of our core. This is where my strategy as a real estate broker started to change."

First, Nashville City Council lifted the ban on developing residential in the downtown core and started planning for mixed-use of the city's centre. The Civic Design Center, which Deutschmann serves as a board member, was founded to develop the Plan of Nashville, the first effort to consider the central city in its entirety, develop a community-based vision, and identify design principles. "I've always been a neighbourhood advocate," says Deutschmann. So Village Real Estate positioned itself to sell mixed-use multi-purpose re-developments, and to manage new developments in downtown Nashville.

Deutschmann says that before he shifted the focus of his business, he concentrated on selling single family residences in suburban Nashville. Today, Village Real Estate involves itself in project development and marketing in dozens of downtown infill projects, and in adaptive re-use of existing structures. And he says that now the company is of a size that it can put more money into the Village Fund, having given away more than $100,000 to community organizations in 2004.

Next, he says, Village Real Estate will work to get residents of urban Nashville to switch to green power through the Tennessee Valley Authority, which consumers can do through Village Real Estate's website. He also says that many of his more than 100 real estate agents are attracted to Village because of the company's values.

Deutschmann says that since 1996, he's seen dramatic change in downtown Nashville. "People are taking ownership of the downtown core. People are becoming aware of the issues that affect this city and their lives. Low income projects are being redeveloped to make them more livable."

Deutschmann considers himself an advocate. "I'm an advocate for downtown Nashville," he says. "I'm an advocate for curbing urban sprawl, for recycling old buildings, for a walk-able bike-able city, and for the river that runs through urban Nashville." [3]

Moving through Change

Challenge and change are a part of our daily lives as leaders and as advocates. How we manage challenge and change can determine our success. I manage challenge and change with movement. I am a movement-oriented person. That's a polite way of saying I have ants in my pants; I have trouble sitting still for more than about half an hour at a time.

For me, there are two kinds of movement. The first is simply that which channels my energy into activity other than foot tapping, seat bouncing, pen flicking, or other charming habits. The second type is more deliberate, and done for the dual purpose of a physical and emotional/spiritual work-out, such as when I practice Tai Chi. This kind of movement shapes my life, allowing and encouraging me to follow the Way and its Virtue consciously.

The *Tao te Ching* teaches us that we have an innate ability – call it the subconscious mind, call it instinct – that sorts through the myriad daily challenges better than our rational, calculating minds can. It also suggests that the best use for that instinct is to apply it to our more pressing challenges. This deeper wisdom gives us a powerful sense of discrimination so that we don't handle urgent decisions with the haste and impulse used to make a choice at the doughnut shop counter.

If we want to harness the power of the Tao's wisdom locked within the energy and matter of our bodies and our brains, we must step back and allow that wisdom to "arise of its own accord." We must allow our *inaction* to give way to the right course of action. Stepping aside – and by this I quite literally mean stepping out of a loaded situation and taking a break, even that vital breath of air – al-

---

3. Visit *villagerealestate.com* to learn more about the company philosophy. Under Villagers, look up Mark's bio to read more about his fascinating efforts to help transform urban Nashville.

lows our minds and, more importantly, our bodies, to sort through the conundrum without the clutter that gets in the way of a sound decision.

The body stores a fantastic wealth of wisdom. Sometimes we fool ourselves into thinking that all of our wisdom is housed in our brains. But I know that my wisdom is not stored only in the grey matter of my cerebral cortex, but also in my heart, my lungs, my blood, my muscle, and my bones. The rhythmic working together of these body parts can unlock possibilities that simply don't occur to us when we are squished into an office chair or clenched in front of a computer.

When we move we encourage the energy in our bodies' invisible network of meridians to flow. This energy is called chi, or qi, and through the practice of martial arts such as Aikido or Tai Chi, we can tune in to that energy and channel it consciously into our lives.

"We can imagine chi as something like a primal vapour," writes Trevor Carolan, "the invisible white of an egg in which physical forms live and function, breathing in the chi that surrounds and nourishes them.... In reality chi cannot be detected by the five senses. Rather, it is intuited through the process of stilling the mind to such a point that our awareness is invoked to a larger Oneness and vitality. Chi, then, is a quintessence."[4]

After graduating from Sir Sandford Fleming College, I took a job with the school to help them design and implement new environmental programs for waste management and energy conservation. It was a great opportunity to learn and grow, and it came with many challenges and a steep learning curve. There's nothing like a college's bureaucracy to temper the enthusiasm of a twenty-one-year-old idealist. In part to sort through these challenges and in part because my office was a cinderblock tomb without windows, I took a walk around the campus every couple of hours. In the winter, I'd swing through the greenhouse and soak in the warm, humid air and greenery, and in the summer, I'd saunter across the school's leafy grounds.

The walks kept me from going squirrelly in my cubby hole, and they often gave rise to interesting ideas and new solutions to prob-

---

4. Trevor Carolan, *Return to Stillness, Twenty Years with a Tai Chi Master*, New York: Marlowe and Company, 2003, p. 42

lems that never came when I sat at my desk. Go figure.

When I work on something that excites or baffles me, I'll leap out of my seat and start to pace back and forth. When I worked at home in the late 1990s, I had a cordless headset phone that allowed me to do laps around the outside of my house while on conference calls. My neighbours thought I was nuts.

There is no one form of movement that is correct. I choose Tai Chi and running, and when I lived in the mountains of Alberta I loved to ski on Nordic trails. My partner Kathleen has practiced yoga for most of her life. I have friends who surf for the same reasons that I run.

When I run I strive to "make it soft" by holding in my mind the image of a standing wave, one that forms at the bottom of a small set of rapids, rises up and rolls over, rises up and rolls over. The river flows through that wave. When I run, I try to flow that way. I'm sure you'd never know it to see it, but I try.

Though I've run on and off since the age of nine, now my running regimen gives me more energy and vitality than ever before. I think that's because of the wave.

Running reduces my stress level. Kathleen jokes that my running is good for *her* health. My running helps me to accept Lao Tzu's teaching more readily.

Dancing is another way of unlocking the wisdom. In my early twenties living in Lake Louise, Alberta, my friends and I went out dancing every week at the local bars. Now I find fewer but more meaningful opportunities to dance; now it's with friends and colleagues that I am learning with during leadership retreats or conferences for social entrepreneurs and activists. (And as an added bonus, now the dance floor isn't a half-inch-deep puddle of beer!)

The place where you really get to understand the Tao and its virtue is in your heart: the physical one and the emotional one. In that muscle and in that idea lies tangled all the understanding we need to follow the Way. Exercising the heart – the physical one, yes, but more importantly the emotional one – is the best way to release an understanding of the *Tao te Ching*.

Gabrielle Roth's 5 Rhythms Dance, taught to me by Soasis Suku-weh at Hollyhock, provides a map which can take us on "an ecstatic journey," opening us to the "inherent wisdom, creativity, and energy of your body." This dance helps me let go of some of the hesitation in my body, which in turn leads to letting go of the strictures in my mind and my life. The more pliable and flexible my body becomes, the more resilient and elastic my attitude is.

Lao Tzu counsels us as activists to let go: of desire, of ego, of possession, of fear, of hatred, of remorse, and of the stories we fill our heads with. That's a lot to let go of just sitting in front of a computer screen. Under the loving guidance of an enthusiastic teacher like Soasis, the 5 Rhythms can be a fulcrum for dislodging so much of what we cling to in our work. Soasis has helped me let go.

Plus, it's a ton of sweaty fun.

> All living things are soft and flexible
> All things in death are hard and brittle
>
> The hard and the brittle will be broken
> the soft and flexible will endure
> (*Tao*, 76)

Running, skiing, and dancing are important to my activism, my parenting, my marriage, to me as a human being. But Tai Chi is the tool that I have used most consistently over the last decade to work through the paradoxes of the *Tao te Ching*.

You can't understand the *Tao te Ching* in your head alone. It's not rational. It's full of contradictions. It's not intellectual intelligence; it's emotional and physical wisdom.

Until I started practicing Tai Chi in the early 1990s, the *Tao te Ching* was just one of many books of wisdom. Tai Chi gave the *Tao's* eighty-one verses physical shape. Now I've begun to understand the *Tao* in my legs and back. I've started to feel the *Tao* in the sweep of my arms, in the twist of my hand, in the deep bow and gentle side step of Tai Chi's ebb and flow. Doing Tai Chi has connected me more closely with the chi – the natural energy – that flows through me and everything in the universe.

"What we are doing in our physical exercise and moving meditation is no less than attuning ourselves to the mysterious energy of the divine," says Trevor Carolan.[5] Tai Chi connects me with my own internal energy, virtue, and power, and with the energy that I feel present in nature. Its movements mimic nature – storks and monkeys, tigers and snakes. Through it, I have connected more deeply with nature than through any other practice.

Tai Chi is a natural flow. One movement blends into the next, so that it doesn't look or feel like 108 postures, just one long complex but flowing movement. Someone who saw me doing Tai Chi on the beach asked if I was dancing. I self-consciously said no, but that's what Tai Chi is. It's a dance set to the rhythm of nature, the harmony of our bodies, and the music of life. My friend Neva Murtha once described her practice of Tai Chi as the rushing and receding of waves on the sea shore.

The Tai Chi of activism follows that same flow. You can let it take you from being an activist working away to make the world a better place to becoming a part of nature, doing what comes naturally.

I used to get angry with myself when I became distracted in my practice of Tai Chi. The physical motion is important for me, but so too is the mental process of focusing for a few minutes a day not on my mind, but on my body and its union with my surroundings. When I make that connection between my body and the Tao, the boundary between my body and my surroundings evaporates, and I am the beach, the woods, or my backyard garden.

This is what I am trying to achieve in every aspect of my life – to dissolve the boundaries that separate me from other people, nature, and the wide world around me. I get glimpses of it two or three times a year – moments of ecstasy where there is no separation. They are my spiritual apex.

But when I get distracted my mind starts to race, I lose focus, and then I lose my place. Where was I? I just finished doing turn and kick, but which turn and kick? I get flustered and then angry with myself for getting flustered, and then angry for getting angry. It's very complex.

But now I can accept that sometimes I get lost. Rather than getting angry with myself, I just let go and see what comes next.

---

5. Ibid, p. 42

Something always does. Sometimes what comes next is that I'm left standing there a little befuddled, but that's okay too.

In our work, sometimes we lose our way. When this happens, don't become angry with yourself. Just trust that you'll naturally flow into the next experience, and allow that to happen.

Do we need to be in motion for these awakenings to occur? No. Not everybody has the ability to move as freely as I do, a gift which I feel deeply blessed to possess. And movement is just one side of the coin. Stillness is the other. Meditation, study, worship, prayer, art – in particular pottery, with its emphasis on centering – and even daily domestic activities, such as cooking or scrubbing the floor, can all provide opportunities for insight.

Seven Year Itch

We are always changing. Our bodies change daily. It is said that every seven years, each cell in our body has been replaced (thankfully not all at once). Maybe that's why yoga teaches that we move through seven-year periods of growth and development throughout life.

Knowing ourselves well enough to move through change effectively is incredibly important to our work as activists, because during transitions we are vulnerable to burnout, loss, and distraction. And any of these things can keep us from doing our work well on behalf of the causes that we serve.

> Knowing what others will do is intelligence
> Knowing what you will do is wisdom
> Controlling others is force
> Controlling yourself is real power
> (*Tao*, 33)

Knowing where we fit into civil society is paramount. Lao Tzu says in the same verse as above: "Find your true role and play it and you will endure."

Each of us must also find our place in our movement. For the last two years, I worked with a group of inspired leaders, mostly from American conservation organizations, brought together by Training

Resources for the Environmental Community (TREC), in a strategic leadership program. Through the course of a year, we supported each other as we faced challenges as leaders of our movement.

All eighteen of us were searching for the role to play in our movement. For most, that means advancing within our own organizations or moving to similar or larger roles in others. During the time we were together, half a dozen people took on executive director roles or senior manager positions. There is tremendous pressure for upward mobility in the conservation movement; the dearth of leadership means that anybody with a knack for it is pushed to the front, ready or not. Most are ready and take on the role with gusto, but some are not and suffer the consequences.

For some, however, finding one's true role doesn't necessarily mean moving up. For some, it means simply settling in. I know several former executive directors who now happily work as campaigners. After experiencing the stress of formal leadership positions, these talented leaders are much happier in less demanding roles. I myself am very relieved not to be in a *formal* leadership position for the time being. But a part of me is preparing for my next opportunity to take on that challenge again.

Three Stages of Activism

While considering these stages in leadership and the changes they bring, I came across a passage in Alan Watts' book, *What is Tao?* that intrigues me. In his chapter on Te, which he refers to as "virtue: skill at living," he says, "In all this you will see that there are three stages. There is first what we might call the natural or the child-like stage of life in which self-consciousness has not yet arisen. Then there comes a middle stage, which we might call one's awkward age, in which one learns to become self-conscious. And finally the two are integrated in the rediscovered innocence of a liberated person."[6]

I am starting to believe that similarly there are three stages of activism. These stages are not an upward progression, but a spiral without a beginning or end. Moving from one stage to the next isn't necessarily succession, but is more akin to the seasonal growth of

---

6. Alan Watts, *What is Tao?* Navoto, CA: New World Library, 2000, p. 49

plants or trees – we must proceed through periods of dormancy in order to flower each spring.

The first stage is what I call "grassroots" activism, when we first discover that something we love in this world is threatened, and alone or with others, set out to make it right. This is an innocent, even child-like (as opposed to *childish*) stage of activism, when we haven't learned to be self-conscious about our actions, or that there are limitations to what we can achieve. We don't really know what we are doing, and so we can do anything!

We often enjoy great success during this grassroots stage: there are no organizational demands to keep us from focusing all of our creative energy on the task at hand. We're not worried about our careers, therefore our egos don't get in our way. We're not constrained by the background chatter in our own heads telling us that "we've already tried this, and it doesn't work."

The second stage is "professional" activism. After our grassroots campaign is completed, we're now driven to take further action to support our movement. In some cases, this means continuing to volunteer for our church group or local grassroots organization, and in others it means applying for a job with formal organizations or groups. We're ready to dedicate our lives to our efforts.

Often at this time we connect with the larger world of civil society. Suddenly we're exposed to new ideas, new methods of carrying out our ideas, and new people. During the early 1990s I got involved with an organization called the Canadian Unified Student Environmental Network (CUSEN). It was rich and rewarding to come together with other young people from across Canada who felt as I did. Until that time, I felt very isolated. In high school and college, I was one of a handful of people beavering away. When I attended my first CUSEN conference in Waterloo, Ontario, however, I discovered a room full of like-minded people. My exposure to CUSEN, and to people like Derek Ball, Mike Gifford, Pat Potter, Catherine Phillips, side-by-side with my good friend Richard Griffith, opened a wider world of advocacy to me.

During this stage we may become convinced that we know what we're doing, and conversely, become disillusioned with our efforts and the progress of our movement within civil society. We spend more time dealing with office politics and raising money. We have to write reports and work in coalitions and have meetings, meetings, meetings.

This is a dangerous time for activists. During this stage we can become disenfranchised, or suffer from burnout. I know many young people who come into our movement with lofty goals and great idealism, but within two or three years, they leave, sick to death of the tedious nature of organizational politics and worn out from failing to make headway on issues that need our attention.

They thought they signed up to save the forests or the salmon or the seals. They thought they were signing on to end global poverty or free political prisoners. Instead they are struggling against complacency, and for recognition, resources, and position. The optimism that they felt when they were volunteering for their local "Friends of the Forest" group, or the community chapter of "Save the Kids," slowly leaches out and is replaced by cynicism and negativity.

It happens often enough that it comes to characterize our approach to advocacy. We can become staid and risk-adverse and bureaucratic in our work.

But it doesn't happen to everybody. I know some seasoned advocates – Cliff Wallis, a long-time volunteer with the Alberta Wilderness Association for one – who have maintained their youthful enthusiasm throughout their careers. These people seem to rise above the petty matters that hamper our cause, staying focused and positive and energized. Or maybe they simply skip the second phase of advocacy and move from the first directly to the third.

The third stage is where we rediscover our creativity, our innocence, our imagination, and our passion. Call it the transcendence phase. Call it enlightened advocacy. Call it returning to our source. In this phase, we remember again that all things are possible. Though office politics, competition for resources, bureaucracy, and funding reports are still present, we can see beyond these necessary evils to our *real* work. Once again, creativity and imagination become our hallmarks. The phrase "We've already tried that and it doesn't work" is not part of our vocabulary.

In this stage, the advocate brings to the workplace an infectious, creative zeal. She helps organizations achieve the greatness that can come when people work together for a cause that inspires them and challenges them and provides them with opportunities to support each other.

Call this stage what you will, but Lao Tzu would say that you are following the Way and its Virtue.

> Those who are in harmony with the Tao
> are like infants
> whose bones and muscles are soft
> but resolve and strength are great
> The child doesn't know about the union of yin and
>   yang
> the basis of its own vital power
> and so it always has power to wield
>
> To know this harmony is to know the deepest
>   satisfaction
> a full life, a gentle heart
>
> The sage activist is like a child
> letting things come and go
> without interfering or trying to control them
> He doesn't force things or dwell on the results
> and therefore is always able to move beyond them
>
> He knows that anticipation leads to disappointment
> (*Tao*, 55)

Don't necessarily turn to the silverbacks in the conservation movement or the elders on the social justice front to find those in the third stage. You'll find as many among the ranks of newcomers as anywhere else. This transcendence doesn't necessarily take a lifetime – it can happen with a flash of insight. Nor, however, does it necessarily last a lifetime. Throughout our careers, we must work through these stages again and again.

This is exemplified by how people at various ages and stages dance. I love to watch my son Rio dance: when he is happy, when he finds a big crab or a sea star, when he eats ice cream. His arms fly up and out, his body twists, and he twirls around, falling down, laughing hysterically. It is artless, and it is beautiful, pure, innocent. Nothing about it is self-conscious. Compare that to watching teenagers dance in a high-school gym. I wish I could forget my seventh- and eighth-grade dances.

Over time, we can find our way back to that place where we dance for the sake of moving our bodies in joyful expression. We learn to let go. And in letting go, we find that anything is possible once again.

Moving through change makes me think of Wave Hands like Clouds. It's lovely to watch and very beautiful to do. It's a graceful side to side motion, the hands floating as if on clouds as they alternatively sweep up from below and push to one side. It's full of movement: we take five big steps sideways during the posture, covering lots of ground. It's full of grace and poise as I wish each of life's transitions could be.

The Book of Changes

Any discussion of how to employ the *Tao* to address changes in our life would be remiss without mentioning the *I Ching*. Among other things, the *I Ching* – the Book of Changes – offers a way to consider a problem or challenge so you can let go of your search for an answer.

Attributed to a sage named Cheng Yi, the *I Ching* is possibly the oldest of the Taoist texts, predating the Lao Tzu book. Like the *Tao te Ching*, its origin is clouded in uncertainty, and it is likely to have been compiled from folk lore and cultural wisdom over many hundreds of years. According to translator Thomas Cleary, the book is over 3,000 years old, and addresses "how to respond to change – in ourselves, in our relationships and in the world at large."[7] The *I Ching* contains the Tai Chi – the familiar circle with the black and white helix – surrounded by a set of eight three-line symbols or ideograms. Some lines are solid, representing yang, while some are bro-

---

7. Cheng Yi, *I Ching, The Book of Change*, trans. Thomas Cleary, Boston and London: Shambhala, 2003, p. ix

ken, representing yin. In the text of the *I Ching*, the eight ideograms are arranged into sixty-four groupings, each with a symbol on the top and bottom, creating arrangements with six lines. In this way, the combination of each of the eight ideograms comes together to create a message, something like a koan, enigmatic riddle, or paradox that challenges the mind to unlock ideas buried deeply in the subconscious. Each arrangement has a name, so that the symbols for "earth" and "heaven" come together to form "tranquility," while "wind" and "thunder" form "constancy."

When consulting the *I Ching*, the reader holds a question in mind and casts a set of yarrow sticks or coins to come up with six results. These are then correlated into the solid (yang) or broken (yin) lines to form the six-line symbol that translates into one of the sixty-four verses of the *I Ching*. The verse offers insight into your question.

This may seem like a sophisticated fortune cookie, and for the longest time I was puzzled by the *I Ching* and put off by the seemingly random nature of the advice that it appears to provide. But recently while undergoing massive changes in my life, I consulted the *I Ching*. It was fascinating. For example, while preparing for my family's move to the west coast, I held the following question in my mind: What is essential about our relocation?

I flipped a coin six times and then consulted the *I Ching*. The top three lines – all yin – symbolized earth. Earth stands for harmony, flexibility, and receptivity in the *I Ching*. The next three lines – one yang atop two yin lines – symbolized mountain – stopping, stabilization, and stillness. Together they form the ideograph called Humility.

The text for this ideogram focuses on lowering oneself below others, and being flexible, open, and trusting. It suggests that true leaders practice humility as a constant and that we must not concern ourselves with the accumulation of wealth. Being flexible and receptive is the message in this ideogram for me.

Did this consultation answer my question? If my question had been too specific – say, what street in Victoria should my family move to – then I'd be pretty disappointed with the answer. But ask an open-ended question – how to approach a problem, or how to seek a solution – and the *I Ching* provides ideas that can help you find the solutions lurking within your subconscious.

"The rituals and calculations of consulting the *I Ching* are a kind of doodling which quiets the repressive anxieties of consciousness and, with luck, allows useful insights to emerge from one's deeper centers," says Alan Watts.[8]

The *I Ching's* answer regarding my family's move is still emerging. I am still coming to grips with the need for humility in my work and efforts. After six nerve-wracking years as executive director of Wildcanada.net, finding harmony and being receptive to stillness and stabilization is a serious challenge, and a deep and profound need.

Once again, common sense is needed when we use tools like the *I Ching*. If you're sitting in your office and a harried staff person enters and asks a routine question, asking him to have a seat while you consult the *I Ching* will not instill confidence or respect. Nor would jumping up and going for a walk around the block or to the local park while you let the right answer "arise of its own accord."

You will know when it's appropriate to step back from a troubling situation to seek clarity by setting the pressing issues of the day aside and allowing your subconscious mind to do its work, unhindered by the chatter and the constant pressure that holds it at bay on most days. You will know this as surely as you will know the solution to the riddle that troubles you when you see it before you.

Making use of these tools for sorting through changes and challenges requires of us a higher level of self-awareness. We're not just being absent-minded. We're not just putting the idea out of our minds with no intent of returning to it. Nor are we abdicating our responsibility to solve the problem while we consult the *I Ching*. We're taking two important steps: we're deliberately *not* reacting, but stepping out of the situation to clear our minds, and then we're becoming aware of our subconscious process that sorts through these problems. In time, we can tune our minds to recognize the solution when it does arise of its own accord. This skill, like any other, takes time, patience, and practice. But also like any other skill, it is very rewarding when learned.

When I lived in Canmore, Alberta, I'd often walk to the Bow

8. Alan Watts, *What is Tao?* Navoto, CA: New World Library, 2000, p. 66

River to reflect on the changes and challenges in my life and in my work. Day after day, the river calmed and centred me as it carved its patient pathway between towering peaks.

The philosopher Heraclites said, "You cannot step twice into the same river, for other waters are constantly moving on."

The only way to keep up in a world that is constantly changing is to let go of attachment, including attachment to change.

There are rocks in the river. In some places, the water is deep and the banks on either side are far away. There are rapids. This is our life. This is our work. Following the Tao as we navigate these waters means not forcing ourselves upstream, but rather letting the current be our guide, trusting that it will see us safely to kinder shores.

11

STEP BACK TO WARD OFF MONKEY

Balancing Leadership, Activism, and a Healthy Life

The Way is like a bow
When drawn it is in perfect balance
its lower tip drawn up
its upper tip drawn down

The Tao seeks balance
adding and subtracting
to keep the world in harmony
(*Tao*, 77)

In 1993, Sir Sandford Fleming College's Earth Issues Club hosted a conference for youth from across Eastern Canada on the topic of sustainable living. We worked hard to create an inspiring and motivating event for the one hundred or so attendees who braved January's blizzards and minus twenty temperatures to attend. Five months of planning by a team of fifteen people paid off, and it was a roaring success. By the end of the weekend, I was too tired to speak.

I was employed by the college at that time. The week after the conference, I had a major report due on environmental sustainability at the school's two main campuses. Promptly after I handed in the report, I crashed. The stress and long hours leading up to the conference, the hard work to complete the report, and the inevitable personal dramas playing out in my life all culminated in a mini-meltdown.

It was just a little burnout. Small flames. I got sick, laid around for a week, and lost some of my motivation to fight and organize and struggle. After a couple of months, I headed back to the mountains for another summer of guiding for Parks Canada, and recovered my pluck. In the nearly two decades that I've been an activist, I think that was the only time I hit the skids.

Until recently.

After five years of intense work with groups like the Alberta Wilderness Association and UTSB Research in Banff, Alberta, in 1999 I worked with my colleague Kevin Scott to start Wildcanada.net, a national conservation group. I didn't realize until I stepped down as executive director in 2005 how close to spontaneous combustion I was. I should have seen it. I thought I knew better.

We all need to understand the forces at work within us that cause us to burn out, and keep us from living a more balanced life. My intent in this chapter is not to duplicate the many resources available to activists to help us cope with chronic stress or burnout. Vast swaths of ancient forests have been cleared to provide books on this topic.[1] Instead, I'm going to address only a few themes that arise from the teachings of Lao Tzu and his contemporaries.

In the *Tao te Ching*, Lao Tzu identifies six things that apply to our work as activists that might lead to burnout: resisting the flow and failing to find balance, clinging to expectations, developing excessive ego, doing too much, failing to step aside when the time is right, and resisting our three treasures: restraint, compassion, and love. He also addresses a number of things we can do as activists to try and find a balance between our advocacy and our personal lives.

As activists, many of us struggle with burnout. We work long hours at jobs that often don't have large pay-packs attached to them.

---

1. This book is printed on Ancient Forest Friendly paper. The publisher, Arsenal Pulp Press, has signed onto the Markets Initiative's campaign promoting the use of AFF paper by Canadian book and magazine publishers. Visit *oldgrowthfree.com* for more information.

Many of us volunteer our time either as the primary way we contribute, or in addition to our full-time positions with organizations. We run businesses that not only have to make a fiscal profit, but a social profit too. Our work is very stressful – we are often in conflict with people on a daily basis. We carry a great deal of responsibility to our organizations, to our families, to our cause. We're often asked to manage or lead efforts without any formal training as leaders. We manage staff, something that we might not be well suited for. We have to ask for money, something that many activists find nerve-wracking. And all of this is set against the backdrop of causes that we consider to be so important that we're willing to dedicate – some might say sacrifice – our lives to them.

Finding balance in our lives as leaders, activists, and social entrepreneurs amid those conditions can be a monumental challenge. But the consequences of failing to find that balance are very high.

Case in point: at Wildcanada.net, we worried almost constantly about money and our sustainability. Very early in our work, I became acutely stressed about a difficult financial situation, which resulted in a case of shingles – a very painful nervous system malady that is the result of having had chicken pox as a child and intense anxiety as an adult. The painful rash lasted for about a week, and I think I got off easy, with only one band of nerves in my chest and back affected. But it foreshadowed things to come.

Of all the stresses I encountered while at Wildcanada.net, money was undoubtedly the one that affected me the most. Having to raise between $1,000 and $2,000 a day to run the organization took its toll on me. Finding a way to ameliorate such stress is critical if we're to create the leaders who will be needed to succeed our efforts.[2]

Hooked on a Feeling

If being an activist is so stressful, why advocate? If running an organization or social enterprise is so stressful, why do it? It's true that not everybody finds it as stressful as others.

---

2. Though I've only touched on it in this book, you might have surmised that I think civil society as a whole could use a sound shake-up. Visit *highwatermark.ca/seachange* to read some of my thoughts and contribute your own.

"Sometimes I fantasize about being a clerk in an antique furniture store," says Carole Stark, executive director of the Alberta based Chinook Institute for Community Stewardship. "I read my book. People come in, I chat with them about antiques, they leave, and I read my book. That's my day." That might be the fantasy many of us have versions of, but inside, we all know that after a couple of days of that, we'd be climbing the walls, trying to advocate for better working conditions or more ethical treatment of antique furniture.

And so many of us accept the strain and stress as the cost for standing up for what we believe in. For me, it came down to two things: I wanted to contribute to the protection of nature, and at the time, founding and leading an organization was the way to do it. But it is also true that I was addicted to the stress. I wanted to feel the buzz of adrenaline that came with having dodged another bullet. I wanted the rush of knowing I was responsible for moving an issue forward. Hello, ego.

I didn't realize the price I paid to feel that buzz, to experience that rush. It was only when I saw how badly I was handling the other responsibilities in my life that I realized I needed a big change. That's when I took seriously my own promise to leave Wildcanada.net after five to seven years. I left not solely because my time was up, but because the stress of my work life was affecting my personal life, my family, and my well-being.

When you fail to have the patience and energy to play with your little boy after work, you're getting dangerously close to total burnout. If you're lucky, as I am, to have a loving partner who will point this out to you and enough sense to pay attention, then you can take corrective action.

That's why when I was leaving Wildcanada.net and things were falling apart, I couldn't step back into my former role. It was a monumental effort even to play the small role I did in winding down the organization.

The conservation movement is littered with burnt out leaders. I would guess that other parts of civil society – be it the labour movement, the women's movement, or the social justice movement – are likewise filled with people who have once been on fire and are now simply fried.

Step Back to Ward Off Monkey

If it were only the personal consequences of this burnout that we had to face, it would be bad enough. But burnout means are unable to work for the causes we were once so passionate about. We are losing good people from our movements – people who have the capacity to lead us – and in part the penalty for this is the extinction of species, the loss of equality, the defeat of justice.

There are moments in Tai Chi when we step up – to raise hands, to parry a punch, to kick – and balance for a moment, finding a point of stillness in the motion. In Step Back to Ward Off Monkey, we take a pronounced period of stillness as we ward off an imaginary foe. Our monkey is the one we activists frequently carry on our backs: overwork, burnout, failing health, ruined relationships. If we are to accomplish our goals then we must find a balance to ensure that our lives are long, rich, rewarding, and filled with love.

In my early days as an activist, I believed that I needed to pour everything I had into an effort that would yield quick results and turn the tide on the issues that threatened us. I hoped that if I worked hard enough for a period of time, the momentum would encourage the rest of society to pick up the cause after I had moved on. I hoped that I could secure the kind of results that would let me step aside altogether, at which time I planned to watch daytime television and eat potato chips.

I now know that to protect the things I love will be the work of my entire life. I want that life to be long and rich, filled with the love of my friends and family. In short, I'm in this struggle for the long haul, and know I will need to safeguard my resources in order to be able to draw upon them over the course of many years.

Rolling with the Flow

Once on a flight from Calgary to Toronto, my partner Kathleen was seated next to an officer in the Salvation Army. He was on his way to Ground Zero in New York where the gaping hole in the earth memorialized those who died on the morning of September 11, 2001. He was going to provide relief to Salvation Army workers who had been serving the people of New York since the terrorist attacks. Kathleen asked the man about his work and his life, and then she quizzed him on how he managed to stay positive through all the challenges he had faced. Mixing two common metaphors, he said, "I just roll with the flow."

Lao Tzu could not have said it better.

Certainly rolling with the punches or going with the flow is an attitude that lends itself to long-term survival, but it's not that simple. Jacob Needleman, in the introduction to Jane English and Gia-Fu Feng's translation of the *Tao te Ching,* cautions that the cliché "go with the flow" can be misleading: "Do these words in their popular use mean the same thing as living according to the Tao? Certainly not. The distortions of this phrase that have become popular suggest an unthinking passivity along with a naïve trust in the flow of outer events."[3]

Rather than unthinking passivity, what we might aspire to is a process of conscious decision-making around when to step forward and when to step aside.

Often as activists we want to force things. We need to force things. If not, we feel like we are losing control, which we can't afford, because the things that we are fighting for can't afford to lose much more. Children are dying. Ecosystems are collapsing.

But here is the thing: if we're always forcing, always pushing, always fighting, and never "rolling with the flow," we won't last long. The mark of a sage advocate is to know when to push, and when to step back:

> Know that for everything there is a time
> To be a leader
> to follow
> To take action
> to stand still
> To be strong
> to fade
> To be cautious

---

3. Lao Tzu, *Tao te Ching,* trans. Gia-Fu Feng and Jane English, with a new introduction and notes by Jacob Needleman, New York: Vintage Books, 1989, p. xvi

to take a risk
(*Tao*, 29)

The Bible says much the same thing in Ecclesiastes 3:1-8: "For every-thing there is a season, and a time for every matter under heaven." (If you're humming the tune by the Byrds now, don't blame me. It's in your head and you won't be able to get it out for the rest of the day.)

There is a time to yield no ground in the effort to protect what we love. But there is also a time to yield, to fall back strategically and regroup, or to simply pick our fights with an eye to being around to fight for a long, long time. If all you do is to hurl yourself against the brick wall of the opposition, to "rage against the machine" as some have put it, your energy will be spent and what will you have to show for it?

Sometimes when I'm trying to justify the opposite of this, a line from a Neil Young song runs through my head: "It's better to burn out than to fade away." Another line whose origin I don't know comes to mind: "To burn out you must have once been on fire."

We like that image as activists. We like the idea of "being on fire." It connotes passion and exuberance. We think that if we are on fire, we're making progress and getting things done. Or at least it looks like we are.

We know that in certain ecosystems, fire is a force for renewal. In the wake of a forest fire, lush new growth occurs. Fire produces nitrogen, making it available for plants to feed on, spurring rapid upward growth. But that generation of vegetation is lost to the eco-system and the new forest grows up in a nutrient-rich but single gen-eration landscape.

Compare that with a temperate rainforest. In these ecosystems, old trees slowly topple over as subsequent layers of new growth push up from below. The ancient trees fall to the ground where their nutrients slowly leach into the soil. In many cases young trees grow straight out of the fallen nurse logs, so that in time the old trees are absorbed into the new trees and you can't see the difference between the two.

Both systems are natural. Both spawn new growth. In the latter example, the saplings feed from the nutrients of the elders. But in civil society, fire purges the landscape every so often, leaving skeletal remains in its wake and new shoots struggling up through the ashes. I think if we want to have long-term successes we'll need to start behaving like the temperate rainforest, where we nurture each generation of activists to create perpetuity.

Look to the Source

Part of why activists experience burnout is that much of our drive and energy comes from our anger or fear. Early in this book, I wrote about acting from a place of compassion and love. It will make us more effective advocates, and it will help us be effective for much longer. Remembering our three treasures – restraint, compassion, and love – will help us advocate from a part of our hearts, our bodies, and our minds that renews us.

In the yoga tradition espoused in the *Bhagavad Gita*, there are three basic energy sources: *Raja* (passion, aggression, willpower, determination, and drive), *Tamas* (inertia, dullness, passivity, and sleep), and *Sattva* (peacefulness, clarity, and joy). In a May 2005 article in the *Yoga Journal*, Sally Kempton says that the three energetic qualities "are inseparable, like strands of a single rope, and are layered throughout nature as the energetic substratum of everything."

I like this image. Reading this story made me think about the energy and passion with which we as activists go about our work. In the Yogic tradition, it could be argued that much of our work is accomplished from energy derived from *Raja*, from passion, from a drive born of determination and even aggression. In the Taoist tradition, this might be seen as energy flowing from Yang – the masculine, the light (or bright, as in fiery) side of the Tai Chi.

Kempton says that energy born from this sort of source can be creative and efficient, but there's an edge to it because it's fueled by restlessness and the fear of losing or being left behind. "*Sattva* is born in stillness," says Kempton. "True *sattvic* strength arises out of a willingness to wait, to allow actions to unfold out of the quiet of your center." Doesn't this sound like the concept of *wu wei*, or waiting for the right action to arise of its own accord, that Lao Tzu advocates?

Sattva is akin to yin – the dark or shady side of the mountain, the feminine, the quiet, the restful place that we work from when we are tapping into our deeper connection with our work and with our purpose.

Tamas is the place in between yin and yang – the transition between them, and the expression of each in the other found in the dots of white and black within the fish-shaped half-circles on either side.

Raja fuels us, but if we allow it to burn too hot, it will burn us out. *Tamas* allows us to rest. *Sattva* sustains us for the long haul. It is the power of the heart.

These three strengths are simply another way of expressing the universal truth found in the Tai Chi, or yin/yang polarity. There is no judgment in the *Bhagavad Gita*, nor in the *Tao te Ching,* that one is better than the other. They are inseparable, and the key to success and happiness is to find a place where we can live with both yin and yang in balance.

"Rolling with the flow," and finding a balance or harmony between the light and dark sides of the mountain, is almost certainly the first step in warding off the monkey. But there are barriers to this; one of the most difficult to overcome is our own expectation of success, and the part of our ego that drives us towards it.

What to Expect When You're Expecting

The *Tao te Ching* says "Because the sage activist has let go of expectation and ego she is able to be confident and content." Here I take expectation to mean the formulation of a desired or preconceived outcome. This could mean that as we develop a strategy we anticipate its successful execution. Or when we develop a fundraising plan we expect it to succeed. We have a legislative agenda and expect that we'll accomplish our lobby efforts. We expect our business plan will almost certainly bear fruit.

Lao Tzu says that the sage "knows that anticipation leads to disappointment."

Stephen Mitchell translates this passage as, "He never expects results; thus he is never disappointed."[4]

---

4. Lao Tzu, *Tao te Ching: A new English Translation*, trans. Stephen Mitchell, New York: HarperCollins, 1989

The Buddha said much the same thing in the *Dhammapada*: "Expectation inevitably creates disappointment."

If we develop our plans and strategies with the expectation that they will succeed, our disappointment when they don't will cause us to suffer.[5] This suffering is a result of our attachment to the outcome. But if we develop our plans and strategies and let go of our expectations of them, we can sit back and watch them unfold objectively. If they succeed, great – but if they don't, we are free to adapt those plans or re-craft those strategies and try again. As such, we don't waste precious energy on anxiety over our "failure." Instead, we hold that energy in reserve for our next effort.

I fear that in civil society, some of us have replaced expectations for success with the acceptance of defeat. We get knocked down enough times to know that we must get back on our feet again and continue our work. But if you've been knocked to the mat time after time until you're punch drunk and staggering, you're inclined to simply stay there after a while. Abandoning hope is not the same as abandoning expectation.

> When the movement loses the Way
> we carry on as a matter of routine
> without passion or hope
> (*Tao*, 18)

His Holiness the Dalai Lama says that there are two kinds of desire, or expectation. He says, "One is the aspiration to be of benefit to all sentient beings and the other is the aspiration to attain fully the enlightened state for that purpose. Without these two types of aspiration, the attainment of full Enlightenment is not possible."[6]

By setting aside our expectations, we can hold onto our larger hope that the world and all of its creatures – humans among them – can thrive and succeed. If we are attached to the outcome of our efforts, anticipating success or failure, we cannot serve our cause.

---

5. In the Buddhist tradition, suffering forms the backbone of the Four Noble Truths: 1) that there is suffering; 2) that suffering has cause; 3) that there is cessation of suffering; and, 4) that there is a path to such freedom.

6. His Holiness the Dalai Lama, *The Art of Living: A Guide to Contentment, Joy and Fulfillment*. London: Thorsons Publishers, 1995, 2001

Letting go of both positive and negative attachment, we can be open to opportunity and nimble in our response to change.

Just as important as the need to release expectations of success is to let go of our expectations of failure. There is a middle ground between these two extremes: we should cling neither to hope of success nor expectation of failure, but instead do our work unattached to the outcome.

> Understand attachment
> yet remain unattached
> Accept things as they are
> and the Tao will well up inside you
> and you will return to the origin of the Way
> (*Tao*, 28)

In "returning to the origin of the Way," we can use the strength, passion, and hope of our cause to find the true path to success. That true path will weave its way back and forth between our triumphs and our defeats, and by following it we can remain vital and resilient, never losing our optimism to defeat or giving into the cynicism that it breeds.

In doing so, we can ease the suffering we feel as a result of our attachment, which in turn might ease the chronic stress and potential for burnout that can arise with defeat.

Hello, Ego

Our egos keep us clinging to our expectations. I've written a lot about ego in this book, and that is because in studying the *Tao te Ching* and examining my own work as an activist, I believe that ego is among the chief ills that keeps us from living happily and accomplishing our work as activists. Ego prevents us from making the choices and decisions required of us to be successful in our cause.

Our pride and self-worth can sometimes become tangled up in our expectations for our campaigns, be they fundraising efforts or the execution of a political strategy. We often see ourselves as the culmination of our efforts, and so we understandably create expectations in order to serve our egos.

> If you want to become complete
> first accept that you are unfinishable
> If you wish to follow a sure path
> first accept that the Way is winding
> If you want to be fulfilled
> first relinquish your ego
> (*Tao*, 22)

Finding a healthy state of equilibrium between appropriate pride in oneself and the corrosive force of exaggerated self-importance and conceit is neither easy nor a luxury. In fact, it is critical to our work as activists.

Sometimes our passion for the cause drives us to work until we are exhausted. But while our passion drives us, as often as not it's our ego that keeps us from realizing that we're in trouble. I've seen this in many of my colleagues, and in myself. We believe that nobody can do the work that we do as well as we can. We don't share the burden, the work load, or the responsibility because we fail to recognize in others the possibility that they might do the job as well or better than we can. So we cling to the myriad tasks and work long days, and in doing so, sometimes fall on our faces.

We must address what drives us to hold onto that control. We need to confront what creates the need to hold onto the spotlight, to be at the front of the line. "Daring not to be first" is how many translations of the *Tao te Ching* characterize what I have called restraint. To dare not to be first means to find the courage to address what it is in us that needs that type of recognition. Daring not to be first means restraining our impulse to always be at the front of the line, in the spotlight. It means stepping back.

Remember, "The sage acts without expectation, succeeds without recognition / and steps aside when his work has been done."

Some will say that this recognition is about our effort to build power. Decision-makers fear only those with enough power to cause them harm – at the polls or in the marketplace – and as activists, all we have is the force of our presence in the media and our sway with our organizations and the general public to generate that power.

How can we do this without gaining recognition? How can we do this without "being first"?

As discussed throughout this book, this view of power is antithetical to the teaching of Lao Tzu. It's the argument that we need to meet force with force, and that somehow, if we build up enough power, enough force, we can enact a systemic change that will solve all of the world's problems. But it hasn't worked so far. It's a disingenuous argument, one that massages our own ego.

For me, seeing my name in a newspaper story or my dour mug on television gave me a sense of self-worth and gratification that I could not get otherwise. Plain and simple, being in the spotlight gave me pleasure. Seeing my name on the cover and spine of this book will no doubt do the same thing.

Am I advocating for a complete abandonment of recognition? Do I think that we should somehow buck human nature and find a way to obliterate human ego? Even if I did, it couldn't be done. But controlling our ego and recognizing it when it affects how we work and the decisions that we make is essential to our success – as a movement, and to our own well being.

There is a big difference between seeking fulfillment from our work, something that is healthy and appropriate, and needing to prove ourselves.

> The sage doesn't need to prove herself
> Those who must prove themselves are not wise
> (*Tao*, 81)

For me, stepping aside as an executive director meant giving up the recognition that came with that position. And not stepping back into that role when things got rocky for the organization that I helped create meant quelling my ego and accepting that I had to move on.

Doing so has given me more space in my heart. For the first time in a couple of years, having relinquished that control and position, I feel human. Not having to feed the voracious appetite of my ego, at least for a little while, has helped me find some peace and balance in my life.

What Cost, Burnout?

Not stepping aside, even as we face chronic stress and burnout, can have long-term and detrimental effects on our health. But I know activists who consciously work until they literally crash, at which point they take some time off, get caught up on sleep, and get right back at it.

How long can that last?

For most, not very long. But how long will it take us to triumph over the AIDS epidemic? How long to find a cure for cancer? How long to thwart the effects of climate change? We need activists who are willing to give their entire lives to this work. To do so, we've got to relinquish some of the responsibility and control over our organizations, our campaigns, and our programs. To do that, we need to set aside our own egos and believe that others, with some guidance and assistance, can do as good a job or better than we can. Different, yes, but certainly as good.

Think about this. Do you know what happens when you burn out? I was horrified to learn that when I experience very stressful events and respond with anger and rage, I actually lose brain cells. It takes a long time to recover from stress. And then, when we do try, we find that we've operated on stress so long – on the chemicals that our bodies produce when we are stressed – that we can't really rest, and we don't recover very quickly, or very well.

Research into how the brain responds to prolonged periods of stress shows that the hippocampus (not to be confused with the 8,000-pound throwback to the Jurassic that lives in Africa) can be affected by the excessive production of cortisol that corresponds to chronic stress.

The hippocampus is the part of the brain responsible for, among other things, storing memory. Don't forget that.

According to the Society for Neuroscience, "Accumulating research indicates that continuous or intense stress may sometimes negatively influence the brain and its function. Studies find evidence that severe stress may sometimes alter brain cells, brain structure, and brain function. As a consequence, memory problems and the development of some mental diseases, including depression, may erupt. On the positive side, research also suggests that methods under investigation may be able to help ward off or even possibly reverse some of the stress effects."

Stress is normal. We all experience it, and the production of adrenaline and cortisol help us respond quickly to risk. But prolonged stress results in the circulation of these hormones into nearly every cell in our body, and after a time they can have a dramatic effect on our health and even on our brains.

During long, drawn-out periods of stress, the body produces large amounts of cortisol which puts us into a catabolic state. Even after the stress ends, the effects may continue. With a prolonged exposure to elevated levels of cortisol, the brain loses its sensitivity to the hormone and can no longer monitor its circulation level. The brain therefore becomes powerless to down-regulate cortisol production. A continual state of stress response, with elevated cortisol, becomes the norm.

Once, in 1997, after an acutely stressful episode when I screamed at and threatened with violence my old 286 desktop computer, it took me almost two days to relax and bring my heart rate back to normal. I don't need the Society for Neuroscience to tell me that's not good for me. (It's also a little embarrassing.)

Abnormally high levels of cortisol interfere with our brains in a number of ways. According to one web resource: "Cortisol impairs glucose transport and utilization by brain cells. Glucose or blood sugar is the main energy source of the brain. When the brain's fuel supply is interrupted by high cortisol levels, impairment of learning, memory, and mood can result. What's more, this reduction in energy supply to brain cells weakens them, making them more vulnerable to toxic insult."[7] This toxic assault can damage our friend the hippocampus to the extent that some studies now link Alzheimer's disease with these elevated levels of cortisol.[8]

The cortisol and adrenalin have changed our body's ability to relax, respond to stress, and recover after the stress has ended. Some-

---

7. Dr. Joseph A. Debé, web-published material at *drdebe.com/STRESS.htm*

8. For more information on the impact that stress can have on the brain, visit the Society for Neuroscience's web page at *http://apn.sfn.org* or visit *brainsource.com/stress_&_health.htm*

times, we don't recover from our burnout. I know a number of good activists who have been lost to our movement because of this. I also know of others, suffering from the depression that arises from the cycle of burnout and recovery, who have taken their own lives.

Our passion, our determination to make a difference in the world, our sense of obligation, and our ego propel us to work long, and to work hard. But we also have to work smart. We will never be able to pour the kind of energy – in terms of human power and financial resources – into our cause that those who oppose us do. What we can do is work smarter, and in doing so, reap unexpected benefits: better health and more effective strategies.

> If you try to do too much
> you will fail at all things
> If you don't achieve a balance between your work
> and your rest
> you will not be an effective advocate
> If the only thing that matters is success and victory
> you will find nothing but disappointment
> If you seek only the approval of others
> you will never be fulfilled
>
> Do your work well, and then step aside
> This is the way of the Tao
> (*Tao*, 9)

Of course, there are times when we must work late into the night to prepare a report or get ready for an event. But if as a habit you routinely find yourself at the office or hunched over the kitchen table late into the evening, beware.

When I was a volunteer for the Alberta Wilderness Association in the mid-1990s, I would start my efforts to protect places like Alberta's Kananaskis Country after I had finished my regular work day. I was living in Lake Louise then, and once and sometimes twice a week I drove my little Pontiac Firefly to Calgary, a round trip of nearly four hours, to attend meetings. It was not uncommon for me to work until after midnight each night on various tasks.

When I began work with Wildcanada.net I had to reduce some of my volunteer duties and eliminate some of the long hours. But even then I remained on the board of directors of four organizations, and on many weekends would find myself in such exotic locals as Fernie, British Columbia or Victor, Idaho. After my first son was born, I started paring down my board responsibilities. In late 2004, I stepped down from my last board post.

Because burnout is so prevalent in the conservation movement, we're starting to talk about it more openly. It's no longer the status quo to simply toil in quiet desperation. We're starting to look out for each other. Programs like Strategic Leadership Development of Training Resources for the Environmental Community (TREC) help prepare leaders to manage stress and burnout. A few years ago, I went through the Hollyhock Leadership Institute's Environmental Leadership Initiative, and it was this training that convinced me to immediately step down from three of the four boards that I was sitting on. It came down to Lao Tzu's message: "If you try to do too much you will fail at all things." I had to focus on the role that I felt was most important to play, and play it well.

I think one of the reasons that we try to do too much is that we're not really certain what is best for us to do. Many people come to civil society filled with passion, but lacking experience. We gain that experience as volunteers or on the job, which can be a frustrating process. The internal and inter-organizational conflicts that afflict the movement drain our energy, and the constant loss of what we are charged with protecting wears us down. It's a bad combination.

The way around it isn't simple. We've talked elsewhere about some of the things we can do in our organizations to reduce these conflicts and eliminate this stress from our work. Developing more skillful time management, project management, and strategy implementation will make us more likely to win our campaigns and create the long-term systemic change that we are seeking.

Refusing to allow ourselves to be distracted by petty or unimportant things when we are focusing on our work as activists can create much more time in our day for what is really important.

Letting Go

We need to know when to let go. Again and again in the *Tao te Ching*, Lao Tzu counsels us to "step aside when our work is done." Sometimes it's not so easy to know when that is. How do we know when a campaign is complete? When we win? By now we all know that our work to protect what we love will never really be complete. We must be vigilant in our efforts to defend our successes.

The mark of a true leader is knowing when to say that you've taken a particular effort as far as you can, and to hand it over to another set of capable hands. This is something we have to become much better at if we're going to succeed. Leadership transitions are fraught with peril, failing as often as they succeed. We should be investing much more time in leadership development within our organizations, building a pool of capable people that we can draw from to ensure continuity. *Then* we can feel confident stepping aside before we burn out.

In the *Tao te Ching*, Lao Tzu counsels us to find a middle ground so we can avoid the pitfalls of the extremes, whether it is burnout from overwork or complacency from setting the bar too low. He says:

> Close your mouth
> Dim your senses
> Dull your sharpness
> Untangle your lines
> Soften your gaze
> Settle the mud in your waters
> and find your true identity
> (*Tao*, 56)

And remember, even in trying to find balance, we must exercise common sense: trying to live a disciplined and perfectly balanced life can lead us to create rules that become impossible to live by. Then we create stress when we can't follow them unerringly.

Though no Taoist (he was a recovering Calvinist), writer and activist Edward Abbey offered advice that adorns many office walls: "Do not burn yourselves out. Be as I am. A reluctant enthusiast and part-time crusader. A half-hearted fanatic. Save the other half of yourselves for pleasure and adventure. It is not enough to fight for the west. It is even more important to enjoy it while you can, while it's still there. So get out there, hunt, fish, mess around with your friends, ramble out yonder and explore the forests, encounter the griz, climb a mountain, bag the peaks, run the rivers, breathe deep of that yet sweet and elusive air. Sit quietly for a while and contemplate the precious stillness of the lovely, mysterious, and awesome space."[9]

The Three Treasures: Unplugged

The *Tao te Ching* tells us to let joy and anger arise of their own accord, to embrace them and then let them go. So too must we allow ourselves to be both reflective and exuberant, lazy and energetic, melancholy and ecstatic if we are to find balance in our work, our families, and our lives. "Taoism is not a philosophy of compelling oneself to be calm and dignified under all circumstances," says Alan Watts. "The real and astonishing calm of people like Lao-tzu comes from the fact that they are ready and willing, without shame, to do whatever comes naturally in all circumstances."[10]

The Tao is the Way of the universe. It is the natural pattern of life. It is the way the energy – the chi – of the universe flows. To follow it, all we need to do is stop resisting. It can be a part of every aspect of our lives, our work, our play, our worship.

> Let the Tao be a part of your life
> and you will know peace
> Let the Tao be a part of your family
> and you will know joy
> Let the Tao be a part of your community
> and it will be an example for others to follow

---

9. Edward Abbey quoted in *The Earth Speaks*, edited by Steve Van Matre and Bill Weiler, Greenville, WV: Institute for Earth Education, p. 57

10. Alan Watts, *Tao: the Watercourse Way*, New York, Pantheon Books, 1975, p. 122.

> Let the Tao be part of the world
> and things will find their balance
>
> How will you know that the world works like this?
> Simply watch
> (*Tao*, 54)

Simply watch. Put the book down and step outside. Watch how moving water works on the bones of the earth and against any obstacle in its path. This is *wu wei*, acting without action. Simply watch how the natural world works and learn all you need to know about the Way and its Virtue. Then you can follow those patterns in your lives.

It is inevitable that we will become lost along the way. We'll stumble from time to time on our journey. It's a hard road that we have chosen to walk. If it were easy, we would have already been able to make the changes in our society necessary to achieve our goals. But we haven't, and sometimes we grow weary.

So spend time with family and friends who will let you talk about whatever you feel is needed to make your journey as an activist a life-affirming one. Let them bring you peace. Turn to nature for solace. Love one another.

> Good deeds and virtue can be accomplished
> following the Tao
> but just because you stray from your course
> doesn't mean that you can't return again
> (*Tao*, 62)

The path to becoming a sage activist and a responsible member of society is long and winding. If it wasn't, it wouldn't be the Tao. Those who pursue it can make it the work of a whole life.

> All of our work has a common source
> All of our effort returns us to that point
> If you know this in your heart
> you will be patient

tolerant of others
respectful of their opinions
amused by the uproar
able to respond with dignity

Knowing that the Tao is the source of our efforts
we can have faith that we will not fail
(*Tao*, 16)

My visits to Hollyhock on Cortes Island, or when I spend precious days with peer leaders at the B Bar Ranch just outside Yellowstone National Park, are sacred times for me, coming together with people with whom I have a deep and resonant connection. During these visits – in a beautiful place, and in consideration of the intense work that we do as social entrepreneurs, advocates, and leaders – I sometimes gain sudden insights like a blinding flash. More likely, though, I get a nudge that leads to a gentle understanding of some deeper purpose or a clue on how to move forward through a particular challenge.

Like trying to see the Pleiades, it most often happens when I'm looking away.

Friendships are forged easily in these caring and supportive environments, and after a few days it's like we've known each other for a lifetime. We see in each other what we feel in our own hearts – the aching loss that we each suffer as the things we cherish on this earth slip away, and the passion to make our lives stand for their protection.

When we say farewell, I return to my family and my work. The days immediately following such an intense learning experience are often difficult. I want to bask in the glow of enlightenment and the embrace of friends; instead, there are countless phone messages, a thousand emails, and reports that are past due.

Once, after a retreat, I read the first few pages of a book by Buddhist writer Jack Kornfield. It was a good book, but I kept turning back to the cover for solace. The title of the book was all I needed:

After the Ecstasy, the Laundry.[11]

Remember, we are a blessed generation. As my friend and mentor Brock Evans recently reminded me, "We are the generation who can choose to make a difference." We know that the work is hard. We can do it mindfully, with loving and compassionate hearts. We know that we will sometimes falter. We can help each other up. And we know that we will fail as often as we succeed. We can forgive ourselves and find peace in the knowledge that we are part of the great balancing equation of the universe – part of the Tao, the Way and its Virtue, here to do the work that is right and just and good.

> To know this harmony is to know the deepest
> satisfaction
> A full life, a gentle heart
> (*Tao*, 55)

---

11. Jack Kornfield, *After the Ecstasy, the Laundry: How the Heart Grows Wise on the Spiritual Path*, New York: 2000, Bantam Books

ACKNOWLEDGMENTS

Above all else, my thanks to Kathleen Wiebe, partner of ten years, counsel, guide, teacher, mother to our boys – Rio Bergen and Silas Morgen – and editor of my badly misspelled writing. During the six months that I was working on this book, Kat provided me with the time and space to learn and grow and struggle through this process, all the while contributing indispensable feedback and encouragement. This while moving to Victoria, enduring my change in employment, having a baby, and caring for our four-year-old son. She is an inspiration and an embodiment of the Tao.

Thanks to my colleagues at Wildcanada.net: Jason Meyers, Mike James, Nadine Raynolds, Kate Dugas, Val Pissot, Dave Kalbfleisch, Paul Novitski, Julian Hall, Joleen Timko, Dr. Alison Shaw, Jamie Woods, Alan Keane, Michelle Larstone, Dawn Hanna, Susan Maclean, Kevin Scott, David Cadman, Bill Snape, Donna Reel, Lea Ann Mallett, Daniel LeBlanc, Mark Surman, Jeff Gailus, Mark Barker, Ian Morrison, and Christopher Wilson. I am indebted to you for your service to this planet, and deeply grateful for your patience with my mistakes and follies.

My thanks also to Mike and Diane McIvor for your inspired and passionate leadership for more than thirty years. I am indebted to my friend and mentor Brock Evans for his gentle guidance and leadership throughout the process of writing this book.

Deep appreciation to my good friend Mark Holmes, whose drawings provide lively visual touchstones for some of the *Tao te*

Ching's more challenging paradoxes. Thanks to Dr. Jim Butler for his graceful foreword, and for his extraordinary service to humanity throughout his storied life.

My deep and sincere appreciation to David Thomson, Senior Associate for Training Resources for the Environmental Community, who since 2003 has been my coach, friend, and mentor. And to Dyan Oldenburg, executive director of TREC, and the staff and trustees at the Wilburforce Foundation who support TREC's programs.

To all of the participants in the 2003 Strategic Leadership Development Program, without whom I don't know what I would do: Deb Kmon Davidson, Mayre Flowers, Jeff Emmett, Carolyn Campbell, Yossie Cadan, David Chambers, Grace Potorti, John Wallin, Erika Pollard, Barb Cestero, Stephen Capra, Penny Lind, Arthur Hussey, Mark Preiss, Robyn King, and to the founders of Team Tequila: Deanna Spooner, Matt Skroch, and Chelsea Reiff Gwyther.

To Madeline Stanionis of Donordigital for her insight into the application of the Tao to fundraising, and Jodie Tonita, for helping me with ideas on organization as identity.

My appreciation to Jason Mogus, who gently but persistently urged me to re-engage with Wildcanada.net and ActionWorks.ca after I had stepped down as executive director, and for introducing me to Hollyhock in 2001. Deep gratitude to all of the amazing folks associated with Hollyhock, and especially to Dana Bass Solomon and Joel Solomon for their steady leadership as CEO and Board Chair. My thanks to Joel for his thoughts on our relationship with money and power, and to Carol Newell, his business partner at Renewal Partners, for hers.

Thanks to Julian Griggs for his expert advice on collaborations, and Gideon Rosenblatt for the excerpts from *Movement as Network*.

I am indebted to Cloudwalking Owl, a Taoist and activist, for his incalculable guidance and advice in crafting this book. A special thanks to Ed Whittingham who, several years ago, was the first to review and provide feedback on a chapter that has found its way into this book. Also thanks to Jenn Hoffman, who showed great enthusiasm for my initial scribing on leadership and the Tao.

My thanks to Karen Mahon, Tzeporah Berman, Darcy Riddell, and Andrea Reimer for the discussion on compassion and the notion of capturing your opponent whole. It is an honour to know you.

Thanks to Rob Sinclair for his story about the spring bear hunt; David LePage of Fast Track to Employment, Mark Deutschmann of Village Real Estate, and Maia Gibb of Dusting Divas for their inspirational stories of social enterprise; Neva Murtha for her inspired view on Tai Chi; and Carole Stark for her antique furniture story.

My deep gratitude to Matt (Mad) Jackson for his advice on marketing and touring; his book *The Canada Chronicles* is an inspiration. Thanks to Jill Kirker, Mae Burrows, Nola Poirier, Penny Lind, Cliff Wallis, Peter Lee, Red Sara, Rex Weyler, Lorna Visser, and Dena MacMynowski for various feedback.

My gratitude to Brian, Robert, Shyla, Janice, Tessa, Nicole, Beth and Linda at Arsenal Pulp Press. You can't know, after more than a decade of effort, how good it feels to finally publish a book. Any book. This book. Thanks for taking the chance on me.

And finally, an acknowledgment to you, gentle reader, for making it this far. We're only just getting started.

INDEX